Counseling

"*Counseling in a Gender-Expansive World* is an excellent in-depth look at the world of gender outside of the binary. The authors help readers understand their own concepts of gender with reflection questions for class discussions and to help students understand their own perceptions of gender, gender identity, and more. The authors challenge students to grow in their understanding of gender in our society. This book is a helpful tool for furthering the development of mental health professionals in understanding affirmative practices for all gender identities."

—Beck A. Munsey, Tarleton State University, Fort Worth

"I fully recommend this book to anyone wanting to better support the gender-expansive community. It is a through, detailed, and helpful exploration of gender identity and its impacts on people. It provides a great overall picture of the experiences and needs of gender-expansive clients, and guides students and clinicians alike in developing their ability to be supportive and culturally sensitive professionals working with this community. Case examples, self-as-therapist exploration, clinical recommendations, and summaries for each chapter contribute to this excellent resource for counselors interested in working with the gender-expansive community.

Beyond assisting those in traditional helping professions, the authors have taken care to demonstrate an inclusive definition of human service professions. This air of inclusivity is present throughout and provides an important reminder that we are all human beings with the ability to help create a better world—and that much of this involves accepting and supporting one another."

—Alicia A. Bosley, assistant professor of counseling
and mental health professions, Hofstra University

"This is a timely, comprehensive textbook for learners in the health professions seeking to understand gender-expansive identities and issues of providing affirming, competent care. It is nuanced in its discussion of intersectionality, social justice, oppression, and privilege. This is a great resource for educators, learners, and professionals, especially those new to providing gender-expansive care."

—Lara Stepleman, Augusta University

"This resource offers both students and clinicians an overview of gender-expansive people, their identity development over the lifespan, and how clinicians and mental health professionals can benefit from adopting affirmative counseling with LGBTQIA+ clients."

—**Mari Alschuler, Youngstown State University**

"Douglas Knutson, Chloë Goldbach, and Julie M. Koch's book *Counseling in a Gender-Expansive World* presents the most comprehensive offering on working with gender-expansive clients to date. Therapists will come away feeling more confident and culturally competent in their work with TGNCNB (transgender and gender nonconforming nonbinary) folx and be better equipped to build stronger therapeutic alliances with these marginalized clients."

—**Ivan Diller, LCSW-R, founder and clinical director, Omni Psychotherapy**

"*Counseling in a Gender-Expansive World* is a great introduction to terminology used within and to describe transgender communities. This book encourages current and future mental health practitioners to think about their own relationship to gender and how their own gendered biases may impact their ability to work with and support trans clients. This isn't just a textbook—it's a toolkit. Each chapter has self-reflection questions at the end that are thought-provoking and push you to reflect on who you are and want to be as a provider. This is an important read for cisgender providers generally but especially those who want to work with trans and gender-expansive clients."

—**Brendon T. Holloway, MSW, doctoral student and graduate research assistant, University of Denver, Graduate School of Social Work**

COUNSELING IN A GENDER-EXPANSIVE WORLD

Resources to Support Therapeutic Practice

Douglas Knutson
Oklahoma State University

Chloë Goldbach
Southern Illinois University Carbondale

Julie M. Koch
University of Iowa

ROWMAN & LITTLEFIELD
Lanham • Boulder • New York • London

Executive Acquisitions Editor: Mark Kerr
Assistant Acquisitions Editor: Sarah Rinehart
Sales and Marketing Inquiries: textbooks@rowman.com

Credits and acknowledgments for material borrowed from other sources, and reproduced with permission, appear on the appropriate pages within the text.

Published by Rowman & Littlefield
An imprint of The Rowman & Littlefield Publishing Group, Inc.
4501 Forbes Boulevard, Suite 200, Lanham, Maryland 20706
www.rowman.com

86-90 Paul Street, London EC2A 4NE

British Library Cataloguing in Publication Information Available

Library of Congress Cataloging-in-Publication Data
Names: Knutson, Douglas, 1984– author. | Goldbach, Chloë, 1990– author. | Koch, Julie M., 1970– author.
Title: Counseling in a gender-expansive world : resources to support therapeutic practice / Douglas Knutson, Chloë Goldbach, Julie M. Koch.
Description: Lanham : Rowman & Littlefield, [2023] | Includes bibliographical references and index.
Identifiers: LCCN 2022034023 (print) | LCCN 2022034024 (ebook) | ISBN 9781538129418 (cloth) | ISBN 9781538129425 (paperback) | ISBN 9781538129432 (epub)
Subjects: LCSH: Transgender people—Counseling of. | Gender-nonconforming people—Counseling of. | Gender identity. | Counseling. | Psychotherapy. | Counselor and client. | Psychotherapist and patient. | Cultural competence.
Classification: LCC HQ77.9 .K63 2023 (print) | LCC HQ77.9 (ebook) | DDC 306.76/8—dc23/eng/20220915
LC record available at https://lccn.loc.gov/2022034023
LC ebook record available at https://lccn.loc.gov/2022034024

Brief Contents

Acknowledgments   xvii

Introduction   1

SECTION I   LAYING THE FOUNDATION FOR AFFIRMATIVE WORK

1 Building an Understanding of Gender   11

2 Exploring Your Gender Identity   21

3 Gender Identity and the Intersectional Self   31

4 Gender Identity and Lifespan Development   45

5 Gender Identity and Geographic Location   57

SECTION II   ELEMENTS OF AFFIRMATIVE PRACTICE

6 Relationship Building   73

7 Assessment and Diagnosis Frameworks   85

8 Ethics and Professional Standards   99

9 Transitions, Care Teams, and Clinical Processes   111

10 Resources and Letter Writing   123

SECTION III   AFFIRMATIVE CARE IN CONTEXT

11 Affirmative Work in Various Settings   135

12 Partners and Families   147

13 Groups   161

14 Sex, Sexuality, and Romantic Attraction   175
   Dannie Klooster

15 Supervision   187

Conclusion   199

Appendix A: Resources Table   201

Appendix B: Letter of Recommendation for Hormone
   Replacement Therapy   203

Appendix C: Letter of Recommendation for Surgery   205

Appendix D: "Carry Letter"   207

Appendix E: Clinician Action Steps   209

Bibliography   211

Index   221

About the Authors   233

Contents

Acknowledgments   xix

Introduction   1

The Importance of Making a Difference   2

An Inclusive Vision   2

Sociocultural Context   3

Resilience and the Fight for Justice   5

Cases   5

Bill   6

Molly   6

Rowan   6

Gender-Expansive Care   7

Thank You   7

References and Suggested Readings   8

SECTION I   LAYING THE FOUNDATION FOR AFFIRMATIVE WORK

1 Building an Understanding of Gender   11

Bill   11

Molly   12

Rowan   12

Gender Terminology   12

Gender Binary   12

Gender Identity   13

Gender Expression   13

Gender Continuum   14

Gender Identities   14

Cisgender   15

Transgender   16

Nonbinary   16

Intersex   17

Transsexual   18

Pronouns   18

Summary and Recommendations   19

Reflection Questions   19

References and Suggested Readings   20

2 Exploring Your Gender Identity 21
   Bill 21
   Molly 21
   Rowan 22
   The Unexplored Life 22
      Cisnormativity 23
      Misgendering/Mispronouning 23
      Deadnaming 24
   Gender Identity and Your Environment 24
      Family and Friends 25
      Workplace 25
      Community 26
   Privilege 26
   The Binary and Me Exercise 27
   Summary and Recommendations 28
   Reflection Questions 29
   References and Suggested Readings 29

3 Gender Identity and the Intersectional Self 31
   Bill 32
   Molly 32
   Rowan 32
   Client Intersectionality 33
      Privilege and Power 34
      Race and Ethnicity 34
      Sexual Orientation 35
      Disability Status 35
      Socioeconomic Status 36
   Human Service Professional Intersectionality 36
      Gender Identity 37
      Exploring Intersectional Gender Identity 37
      Connecting with Others 38
   Client-Professional Interactions 39
      Points of Interaction 40
         Socioeconomic Status 40
         Sexual Orientation 40
         Race 41
         Social Support 42
         Age 42

Summary and Recommendations   43
Reflection Questions   43
References and Suggested Readings   44

4 Gender Identity and Lifespan Development   45
   Bill   46
   Molly   46
   Rowan   46
   Early Awareness   47
     Gender Assumptions   47
   Childhood and Adolescence   48
     Childhood   48
     Adolescence   49
     Puberty   50
     School   51
   Early Adulthood   52
     Work   52
   Middle to Late Adulthood   53
   Summary and Recommendations   54
   Reflection Questions   55
   References and Suggested Readings   55

5 Gender Identity and Geographic Location   57
   Bill   57
   Molly   58
   Rowan   58
   Cultural Nuance   58
     Teletherapy   59
   Urban Areas   60
     Transportation   61
     Violence and Safety   61
     Fees for Service   61
     Discretion   62
     Family, Partners, and Friends   62
   Positive Aspects of Rural Areas   62
     Proximity to Family   63
     Faith, Friends, and Church   63
     The Beauty of Nature   64
     Access to Services   64

Limiting Aspects of Rural Areas   64
   Proximity to Family   64
   Faith, Friends, and Church   65
   Seclusion   65
   Internet Access and Remote Connections   65
   Travel and Resource Access   65
   Access to Competent Providers   66
Semi-Rural and Semi-Urban Areas   66
People Who Immigrate   67
General Guidelines   67
   Explore the Geographic Culture of Origin   67
   Assess Distance and Physical Access to Resources   68
   Explore Spatial Connections to Community and Religion   68
   Address Family Businesses, Ties, and Expectations   68
   Explore the Impact of Local Laws and Policies   68
   Assess Availability, Longevity, and Commitment   69
Summary and Recommendations   69
Reflection Questions   69
References and Suggested Readings   70

SECTION II   ELEMENTS OF AFFIRMATIVE PRACTICE

6 Relationship Building   73
   Bill   73
   Molly   74
   Rowan   74
Prior to Meeting a Client   75
First Appointment   77
Early Stages of the Relationship   78
Strengthening the Relationship   79
Termination and Beyond   81
Summary and Recommendations   83
Reflection Questions   83
References and Suggested Readings   84

7 Assessment and Diagnosis Frameworks   85
   Bill   85
   Molly   86
   Rowan   87

A Brief History of Mental Health Diagnostic Categories   87
Assessment   88
   Formal Measures   89
   Informal or Interview-Based Assessment   91
   Intake Protocols   91
Diagnosis   92
   Default Diagnosis   92
   Differential Diagnoses   93
   Stabilization   93
   Diagnoses as Permission or Endorsement for Treatment   93
   Ethics and Diagnoses   94
Common Pitfalls   95
   Refusing to Write a Letter   95
   Ignoring Gender-Expansive Identities and Intersections   95
   Homogenizing the Population   96
   Being Unprepared to Provide Affirming Services   96
Summary and Recommendations   96
Reflection Questions   97
References and Suggested Readings   97

8   Ethics and Professional Standards   99
   Bill   99
   Molly   100
   Rowan   101
Positive Ethics   101
   Taking a Positive Ethics Approach   102
   Positive Ethics and Decision Making   103
   Nonmaleficence and Positive Ethics   103
Ethics and Legal Issues   104
   Conversion Therapy   105
Ethics and Practice Concerns   106
   Multiple Relationships with a Single Client   106
   Relationships with Client Families   106
   Rural Considerations   107
   Informed Consent   107
   Competence   107
Multicultural and Social Justice Practice   108
Summary and Recommendations   109
Reflection Questions   109
References and Suggested Readings   109

9 Transition, Care Teams, and Clinical Processes   111
  Bill   111
  Molly   112
  Rowan   112
  Transitions   113
    Social Transition   114
    Medical Transition   115
    Gender Dysphoria   115
      Diagnosis and Access to Care   116
    Gender Euphoria   116
    Passing   117
    Diverse Pathways   118
  Care Teams   119
  Clinical Processes   119
  Summary and Recommendations   120
  Reflection Questions   120
  References and Suggested Readings   121

10 Resources and Letter Writing   123
  Bill   123
  Molly   124
  Rowan   124
  Resources   124
  Letters   125
    Affirming Hormone Therapy   126
    Affirming Surgeries   126
    Carry Letters   128
  Other Resources   129
    Competence-Building Resources   129
    Transition Care Resources   129
    Web-Based Resources   130
  Summary and Recommendations   131
  Reflection Questions   131
  References and Suggested Readings   132

SECTION III   AFFIRMATIVE CARE IN CONTEXT

11 Affirmative Work in Various Settings   135
  Bill   135
  Molly   136
  Rowan   136

General Considerations   137
  Leadership   137
  Support Staff   138
  Operating Systems   140
Location Specifics   140
  Schools   140
  College or University Counseling Centers   142
  Private Practitioners   143
  Corporate and Large Companies   143
Conclusion   144
Summary and Recommendations   144
Reflection Questions   145
References and Suggested Readings   145

12 **Partners and Families   147**
  Bill   147
  Molly   148
  Rowan   148
Foundations and Key Concepts   149
  Deconstructing Negative Biases   149
  The Power of Acceptance   150
Gender in Family Dynamics   150
  Gender Fixation in Families   151
Components of the Family System   152
  Supporting Gender-Expansive Children   152
  Supporting Gender-Expansive Parents   153
Gender Transition and Romantic Relationships   154
  Partners and Relationship Dynamics   154
  Transitioning in Close Relationships   155
  Polyamorous Relationships   156
Summary and Recommendations   157
Reflection Questions   157
References and Suggested Readings   158

13 **Groups   161**
  Bill   161
  Molly   162
  Rowan   162
Group Stages   163
  Group Formation   163
  Group Member Selection   164
  Forming   165

Storming   167
Norming   168
Performing   169
Termination   170
General Suggestions   171
Summary and Recommendations   172
Reflection Questions   173
References and Suggested Readings   173

14 Sex, Sexuality, and Romantic Attraction   175
Dannie Klooster
Bill   175
Molly   176
Rowan   176
Historical Perspectives on Sexual Health   177
Gender-Affirming Approaches   177
Gender-Expansive Clients and Sex Education Myths   178
Toward a Sex-Positive Framework   179
Body Positivity   179
Eroto-Positivity   180
Kink Positivity   180
Relationship Positivity   181
Additional Considerations   184
Conclusion   184
Summary and Recommendations   184
Reflection Questions   185
References and Suggested Readings   185

15 Supervision   187
Bill   187
Molly   188
Rowan   188
Lisa, LPC, and Austin, Master's Trainee   189
Supervision and Contextual Factors   190
Group Supervision   190
Identity Differences   190
Power Dynamics   191
Constructive Feedback   192
Supportive Feedback   192
The Supervisory Relationship   193

Self-Disclosure   193
Boundaries   194
Parallel Process   194
Ruptures and Conflicts   195
Supervision as a Professional Role   195
Qualification Compatibility   195
Consultation   196
Continuing Education   196
Future Developments   196
Summary and Recommendations   197
Reflection Questions   197
References and Suggested Readings   198

Conclusion   199

Appendix A: Resources Table   201

Appendix B: Letter of Recommendation for Hormone
Replacement Therapy   203

Appendix C: Letter of Recommendation for Surgery   205

Appendix D: "Carry Letter"   207

Appendix E: Clinician Action Steps   209

Bibliography   211

Index   221

About the Authors   233

Acknowledgments

We want to express heartfelt gratitude to Daniel Walinsky for his contributions to the early stages of this project. We are also grateful to the many mentors, clients, research participants, advisers, scholars, researchers, and collaborators who provided valuable insight, feedback, and guidance that shaped this text.

Introduction

This is a book for everyone who is interested in making a positive difference for gender-expansive people. You may have read the title and thought, "I'm not a licensed mental health provider, so I probably won't get anything out of this." On the contrary, we hope that all people who pick up this book and leaf through its pages will gain a deeper understanding of themselves and the world around them. We hope that you, regardless of your training and background, will learn new ways to help gender-expansive people thrive in your corner of the world.

Toward that end, we challenge you to think of yourself as a human service professional. In other words, we encourage you to take what you are good at (your profession) and consider the ways that it makes a positive impact on the world (it is a service to humans). For example, if you work as a cashier, you help people gain access to goods that they need in order to live. If you think of yourself as serving others through your profession, you can probably come up with lots of ways that you could use your expertise to support the gender-expansive people around you. For one thing, smiling and affirming people of all genders as you ring up their purchases is a small but very impactful way to improve their lives (as you will discover while you read this book).

In countries around the world, the terms used to refer to human service professionals such as counselors, psychologists, therapists, social workers, or coaches, vary widely. Similarly, the types of licenses and the scope of practice granted different professionals can be vastly different in different areas of the globe. In an effort to be as inclusive as possible and to broaden the scope of this book to include anyone who may provide care for gender-expansive people, we use the term *human service professional(s)* or the abbreviated version, *professional(s)*. In keeping with the theme of inclusivity, we also refer to recipients of human services as *clients*. In other words, we are talking to you, and we are discussing ways to improve your work with the people you serve.

The Importance of Making a Difference

Gender-expansive people, such as those who identify as transgender and nonbinary, are increasingly becoming the focus of media, politics, legislation, research, and public conversation. Current estimates place the population of gender-expansive people in the United States at approximately 1.4 million (Flores et al., 2016), and if that trend holds globally, there are about 76.7 million gender-expansive people around the world. With increased attention comes greater visibility, and current estimates of gender-expansive populations are likely underestimates. The number of people who identify as gender expansive is expected to continue to rise. Human services professionals are now, more than ever, likely to provide services for someone who identifies as gender expansive. However, many professionals have not received specific training in the skills, knowledge, and awareness necessary to provide affirming, informed care for gender-diverse populations.

As the focus on gender-expansive people grows, so do the number of affirmative practice resources available for people in a variety of professions such as counseling, social work, and nursing. Affirmative practice is supportive, informed care provided for gender-expansive people by a competent professional. Right now, writers tend to write about specific professional roles and specific settings, such as doctors in hospitals or psychologists in rural areas. However, affirming practices tend to be similar across disciplines, regardless of a given job or field. That is why we wrote a book on affirmative care that spans professions. We know that affirmative care makes a difference, and we want everyone to have the chance to provide better care, regardless of their context or job.

An Inclusive Vision

In this book, whenever possible, we zoom out to provide an overview of the broader professional landscape of affirmative, gender-expansive care. Within that broad overview, readers are provided the opportunity to engage in self-exploration, to apply content to specific cases, and to amass specific tools and approaches that support competent care (see Appendixes for specific tools and templates). The book is designed so that each chapter builds on the one before. We recommend engaging with the chapters in order; the cases we provide in this introduction are revisited and further developed in subsequent chapters. Of course, this text will not replace the need for professional training in gender-diverse care, but we hope that readers who engage with the full text will become far more competent and informed providers.

We encourage you to interact with this text, highlight important passages, and take notes. The chapters in this book focus on specific topics and/or areas of care so that you can return to them as needed. They may also be referenced by providers who need a quick refresher or by well-trained affirmative providers who are in search of additional tools and resources related to a specific subject area or treatment modality.

The chapters are organized to optimize indexing and to facilitate quick access to specific content. Each chapter opens with a series of cases, followed by general information related to the chapter topic and relevant to the case information provided. The general information is followed by specific resources, tools, templates, and/or guidelines that apply the content of the chapter. Last, summaries, reflection questions, and additional readings are provided to facilitate deeper thought about and engagement with the chapter topic and content. The bibliography at the end of the book collects all of the resources in a single location to give professors, readers, researchers, and students a centralized place to go to source key readings and high-impact articles without having to search through individual chapters.

Readers will notice that this book is very inclusive, but that it has some limitations. For example, the text defaults to a focus on adults, speaks mostly to cisgender readers, and skews toward mental health professions. It is impossible to cover all aspects of gender affirmative care for all populations in all contexts at all times in a single book. Wherever possible, we try to incorporate lifespan, cross-disciplinary, developmental approaches, but we cannot cover everything. We hope that readers will use the bibliography and other sources to supplement their knowledge as they read this book. We hope this book inspires readers to begin or continue their journey of gender exploration. Put simply, we hope you will continue to read and learn about gender-affirming care and gender identity long after you have closed the cover on this book and stowed it away on a bookshelf (or have archived it in your online library).

Sociocultural Context

Before launching into the specifics of the book, it is important to take a moment to consider the sociocultural and global contexts of the present work. Through a historically Western, colonized lens, gender expansiveness is generally considered abnormal (West & Zimmerman, 1987) rather than celebrated, although we also know that societies around the world have had long histories of celebrating gender diversity. At present, many of the leading diagnostic manuals, such as the American Psychiatric Association (APA) *Diagnostic and Statistical Manual of Mental Disorders 5* (APA, 2013) and the *International Statistical Classification of Diseases and Related Health Problems*, 10th edition (World Health Organization, 2016), characterize gender expansiveness as a source of distress. The approach to gender expansiveness as tied to a mental health diagnosis has touched off an intense debate that is discussed in Chapter 7.

Regardless of where perspectives on gender expansiveness come from and despite how they may be formalized in the manuals of human service professionals, the truth is that gender-expansive people face widespread oppression and discrimination (James et al., 2016). Oppression, discrimination, and violence experienced by gender-expansive people is often further exacerbated for individuals who also hold additional marginalized identities, such as transgender women of color, gender-expansive people living with disabilities, and neurodivergent gender-expansive people. The mental, emotional, and physical health concerns resulting from rejection and experiences of cruelty are well documented (e.g., Puckett et al., 2020). For example, researchers continue to find elevated rates of depression, anxiety, and suicidal ideation in gender-expansive populations (e.g., James et al., 2016). This distress is one focus of affirmative therapy, and it is our hope that, after reading this book, helping professionals will feel more equipped to help reduce distress in gender-expansive clients.

Scholars are beginning to emphasize the strong community connectedness and remarkable adaptability of gender-expansive individuals (Puckett et al., 2019; Stone et al., 2020). The sociocultural climates in which gender-expansive people find themselves, announce who they are, and come to know themselves are often oppressive and dangerous. Nevertheless, many gender-expansive people continue to fight for justice, and help to produce cutting-edge research on gender and affirmative care. It is important to recognize that combating injustice and improving gender affirmative care is everyone's responsibility, not a task for just gender-expansive people. As professionals, we are called to participate in and to cultivate resilience-building endeavors if we are to provide maximally effective affirmative care. This book takes a resilience/liberation focus that emphasizes strengths and possibilities over oppression and discrimination. However, it is important never to lose sight of the struggles and setbacks that gender-expansive people face in the fight for justice.

Resilience and the Fight for Justice

Some of the most oppressed and marginalized members of gender-expansive communities have been among the most powerful advocates for equity and justice. Gender-expansive people like Marsha P. Johnson and Sylvia Rivera were pivotal figures in early lesbian, gay, bisexual, transgender, and queer (LGBTQ+) rights movements. At the same time, transgender and gender-expansive women of color are murdered daily around the world. We hope that books like this one honor the memories of those who fight and who fought for gender justice. This work is intended to be an extension, however small, of the efforts to combat oppression, discrimination, and violence that many gender-expansive people frequently experience.

We invite you to locate yourself within the fight for justice as you engage with this text. As a current and/or future affirmative provider, you are a warrior for justice too. We hope you will keep a resilience mindset as you reflect on the injustice and the need for change outlined in this text. In other words, we hope that you consider all the ways in which gender-expansive people are resilient and strong, and not focus just on barriers they may face, although these are important to consider also. We also hope that you will walk away from this book energized to continue the fight for justice for gender-expansive people everywhere.

Cases

We introduce three case examples, based on our work with gender-diverse populations, that we then integrate into the chapters that follow. With the exception of the self-exploration chapters, each chapter will further extend and expand on the biographical data presented here. This text is designed to help readers apply the knowledge they gain to work with gender-diverse clients who hold a wide range of identities. It is not possible to capture the full scope of gender-diverse experiences in only three case studies. Here, we present profiles of people who identify as a trans man, a trans woman, and a gender-fluid individual. Please note that the cases are synthesized from our combined experience and any resemblance they hold to real people is purely coincidental.

Bill

Bill (he/him) is a 28-year-old who identifies as White, heterosexual, and as a trans man. Bill was assigned female at birth. He is partnered and has never been married. Bill works as an information technology specialist at a large law firm in Boston, Massachusetts. Bill served in the US Army and he used his GI bill to pay for a bachelor's degree in information technology. He is very connected to the LGBTQ+ community in his area and he coleads the transgender and nonbinary support group at a local community center on Saturday afternoons. Bill came out to his parents as a lesbian when he was 15 and then later came out as a trans man when he was 25. Bill's parents have been generally supportive and have expressed a desire for Bill to be happy. Bill reports that others think he "has it all together" and he is a role model for many of the men in his community. Few people know that Bill experiences panic attacks and suffers from generalized anxiety disorder.

Molly

Molly (she/her) is a 60-year-old who identifies as Latina, lesbian, and as a trans woman. She was assigned male at birth. Molly married a cisgender woman, Rebecca, when Molly was 22 and the two remained married until Molly came out at 35. Molly has one child, a daughter who is 35 years old. Molly's divorce was amicable, and she has a relationship with both her daughter and her ex-wife. Molly is disabled and she depends on a monthly social security check to cover her bills. She lives in rural North Dakota, where she feels isolated and alone. Molly is beginning to experience intensifying suicidal ideations.

Rowan

Rowan (they/them) is an 18-year-old who identifies as Black, panromantic, and as gender fluid. Rowan attends college in Thousand Oaks, California. They are majoring in pre-veterinary science (biochemistry and molecular biology) at California Lutheran University because they love animals, but they are not doing well in classes. Rowan is not out to their classmates. They fear that their professors and fellow students would discriminate against Rowan if Rowan came out. Rowan is very afraid of failing all of their classes this semester. If they do, they will be placed on academic probation and will lose their scholarships. The worse things get, the less motivated and more worried they become.

Gender-Expansive Care

In the chapters that follow, you will build skills, knowledge, and awareness necessary to provide affirming care for gender-expansive people. Section I will help you lay the foundation for affirmative work by guiding you through a process of self-exploration and discovery. The section is designed to help you build empathy, to assist you with identifying biases, and to ground you in your own gender story. This exploration process is fundamental to providing competent, affirming care.

Section II will address general elements of affirmative practice. The section will assist you with thinking through ethical considerations, the application of professional standards, documentation, and interdisciplinary collaboration. Some of the content is clinical in focus, but we hope you will be able to apply the general principles we present to your own human service role.

Section III focuses on specific populations and/or services that are specializations for some human service professionals. Although this book is designed to be read in its entirety, readers may skip some chapters in Section III if those sections do not apply to their current work. However, we strongly encourage readers to review Chapters 11, 12, and 14. It is important for all affirming professionals to have a working understanding of how gender-expansive clients may experience intimate relationships, family dynamics, sex, and sexuality.

Thank You

Thank you for picking this book up from the shelf or adding it to your electronic library. We hope you will find the content helpful as you strive to provide more effective services for gender-expansive people. Affirmative work can be hard at times, but it is vitally important. We are glad you are taking this important step toward greater understanding and competence.

References and Suggested Readings

American Psychiatric Association (2013). *Diagnostic and statistical manual of mental disorders* (5th ed.). https://doi.org/10.1176/appi.books.9780890425596

Flores, A. R., Herman, J. L., Gates, G. J., & Brown, T. N. T. (2016). How many adults identify as transgender in the United States? http://williamsinstitute.law.ucla.edu/wp-content/uploads/How-Many-Adults-Identify-as-Transgender-in-the-United-States.pdf

James, S. E., Herman, J. L., Rankin, S., Keisling, M., Mottet, L., & Anafi, M. (2016). *The report of the 2015 U.S. Transgender Survey*. National Center for Transgender Equality.

Puckett, J. A., Maroney, M. R., Wadsworth, L. P., Mustanski, B., & Newcomb, M. E. (2020). Coping with discrimination: The insidious effects of gender minority stigma on depression and anxiety in transgender individuals. *Journal of Clinical Psychology, 76*(1), 176–194. https://doi.org/10.1002/jclp.22865

Puckett, J. A., Matsuno, E., Dyar, C., Mustanski, B., & Newcomb, M. E. (2019). Mental health and resilience in transgender individuals: What type of support makes a difference? *Journal of Family Psychology, 33*(8), 954–964. https://doi.org/10.1037/fam0000561

Stone, A. L., Nimmons, E. A., Salcido, R., Jr., & Schnarrs, P. W. (2020). Multiplicity, race, and resilience: Transgender and non-binary people building community. *Sociological Inquiry, 90*(2), 226–248. https://doi.org/10.1111/soin.12341

West, C., & Zimmerman, D. H. (1987). Doing gender. *Gender & Society, 1*(2), 125–151. https://doi.org/10.1177/0891243287001002002

World Health Organization. (2016). *International statistical classification of diseases and related health problems* (10th ed.). https://icd.who.int/browse10/2016/en

SECTION I

Laying the Foundation
for Affirmative Work

Building an Understanding of Gender

One of the first steps toward being a competent, affirming provider is to learn, or return to the basics. Even seasoned professionals regularly return to Gender 101 in their scholarship and practice. Terms, identities, and experiences that gender-expansive people talk about are constantly changing, developing, and fluctuating. That is because gender is a construct and, as a lived experience, it is dynamic and varied. In this book, we use the umbrella term *gender expansive* to capture the rich range of gender identities and expressions with which clients may identify. Please note that some professionals use TransGender and Gender Nonconforming (TGNC) or transgender and nonbinary (TNB) to serve the same purpose.

In the introduction, we noted that gender identity and gender expression may fall under the umbrella of gender expansive. For example, a person may identify as a woman, but may exhibit what are considered traditionally masculine behaviors and/or attributes (e.g., getting a buzz cut, working on heavy machinery). In this chapter and throughout the book, you will notice that unless we are specifically referring to someone who uses other pronouns such as he/him or she/her, we will use they/them in the singular in order to be inclusive. As you read the cases that follow, consider how gender is uniquely experienced and expressed by Bill, Molly, and Rowan. These cases will be extended through the entire book, so please pay close attention to the introductions below.

Bill

Bill uses the pronouns he/him/his. He strongly identifies with the label *trans man*. For him, identifying as a trans man honors his journey from being assigned female at birth to embracing his identity as a man. Bill is open about his transgender journey, and he feels as if sharing his identity openly allows him to engage in teaching moments with others. He does not mind sharing or answering questions about his journey, but he corrects people when they ask questions that are too private or invasive. He feels bonded with transgender and gender-expansive communities.

Molly

Molly uses the pronouns she/her/hers. She identifies with the label *woman*, and she does not feel it is necessary for her to use the adjectives *trans* or *transgender* in front of her identity as a woman. When Molly transitioned, she left her old life behind. She does not feel connected to her pre-transition self; she got rid of many of her old photo albums in which she was pictured presenting as a man, except for those that include her daughter. Molly is not open to answering questions about her transition experience and she is most comfortable in spaces in which she is recognized and interacted with as a woman.

Rowan

Rowan uses the pronouns they/them/theirs, but they are not out at school. Because they present as androgynous, people usually seem confused about how to respond to them and/or about what pronouns to use when referring to them. Rowan feels sad when people fail to use their pronouns, but they do not feel comfortable correcting others. They are faced with the constant awareness that most of the people around them do not understand gender fluidity. At a fundamental level, Rowan feels misunderstood. It means a lot to them when people use they/them pronouns to refer to Rowan.

Gender Terminology

In this chapter, we explore a wide range of terms and concepts related to the notion of gender. Please note that our focus is purely on gender identity; we only mention sex as it relates to gender identity. For more information about sex and sexuality, please refer to Chapter 14.

Gender Binary

The gender binary refers to the traditional classification system that divides gender (and sex) into two distinct and "opposite" categories of male/men and female/women (American Psychological Association [APA], 2015; Fausto-Sterling, 2012). Many cultures and countries, including the United States, operate on the assumption that gender is dichotomous and therefore only two categories for gender (male and female or men and women) exist. Thinking of gender as only having two categories excludes and erases the existence of individuals who do not strictly identify as only a man or only a woman or who identify as a gender outside of the man/woman binary. Therefore, we encourage you to conceptualize gender as a continuum, or even as a constellation (see definition of gender continuum below), in order to best serve clients who identify as gender expansive.

Gender Identity

Gender identity refers to how an individual conceptualizes their own gender in terms of identifying as a man, woman, nonbinary, and/or any other gender outside of the gender binary (APA, 2015). In the United States, sex is assigned at birth and a baby is typically designated as either male or female. Gender is often assumed by the public to be aligned with that sex designation such that the male babies are declared to be boys and female babies are declared to be girls. Intersex babies are generally surgically designated female and then socialized as girls.

When a person's gender identity is aligned with what is culturally expected, based on sex assigned at birth, they are referred to as *cisgender*. When a person's gender identity is different from what is culturally expected, based on sex assigned at birth, they are referred to as gender expansive. The assumption that sex determines gender is very problematic and harmful. Just as with many other things, there are both biological and social contributors to gender identity (a combination of nature and nurture). Sex assigned at birth and gender identity are not the same thing, and the development and acceptance of one's gender identity is not inherently related to or determined by one's sex assigned at birth.

Gender Expression

Gender expression refers to how we show or communicate our gender to the world around us (Stryker, 2017). Gender can be externally communicated through behaviors, clothing, appearance, voice, and more. Expressions of gender are most often seen as being masculine, feminine, or androgynous. Gender expression is not the same thing as gender identity. Gender expression and gender identity are often aligned, such as someone who identifies as a woman and has a feminine gender expression, but this is not the case for everyone. People may express their gender in a certain manner, but this does not dictate what their gender identity is. Therefore, it is important that you do not assume someone's gender identity or pronouns based on their appearance or mannerisms. Assumptions lead to mistakes and mistakes cause distress, as demonstrated in Rowan's case vignette.

Gender Continuum

Take a moment to imagine a sky full of stars. Because humans like order, we usually try to group things together. For example, we say, "That group of stars is the Milky Way," even though the Milky Way stars are all different sizes, colors, and luminosities. We do the same with gender. We look at a grouping of people with seemingly similar gender identities and say, "That group of people are men." In reality, the unique ways that humans understand, identify with, and embrace gender are as different as the stars in the sky. As affirming professionals, our job is not to try to label clients as Venus or Mars. Rather, we have the opportunity to provide services for each individual client as they embark on a journey to discover their own gender identity and expression.

Conceptualizing gender as a continuum means that we can think about gender identity in an infinite number of ways rather than only as members of a male/female or man/woman dichotomous category. In a continuum of gender, people can identify as male, female, a combination of male and female, agender, nonbinary, or any other gender identity beyond the gender binary. Sometimes the terms *gender constellation*, *gender universe*, or *gender galaxy* are used instead of *gender continuum*. Conceptualizing gender as continuum ensures that individuals who do not identify within the gender binary are not excluded or erased. A gender continuum also helps break down strict societal norms that surround gender identity and gender expression, and provides a place for individuals to identify and express themselves when they do not fit neatly into societal norms for gender identity, gender expression, or gender roles.

Gender Identities

Because our understanding of gender continues to evolve over time, it is not possible to provide an exhaustive list of gender terms. Instead, in an effort to create a foundation for conversation and for competence, we list the most current, common terms relating to gender-expansive individuals with the caveat that some gender-expansive individuals may have gender identities, pronouns, or experiences that have not been captured here. As demonstrated in the case vignettes in this chapter, clients have strong feelings and experiences tied to the gender identity they embrace and identify with. It is important to also remember that the numerous other identities (e.g., race, ethnicity, ability status, social class, sexuality) held by a gender-expansive person can shape their understanding of their gender identity and influence privileges and oppressions experienced in countless social contexts. Many mistakes are made when professionals make broad assumptions about a client's identities and/or experiences based on an identity label or pronoun.

Cisgender

Many of the readers of this book will most likely identify as cisgender. The term *cisgender* is used to describe individuals whose gender identity is aligned with what is culturally expected based on sex assigned at birth (APA, 2015; Brammer & Ginicola, 2017). Because we rely so heavily on binaries, cisgender is generally an umbrella term that is assumed to encompass anyone who does not identify as gender expansive. However, as we discussed in the introduction, gender identity is far more varied than blanket terms imply. There is a lot of variety under the cisgender umbrella that we will begin to unpack in Chapter 2.

Cisgender, like transgender, is an adjective that precedes the nouns, "woman" and "man." Cisgender men and cisgender women are generally considered the norm by society and cisgender identities carry a lot of privilege. Cisgender people do not have to consider that they possess one of many possible gender identities and they usually drop the adjective "cisgender" when referring to themselves. We recommend that affirming professionals add cisgender as a qualifier when talking about themselves or others who have self-identified as cisgender. This practice challenges the assumption that cisgender individuals are the norm or are "normal," which reduces the "othering" of gender-expansive individuals. Using transgender woman and cisgender woman (instead of transgender woman and woman) implies that both of these individuals are women but neither one is implied to be the norm—they are just different and equal gender identities within the continuum of gender.

Transgender

The term *transgender* refers to individuals who have a gender identity that is different from what is culturally expected based on sex assigned at birth. The term transgender is an adjective, so the use of terms such as "transgenders" (noun) or "transgendered" (verb) is incorrect. Transgender may be used as an umbrella term (like gender expansive), but many gender-expansive people may feel left out when the term is used. Therefore, we recommend using gender expansive or other more inclusive terms instead.

Transgender women may use the term MTF (male-to-female), and transgender men may use the term FTM (female-to-male). In the vignette above, Bill referred to himself as a trans man. It was important for him to identify as a man, but to also recognize his transgender journey. Other transgender people may use the terms *transman* or *transwoman*, but make sure you follow a client's lead. Some clients may feel that removing the space between trans and man, for example, erases the fact that the client is truly and fully a man. You will also hear people use the abbreviated form, *trans*.

Nonbinary

Nonbinary is an umbrella that captures gender identities that are outside the gender binary and/or that rest outside of the concept of gender entirely (Richards et al., 2016). The nonbinary umbrella encompasses those who identify as nonbinary, genderqueer, gender fluid, agender, a combination of male and female, neither male nor female, or any other gender identity outside or beyond the gender binary. Individuals who identify outside of the gender binary may self-identify as nonbinary and/or with a variety of other terms.

Additionally, even though transgender is sometimes used as an umbrella term to capture all individuals whose gender identity is different from what is culturally expected based on their sex assigned at birth, not all nonbinary individuals self-identify with the term *transgender*. Be sure to confirm with each individual the terminology that they prefer and self-identify with.

Cisnormativity (defined in Chapter 2) and the gender binary often lead to the exclusion or outright erasure of nonbinary individuals and identities (Hyde et al., 2018; Richards et al., 2016). Therefore, we urge you to challenge any assumptions or biases you may have regarding gender and acknowledge that the gender identity of any individual is valid, regardless of whether it is within or beyond the gender binary. We will take up this work, in earnest, in Chapter 2.

Intersex

Intersex is a term used to describe individuals who have ambiguous (i.e., not clearly male or female) sex characteristics (Ferrara & Casper, 2018). When most people hear the word intersex, they may think of ambiguous genitalia. In reality, ambiguous genitalia are not as common as other intersex presentations, including genetic, hormonal, or gonadal differences (Fausto-Sterling, 2000).

Discussion of people who are intersex is important in the context of this text because intersex people may also identify as gender expansive. At some point during your career, it is likely that you will work with someone who reports both working through their intersex experience and also working toward understanding and accepting their gender identity.

It is important to note that it has been common practice for physicians in Western countries to perform surgical procedures on infants with ambiguous genitalia in order to make a binary male or female sex assignment (Carpenter, 2016). Activists have proclaimed that such procedures are very problematic because individuals who are intersex often cannot consent to surgical procedures due to the age at which they are typically conducted (Carpenter, 2016; Davis & Evans, 2018). Because intersex surgical procedures are often performed shortly after birth, it is impossible to know the gender identity of the child at the time of the procedure.

Doctors and families are making an arbitrary decision with regard to sex assignment, a sex assignment that may be different from the gender identity that the child will later be able to articulate. This further highlights the importance of differentiating sex from gender identity. Some countries in Europe have begun to ban these procedures in infancy and do not assign sex at birth when children are born with ambiguous genitalia.

It is important to provide the opportunity for intersex individuals to choose for themselves whether they wish to pursue surgical options, especially because intersex procedures often serve no functional purpose and are therefore medically unnecessary (Carpenter, 2016). They are often designed for the sole purpose of creating genitalia that conforms to social norms in terms of how physicians define what makes certain genitalia "male" or "female." Therefore, we recommend the same approach for intersex individuals as we do for gender-expansive individuals: support intersex individuals by allowing them to choose the steps and procedures that best meet and affirm their individual needs, goals, and identities.

Transsexual

Transsexual is now widely considered to be an out-of-date term previously used to describe some gender-expansive individuals, but some clients may identify with the term (e.g., identifying as a transsexual woman or as a woman of transsexual experience). It often has a medical connation in that transsexual is sometimes used to describe transgender individuals who have undergone sex reassignment surgery (SRS). Because the term transsexual is outdated and can be considered stigmatizing, we do not recommend using the term unless an individual self-identifies as transsexual. Even then, the individual may benefit from information and/or discussion about newer terminology.

Pronouns

In reference to someone's gender identity, an individual may use he/him/his, she/her/hers, they/them/theirs, or a variety of other nonbinary or gender-neutral pronouns (see Knutson et al., 2019). Likewise, people may use the gender-neutral honorific Mx. before their name in place of Mr., Mrs., or Ms. Gender-neutral pronouns may be encountered when working with nonbinary individuals. It may be uncomfortable to use singular "they" or other pronouns that you are unfamiliar with when referring to someone, but it is important to use the pronouns that correctly align with an individual's gender identity. Remember that singular they is grammatically correct. We use the singular they much more than we realize, such as when we are referring to someone without knowing their gender identity. We recommend using the term *pronouns* as opposed to *preferred pronouns* because the pronouns that someone uses reflect their actual identity, not a preferred identity.

It would be easy to assume that people who identify as men use he/him pronouns, that people who identify as women use she/

her pronouns, that people who identify as nonbinary use they/them pronouns, and so on. However, the pronouns a person uses and the gender with which they identify are not necessarily connected. Again, it is important to check in with clients and to understand the ways they identify. Professionals can learn a lot from setting aside assumptions and by remaining curious about each individual client's feelings and experiences. We have noticed lately that the younger generation (under 25) often refer to anyone, regardless of assumed gender identity, using "they/them."

Summary and Recommendations

* Sex assigned at birth does not determine a person's gender identity.
* A person's pronouns are not the same as their gender identity.
* Gender expansive is an umbrella term that captures gender identity and gender expression.
* It is important to ask any client, but especially gender-expansive clients, about their unique experiences of gender.
* Mistakes happen when professionals make assumptions about client identities.
* Adding cisgender to man or woman acknowledges gender diversity.

Reflection Questions

1. When it comes to gender identities and expressions, there are no right answers. Terms and identity categories are constantly changing.

    * As a provider, how does it feel to be faced with so much ambiguity?
    * How can you stay current and keep up with recent trends?

2. How does it feel to think of yourself as holding one of many possible gender identities?

3. Take a moment to reflect on the case vignettes at the beginning of the chapter.

    * What stands out to you in the case information?
    * What would you find most challenging about working with these clients?
    * What would you find most fulfilling about working with these clients?

4. To people who are not used to interacting with nonbinary people, they/them pronouns may sound grammatically incorrect.

* What is your reaction to they/them pronouns?
* If you feel uncomfortable, what might be behind your discomfort?
* How might you work to increase your comfort level with they/them pronouns?
* Try using they/them pronouns in reference to someone to practice.

    ○ Read this sentence aloud: "Julie asked a friend to go to the library with them; they were too shy to go by themselves."

5. Learning about gender-expansive people is not just something professionals do by reading. How might you gain greater awareness of gender-expansive communities in your daily life?

References and Suggested Readings

American Psychological Association. (2015). Guidelines for psychological practice with transgender and gender nonconforming people. *American Psychologist, 70*(9), 832–864. https://doi.org/10.1037/a0039906

Brammer, R., & Ginicola, M. M. (2017). Counseling transgender clients. In *Affirmative counseling with LGBTQI+ people* (pp. 183–212). American Counseling Association.

Carpenter, M. (2016). The human rights of intersex people: Addressing harmful practices and rhetoric of change. *Reproductive Health Matters, 24*(47), 74–84.

Davis, G., & Evans, M. J. (2018). Surgically shaping sex: A gender structure analysis of the violation of intersex people's human rights. In B. Risman, C. Froyum, & W. J. Scarborough (Eds.), *Handbook of the sociology of gender* (pp. 273–284). Springer International Publishing.

Fausto-Sterling, A. (2000). *Sexing the body: Gender politics and the construction of sexuality*. Basic Books.

Fausto-Sterling, A. (2012). *Sex/gender: Biology in a social world*. Routledge.

Ferrara, M., & Casper, M. J. (2018). Genital alteration and intersex: A critical analysis. *Current Sexual Health Reports, 10*(1), 1–6.

Hyde, J. S., Bigler, R. S., Joel, D., Tate, C. C., & van Anders, S. M. (2018). The future of sex and gender in psychology: Five challenges to the gender binary. *American Psychologist*. Advance online publication. https://doi.org/10.1037/amp0000307

Knutson, D., Koch, J. M., & Goldbach, C. (2019). Recommended terminology, pronouns, and documentation for work with transgender and non-binary populations. *Practice Innovations, 4*(4), 214. https://doi.org/10.1037/pri0000098

Richards, C., Bouman, W. P., Seal, L., Barker, M. J., Nieder, T. O., & T'Sjoen, G. (2016). Non-binary or genderqueer genders. *International Review of Psychiatry, 28*(1), 95–102.

Stryker, S. (2017). *Transgender history: The roots of today's revolution*. Seal Press.

2

Exploring Your Gender Identity

Another foundational step toward providing competent, gender-affirming care is to explore your own gender identity and to recognize ways that your gender identity was shaped. Gender scholars agree that self-exploration is an important practice that should extend throughout a provider's life and work. When a professional fails to examine their own gendered assumptions, they miss the subtle biases, expectations, and oppressive beliefs that they hold. In the case vignettes that follow, we present mock interactions that commonly occur between gender-expansive people and their providers to illustrate the importance of self-exploration.

Bill

You are a professional who is working with Bill. You like Bill and you like working with him. You give Bill lots of praise and affirmation to validate him. When you interact with Bill, you go out of your way to affirm that he is a real man and that you do not see him as being any different from any other guy. One day, you say, "Yeah, you know, guys like you and my dad and my brother." Bill becomes visibly uncomfortable and states, "I am proud of being a trans man. I'm not sure my experience is quite the same as your dad's." You feel thrown off and you have difficulty recovering the conversation.

Molly

You are a professional working with Molly. You know that working with Molly is important and you feel committed to providing her with excellent care. Still, you may sometimes find your work with Molly to be frustrating. Her depression is pervasive and she tends to complain about many things. One day you get really frustrated and you stop attending as closely to what is coming out of your mouth. Without thinking, you accidentally refer to Molly by her deadname.

Rowan

You are a professional working with Rowan. In your mind, Rowan looks male and you have a very hard time using they/them pronouns with Rowan. Trying to remember to say they instead of he takes up a lot of mental space that you would otherwise devote to being present with Rowan. At times, you feel exhausted and worried that you made a mistake. One day, in a particularly intense session, you slip up and refer to Rowan as he. Right after, you apologize profusely. You start saying, "Oh my gosh. I'm so sorry. I didn't mean to do that. I can't believe it." Rowan tries to calm you down and to reassure you that everything is okay.

The Unexplored Life

It is possible that you have not really considered it before, but for your entire life, you have been on a gender journey. Gender (whether you identify with a gender or not) is a powerful force in cultures around the world, especially Western, European-American ones. Please remember that gender, sex assigned at birth, gender identity, and gender roles are all different. We will discuss many of the gender concepts, experiences, and expectations you may have encountered throughout your lifespan. Before reading on, if you need to review key ideas and terms, feel free to go back to Chapter 1 and take a look.

As demonstrated in the cases at the beginning of this chapter, professionals may make mistakes when providing care for gender-expansive people. When professionals fail to explore their own identities, they are more likely to embrace and express biases and counterproductive beliefs. Biased professionals are more likely to fall into destructive practices like misgendering, deadnaming, or assuming that a client is mistaken about their identity. Therapists may also focus so much on gender that they do not recognize what is actually going on for the client or they end up ignoring other salient aspects (outside of gender) of the client's identity and experience. As you read about some of the common destructive beliefs and practices, we encourage you to identify and actively challenge your biases related to gender and gender-expansive individuals.

Cisnormativity

Cisnormativity refers to the assumption that cisgender people are normal and that they are the default identity. In our cisnormative society, this assumption creates behaviors, attitudes, and practices that are biased against gender-expansive individuals. For example, the professional working with Bill assumed that Bill would feel affirmed when the professional compared Bill to the professional's father. The professional may have assumed that Bill wanted to be normalized or seen as just another cisgender man. On the contrary, Bill expressed value for his gender journey, and he pushed back against the idea that being included in the cisgender community was somehow a compliment. Affirmative providers recognize that all gender journeys are valuable and important. That work begins with an exploration of your own gender journey and with a recognition that your gender identity is just one among many.

Misgendering/Mispronouning

Misgendering refers to using the wrong pronouns when talking to or about someone (Ansara & Hegarty, 2014; McLemore, 2015; Sinclair-Palm, 2017). Misgendering is likely to happen at one time or another when working with gender-expansive clients. In the vignettes above, the professional working with Rowan used the wrong pronouns for them. After making the mistake, the professional drew greater attention to the error and eventually forced Rowan into the position of taking care of the professional.

Everyone makes mistakes. When you make a mistake, we recommend simply apologizing, correcting yourself, and moving on. For example, the professional working with Rowan could have said, "I'm sorry, they," before continuing with the appointment or interaction. Please remember that pronouns, gender identity, and gender expression are not necessarily connected. The fact that your eyes have been trained to see a person as he or she does not mean the person uses those pronouns.

One great way to challenge your biases and assumptions is to do so in your everyday life. For example, you may drive down the road, see a big pickup truck, and think, "That guy is driving so slow." Pause for a second and think, "Why did I think a man was driving that truck?" It is possible that the driver does not use he/him pronouns. The more you notice and challenge your biases, the more likely you will be to provide affirming care for gender-expansive clients.

Deadnaming

Deadnaming refers to using a person's birth name instead of their chosen name. When gender-expansive people embark on their gender journey, they may select a name that better reflects their gender identity. In some cases, professionals may be required to obtain a client's legal name for paperwork and/or documentation, but use of the legal name should be held to a minimum if the client has not legally changed their name to their chosen name. For a broader discussion of documentation and paperwork, see Knutson and colleagues (2019).

In the vignette above, the professional working with Molly deadnamed her and it is likely that, as a result, Molly would terminate services and possibly even avoid seeking/securing other similar professional services. It was not necessary, in the case above, for the professional to have used a different name for Molly. When it is absolutely necessary for a professional (e.g., a law enforcement officer, insurance representative) to obtain a legal or birth name, we strongly encourage being clear and upfront about why an alternate name is needed and about how it will be used. A professional may say, "In order to look you up in our database so that we may provide you with excellent care, we have to have a name that shows up in legal records. I will only use your legal name to look up necessary information." Providing context can help to minimize distress experienced by the client.

Gender Identity and Your Environment

The missteps we talked about so far result from unexamined and unchallenged biases and assumptions. Our assumptions about gender are influenced by the people around us, our family, friends, coworkers, our local communities, churches, schools, media, and many other aspects of our environments. For example, a parent may have told you that boys are not supposed to play with dolls. A patient in the hospital may have told you that they didn't trust a male nurse. Julie often shares about an encounter with a family friend who saw Julie's four-year-old son running around with a purple sparkly fairy wand and said, in a disapproving tone, "Do you see what your son is doing?" The point is that gendered expectations are embedded in many interpersonal interactions, but they may go undetected when you are not looking for them or unless they are intense enough to stand out to you. The following sections will help you consider how you may have learned about your gender through interactions with people in your life.

Family and Friends

Take a moment to reflect on the first time you noticed your gender. Think about what it was like the first time you were called a boy or a girl. Recently, this gendering happens before birth. Ultrasound photos are shown around, and gender reveal parties proclaim, "It's a boy!" or "It's a girl!" Expecting parents are asked, "Do you know what the gender is?" Your guardian holds you in their arms and coos, "You're such a beautiful baby _____." Gender expectations are repeated so many times, they tend to fade into background noise. It is not until they are challenged that they make an impression on you.

Think about a time you expressed yourself in a way that violated the expectations of a family member or a friend. Maybe you were a girl who liked playing in the dirt or roughhousing with boys. Maybe you were a boy who cried "too much" or who liked to play dress-up. Consider how your family and friends responded to you. Think about how different you might have been had you been able to identify or express your gender differently, without those norms and expectations being put on you. You might have been more in touch with your emotions, or you might have been able to express yourself more freely.

As you reflect on gender expectations, try feeling empathy and compassion for the child who could have been. Think about the ways you tend to restrict the gender identities and expressions of others. Consider the damage you may cause to people who are simply being themselves and living their lives. At the end of this chapter, we will provide you with questions that will help you further reflect on your gender identity journey as part of a family.

Workplace

Reflect on your current vocation and on how you selected the job you now occupy. Think about ways your gender identity and/or expression may have limited or supported your success at your current job.

Gender messages at work can be subtle or explicit. For example, your workplace may only offer bathrooms for men and women. Consider how the assignment of different spaces affirms or limits the range of options you have.

Think about the dress code or dress expectations at your job. Consider what it would be like if you violated those expectations by wearing work clothes that are reserved for people of a gender different from yours. Reflect on how disrupting gender-based expectations at your job might limit your ability to be promoted or even retained as an employee.

Community

Now take a moment to reflect on your community. Maybe you love going to the local gym or maybe you have a spiritual community in which you are very involved. Consider what it would be like if you violated gender norms in one of your communal spaces. Think about how the expectations, codes, rules, and beliefs in those spaces impact your gender expression and your perspectives on gender.

Pause for a moment and consider whether you are aware of resources for gender-expansive people in your community. Imagine a friend asking you where to get support for gender-expansive concerns. Consider what it is like not to have to seek out safe spaces for you to express and identify your gender in a specific way. Engaging in this exercise (and in the others in this chapter) may help you to identify and confront your privilege.

Privilege

While the questions above may help us to become more aware of factors that influenced our gender identity from a young age, it's also important to understand the roles of other powerful forces in our gendered lives, especially those that advantage cisgender people at the expense of gender-expansive people. We call this type of advantage privilege. Broadly, privilege refers to ways in which members of one demographic group benefit from social advantages *just* because they are members of that group.

Privilege is maintained through powerful processes and systemic structures that uphold dominant ideas about how various groups fit into society. In the United States, White people, cisgender people, heterosexual people, people who identify as men, Christian people,

people whose bodies and/or minds are currently able to do tasks that life requires of them (i.e., nondisabled people and neurotypical people), people between the ages of 18 and 39, people born in the United States, and people who are middle class or upper middle class benefit from fitting into normalized social structures.

The same goes in many ways for cisgender people, and it's this reason that cis people need to be aware of privilege. There are laws, policies, stereotypes, and negative beliefs about trans and gender-expansive people that benefit cis people and disadvantage everyone else. In doing work with gender-expansive people, it's important for cisgender practitioners to be aware of political, health, and educational policies, laws, and experiences of sexual and interpersonal violence that disproportionately impact gender-expansive people.

There are numerous areas of privilege that cis providers hold that they may not think about without doing some intentional reflection. For cisgender providers who are reading this book, take a look at the following questions to see which you identify with. For trans and gender-expansive providers who identify along the binary, some of these statements may apply to you as well.

The Binary and Me Exercise

When you think about your gender identity, do you fit squarely into one of two boxes, male and female? Or does your gender fall outside of one of those boxes? Have you ever thought about what it would mean to not have a gender at all? Whenever we provide services to someone whose identity differs from our own, it is important to be able to empathize with their experience, even if it is not our own. Therefore, before working with gender-expansive clients, providers need to be able to (a) be aware of and understand their own gender identity and (b) empathize and understand with the gender identity of the people with whom they are working. For some folks, that will mean getting out of the binary—really starting to understand gender as a set of fluid ideas and behaviors that will not align with the ways in which many people understand what it means to be a man or woman. For other folks, it may mean needing to empathize with a more binary understanding of gender.

So, let's take a look at the binary. Imagine a wall—a very, very tall wall. On one side of the wall are male gender roles and on the other are female gender roles. Now, imagine the people on both sides. What do they look like? What are they doing? What are they wearing? Have an image in mind? Now think about yourself. To what extent do you fit on one side of the wall or the other?

Some people may find that they do not fit on one side of the wall or the other at all. They find the wall and its two sides to be much too inconsistent with how they understand themselves. That said, many people may find that they fit in on one side of the wall in many ways, but perhaps not in every way. On closer observation, even people who feel like they fit on one side of the wall or the other in many ways realize that there are things about their side of the wall that don't fit for them perfectly.

Now that you have the wall analogy in your head, imagine that there is no wall. Rather, imagine that people express their gender in any of thousands of ways, each expression of gender unique to their own self. When you imagine a world without a gender wall, in what ways would your life look the same as it does now? In what ways might it be different?

Let us also clarify: we are not saying that the wall is bad, or that people who are comfortable living on one side of the wall or the other are living inauthentically. For some people, the wall and its two sides are relatively comfortable! For those people, we support you! However, the two sides of the wall do not represent everyone. For those people who find the wall restrictive and oppressive, we support you!

Summary and Recommendations

- Exploring your own gender journey builds empathy and competence.
- When you make a mistake, apologize, correct yourself, and move on.
- Be thoughtful and intentional when asking for or using a client's legal or birth name.
- Practice challenging your biases and assumptions in your daily life (outside of the office).
- Build awareness of your privilege and how it impacts your behaviors.
- Reflect on the ways that your gender identity and expression were shaped.
- Remain aware of how your gender identity and expression are maintained even now.
- If you want more information, Dr. Anneliese Singh gives a great TED Talk: https://www.youtube.com/watch?v=-onhIoDRMdM.

Reflection Questions

1. When did you first know your gender identity?
2. What do you know about your gender, and how did you learn those things about yourself?
3. Think about your family and close friends.

   - Were there specific people who told you explicit messages about your gender?
   - Were there unspoken messages about gender in your family and/or friend group?
   - If you acted in a way that was outside of gender role expectations, how did people respond?

4. Think about your workplace.

   - How did gender considerations impact the vocation you chose/did not choose?
   - How do gender norms impact how you are treated at work?
   - How are gender messages communicated in your workplace?

5. Think about your community.

   - How are gender expectations communicated by your place of worship, gym, or community center?
   - Are you aware of spaces in your community that affirm gender-expansive people?
   - How would your community respond if you introduced a gender-expansive friend to your communal space?

6. What are your gender-related privileges and how do they benefit you?
7. How do your other identities (such as race, ethnicity, age, ability status, religion, and so on) interact with your gender identity?
8. If you are working with a gender-expansive client and find yourself getting frustrated:

   - What can you do to avoid causing harm (e.g., misgendering, deadnaming)?
   - How can you, as a provider, prevent this type of harm?

References and Suggested Readings

Ansara, Y. G., & Hegarty, P. (2014). Methodologies of misgendering: Recommendations for reducing cisgenderism in psychological research. *Feminism & Psychology, 24*(2), 259–270. https://doi.org/10.1177/0959353514526217

Hoffman-Fox, D. (2017). *You and your gender identity: A guide to discovery*. Skyhorse Publishing.

Knutson, D., Koch, J. M., & Goldbach, C. (2019). Recommended terminology, pronouns, and documentation for work with transgender and non-binary populations. *Practice Innovations, 4*(4), 214. https://doi.org/10.1037/pri0000098

Leikam, K. (2021). *Gender identity journal: Prompts and practices for exploration and self-discovery*. Rockridge Press.

McLemore, K. A. (2015). Experiences with misgendering: Identity misclassification of transgender spectrum individuals. *Self and Identity, 14*, 51–74. https://doi.org/10.1080/15298868.2014.950691

Sinclair-Palm, J. (2017). "It's Non-Existent": Haunting in trans youth narratives about naming. *Occasional Paper Series, 37*, 7.

Testa, R. J., Coolhart, D., & Peta, J. (2015). *The gender quest workbook: A guide for teens and young adults exploring gender identity*. Instant Help.

3

Gender Identity and the Intersectional Self

Kimberle Crenshaw (1989) is credited with first using the term *intersectionality* to describe the process by which Black women are subjected to judgment based on their multiple marginalized identities (their perceived race and gender). Crenshaw noted that Black women are treated (or more accurately, discriminated against) at different times and in different contexts as Black people, women, women who are Black, and as Black people who are women. Years later, intersectionality was expanded and applied to other populations with multiple marginalized identities. At present, the term is used in social work, psychology, and other disciplines to refer to the ways that multiple minority identities such as race, gender, sexual orientation, and others interact within contexts of privilege, power, marginalization, and oppression to create unique experiences for marginalized individuals. Crenshaw argues that intersectionality is more than a sum of a person's parts or identities; it yields unique interactions of experiences. In other words, a Black woman doesn't just experience racism as a Black person that is separate from her experiences of sexism as a woman. Rather she faces (at different times, to different degrees, and in different contexts) racist-sexism and sexist-racism as a Black woman.

In the context of this chapter, we discuss ways that a person's gender-expansive identity may interact with other minority identities in the context of therapy. Building on Crenshaw's (1989) work, we note that transgender women, for example, are often discriminated against as women, transgender people, transgender women, and as women who are transgender. When clients hold additional minority identities, such as racial minority status, it is easy to see how their experiences begin to take on even more complexity. When we add human service professionals, with all of their identities and positional power to the mix, the layers and interactions of identity become mind-bending. Though we realize that discussing all of the interaction patterns and identities that may exist in a therapy session is impossible and is far beyond the scope of this chapter, we frame the discussion as much as possible. We begin by exploring intersectional identities for Bill, Molly, and Rowan.

Bill

Bill is a White transgender man and a military veteran who sadly observed efforts to ban and limit transgender service members under the Trump presidency. Bill has mixed feelings about his involvement in the army. He is proud to have defended his country, but he had mixed experiences in the army. He began service under the Obama administration, but even then, he felt forced to hide his true gender identity in order to stay safe and to fit in. At present, he works and lives in communities that are skeptical of the government and who equate government employees as complicit with anti-transgender legislation and policies. In the military, Bill was pressed to hide his gender identity. Now, in his friend group, he feels he must play down his veteran status.

Molly

Molly is a lesbian mother and a Latina living in a rural area. At the national level, she is impacted by debates over the rights of LGBTQ+ parents and by anti-immigration rhetoric. She finds it depressing that leaders in the United States are working so hard to restrict her rights and to encourage violence against Latinx people. Because Molly is isolated from the LGBTQ+ community in her rural area, she tries to find community online, but she experiences a split between her trans woman and lesbian identities. Some feminists (trans-exclusionary radical feminists) express anger and hatred toward trans women. Molly lacks a place where she can just be herself. She often finds herself having to select which identity to share with which group of people. For example, in rural spaces like the grocery store, she deemphasizes her queer and Latinx identities. In lesbian spaces, she deemphasizes her identity as a transgender woman. Managing her many marginalized identities is exhausting for Molly.

Rowan

Rowan has mixed feelings about their multiple marginalized identities. They are proud to be part of the Black community during such a pivotal moment in history and they are an outspoken supporter of Black Lives Matter. They are proud to attend a historically Black church. They also want to be proud of their gender-expansive and pansexual identities, but their inability to come out leaves them feeling guilty and worried. They know that LGBTQ+ rights are expanding, and they want to be part of the LGBTQ+ community, but they feel held back from doing so. In classes, at church, and in other communal spaces, Rowan experiences disapproval, rejection, and dismissiveness when they advocate for gender inclusion. For them, many spaces feel dangerous and othering. As a result, they tend to silence themselves, to hold back their ideas, and to only celebrate their identities when they feel safe. The rub between pride and imposed shame makes it hard for them to pay attention, to concentrate, and to fully engage with others.

Client Intersectionality

Although approaches to intersectionality do not prioritize one identity over others, scholars generally focus on gender identity when they think about intersectionality with respect to gender-expansive clients. This is because, whatever other identities a gender-expansive person may possess, gender identity remains a part of the constellation of all the marginalized and privileged identities the person may hold. Of course, gender identity is a salient identity for any human, especially in societies that place a great deal of emphasis on gender, such as the United States.

Before we delve into different identities and experiences, we must establish that there is nothing inherently distressing or wrong with identifying as gender expansive. As indicated in the vignettes above, marginalized intersecting identities expose gender-expansive people to distress because marginalized identities are, put plainly, marginalized. Legislation, national policy, classroom climate, communal expectations, and so on, push gender-expansive people to justify their existence, to deemphasize identities that put them at risk, and to fear rejection or physical harm.

Gender-expansive people may identify with a variety of gender identities, and each identity may open doors to some communities while closing doors to others. Molly, for example, identifies as a transgender woman. She is accepted in groups of transgender women, but she is rejected in some groups of cisgender lesbian women. Take a moment to reflect on how Molly's experience would be different if she identified as nonbinary. It is possible that she would suddenly feel out of place in both communities. In short, the specific gender-expansive identity with which a client identifies impacts their experience on multiple levels and in a variety of spaces.

Privilege and Power

When we talk about gender-expansive identities in this chapter, we generally fall into the rut of discussing identity from the viewpoint of the majority culture (e.g., cisgender, heterosexual, White, nondisabled people's viewpoints). To even call a group of people marginalized is to recognize that a majority group exists. It is sad to admit that discrimination is so deeply imbedded in the way we talk, but it is important to recognize the limitations of language even when they cannot be avoided. As a reader of this text, we invite you to reflect on the ways that learning about marginalized people reinforces your power.

Race and Ethnicity

As demonstrated in the case vignettes at the beginning of the chapter, many common experiences or identities may interact with a person's gender minority status. For example, Rowan might not be able to openly express pride about their gender expansiveness at their historically Black church where their identity is considered, by some church goers, to be "not a real thing" or even sinful. Their religious identity and connection to Christianity, however, might not be accepted by some of their LGBTQ+ friends.

Historically, transgender and queer women of color have been at the forefront as outspoken advocates of lesbian, gay, bisexual, and transgender rights (Jackson, 2021; Shepard, 2013), but LGBTQ+ people of color have been under-researched and White gay cisgender men have often been centered in research and advocacy efforts (e.g., Johnson, 2014). LGBTQ+ activists often refer to the "White gay man focus of research," and the problematic assumption that White cis gay men's experiences apply to anyone else who identifies as LGBTQ+. This assumption erases and invalidates the experiences of other LGBTQ+ individuals who also hold other marginalized identities, such as being LGBTQ+ and a racial and/or ethnic minority.

Assuming that White cisgender gay men's experiences are equivalent to the experiences of gender-expansive people and LGBTQ+ people of color ignores the disproportionately high rates of homelessness, violence, unemployment, HIV, and other issues experienced by gender-expansive people, especially gender-expansive people of color (James et al., 2016). Individuals who hold multiple marginalized identities have experiences that are categorically, qualitatively, and quantitatively different from individuals who hold few marginalized identities with many privileged identities. We should note that scholars are working hard to conduct more research with racial minority individuals in the LGBTQ+ community, but it will take time before the results of these studies become widely available.

Sexual Orientation

Gender-expansive people, and more specifically gender-expansive people of color, are not only marginalized in research and in broader society, but they have been historically marginalized in cisgender LGBQ+ communities as well. Even though gender-expansive people may identify as lesbian, gay, bisexual, queer, asexual, and/or one of many other sexual minority identities, they may not be accepted by their cisgender counterparts. In LGBTQ+ spaces, as in other communities, gender-expansive people may be marginalized based on the identity that is viewed as most salient, their gender-expansive experience.

Disability Status

It is estimated that at least 61 million adults in the United States alone live with a disability (CDC, 2020). Unfortunately, people with disabilities are under-researched and they experience significantly greater inequities across numerous domains (e.g., employment, health-care access) compared to nondisabled individuals. For gender-expansive people with disabilities, the inequities experienced are even greater. Unfortunately, advocacy and research tend to focus on cisgender individuals when addressing disability and nondisabled individuals when addressing advocacy for gender-expansive people (Mulcahy et al., 2022).

Gender-expansive people with disabilities may be more likely to experience developmental disabilities and have unmet health-care needs compared to cisgender individuals with disabilities. Although research suggests that rates of autism and other experiences of neurodivergence are higher for gender-expansive people compared to cisgender people, gender identity development and concerns are generally overlooked or ignored for gender-expansive people who also live with disabilities. It is therefore crucial for providers to consider intersections of gender identity and disability status when working with gender-expansive people to avoid the common pitfall of over-looking or dismissing the role disability may play in their experiences.

Socioeconomic Status

Social class or socioeconomic status is often overlooked in intersectional considerations of identity, but it is critical to consider because many gender-expansive people experience significant socioeconomic inequities. Gender-expansive people are significantly more likely to experience underemployment or unemployment, lower levels of education, higher poverty rates, and lower household incomes compared to cisgender people in the general United States population (Carpenter et al., 2020). It is estimated that almost one-third of gender-expansive people in the United States live in poverty, and the poverty rates are even higher for gender-expansive people of color (James et al., 2016). Furthermore, the socioeconomic issues faced by many gender-expansive people often create significant barriers to accessing social and medical transition needs (e.g., gender-affirming surgeries, hormone therapy).

One side effect of focusing so acutely on gender-expansive identities as a society is that people tend to forget that gender-expansive people are mundane human beings, just like them. As with any other human, gender-expansive people have different abilities, levels of resources, sexual orientations, races, ethnicities, and so on. We encourage you to keep this diversity and multidimensionality in mind as you begin to think about your own identities.

Human Service Professional Intersectionality

The majority of professionals are from dominant cultures (e.g., White, nondisabled, heterosexual, cisgender), but many professionals still possess both visible and invisible minority identities (e.g., physical disabilities, racial minority status, sexual minority status, etc.). If you identify as a minority in any way, you have likely experienced discrimination based on the marginalized identities you possess. Throughout our discussion of intersectionality, you may have been thinking, "Yep, that makes sense." You may identify as transgender or gender expansive, and may already be thinking about how the intersectional dynamics we discussed for clients apply to you.

The thing about intersectionality is that identities are not always cut and dried. Not only do individual identities interact in unique ways, but individual identities may be expressed, integrated, and accepted or rejected in a variety of ways. Over the years, scholars have studied the topic of identity integration and have created a number of models of White identity development, Black identity development, LGB identity development, and so on. In general, scholars suggest that a person's relationship with their identity (or constellation of identities) changes and develops over time. At various points in time, a person may accept themselves and their fellow community members, reject their community, and/or reject various aspects of themselves. This is true of professionals, and the degree to which a given professional has reconciled their identities shows up in therapy.

Gender Identity

One dimension of a professional's identity that may be integrated and accepted to a greater or lesser degree is the professional's gender identity. As professionals begin to work with more gender-expansive clients, or even as professionals reflect on their own gender and the genders of others, they may realize that gender is very nuanced and variable. Exploring one's gender, race, sexual orientation, or other identity can generate anxiety and discomfort at first, but exploring identities is important work. Unchecked biases about identities show up in our work, sometimes in insidious ways.

Even when you think you have "checked" your biases, they will likely emerge. Julie recalls a time when she heard a song on the radio and said out loud, "I like this song but can't tell if the singer is male or female." Her teenage daughter gave her a stern look and said, "Why do you have to gender them?" It was a good reminder that even those of us who spend time exploring gender, thinking about gender, and working with gender-expansive people have been socialized with gender norms that are hard to combat. Doing the work to fully explore and embrace the professional's own identity allows a professional to engage in appropriate exploration and acceptance of the identities of others. This is true of both marginalized and privileged identities. Unexplored privileged identities can be terribly toxic in the therapy space.

Exploring Intersectional Gender Identity

Take a moment to think about some of your most salient identities. Consider making a list of identities that come to mind in order of their importance to you. Is it most important for you to identify as a

Christian? Is your racial identity the one you have thought about most lately? Thinking about individual identities can yield important insights.

Next, consider the ways in which some of your identities (e.g., race, socioeconomic status, ability, religion, education level, nation of origin, sexual orientation, etc.) interact. For example, what is it like for you to be a heterosexual White person, if you identify as such? How do both the sexual orientation and gender identity you hold change the ways that people react to you? What identities do you lead with and which ones do you deemphasize or even conceal?

From our perspective, your gender identity develops in its own way, but not on its own. How you understand your gender is influenced by other facets of yourself. In an effort to help you think through this process, we provide a sample biographical sketch about Tim. As you read it, please reflect on how your own experiences may be similar or different. Then consider writing your own biographical, intersectional paragraph.

> I, Tim, am a White, cisgender, gay man. The way that I understand being cisgender is influenced, and even shaped in part, by being gay. There are some very concrete ways in which this shows up for me. I was never particularly interested in lots of the activates that young boys engage in. Sports were something that I was required to do by my parents and school, but they always felt like a chore. I was not particularly artistically talented either. Although I would not have been able to verbalize this as a child (because I did not know the words gay or homosexual), by the age of 10 I was quite aware that I was not fulfilling some of the gender roles that were expected of me. As I began to become aware of being gay (around age 12), I also became terrified that other people would see my clumsiness in sports and tendency to hang out with only girls as evidence that I was gay. The intersection of my gender identity and sexual orientation led to me being quite an anxious and depressed child!
>
> My gender identity was also shaped in part by my religion. Growing up in a Conservative, Fundamentalist Christian home, I recognized that gender roles were important. There were things that men just did and did not do. I began to understand myself as a gendered person partially based on things my parents would say about "effeminate men" and stories my grandfather would tell about beating up "sissies."

Connecting with Others

In its strictest interpretation, intersectionality applies to multiple minority status. At the risk of overextending the concept, we suggest that professionals may benefit from understanding how privilege, the compound experience of multiple majority identities, impacts their work with gender-expansive clients as well. Privileged identities may cause professionals to overlook or to be unaware of client struggles and issues. It can be hard to empathize or connect across gaps of shared experience if a professional has a hard time connecting with what it is like to be disempowered or restricted by a critical society.

Furthermore, we recommend that professionals explore ways that all of their identities are experienced by clients, both minority and majority identities. In therapy spaces, all of a professional's visible and invisible identities may be salient at different times when working with diverse clients. Professionals may also need to make decisions about when to disclose their identities, especially when those identities are not visible or readily available to the client. This can be a sticky issue, especially if professionals disclose identities out of an often well-intentioned desire to connect with clients.

For example, disclosing one's sexual orientation in an effort to connect with a transgender or nonbinary client may be done in good faith, but may do more to marginalize the client than to reassure them. Suggesting that sexual minority individuals understand and embrace gender diversity is historically unsupported, and implying that sexual orientation is similar to gender identity in some way is inaccurate. Professionals should explore their own identities and should be clear about who they are, but should be selective and thoughtful about disclosing this information.

Client-Professional Interactions

Again, it is important to discuss ways that identities interact, not only within the person, but also between people. In particular, it is important for professionals to be aware of the ways that their privileged identities (or minority identities) may interact with their clients' privileged or minority identities. This will allow professionals to begin to better navigate these points of disconnect in the therapy room and will enable professionals to address and affirm client concerns as effectively as possible.

Therapy spaces that mimic "the outside world" or are microcosms of the discriminatory world that gender-expansive clients face daily will not be effective and are unlikely to be places where gender-expansive clients are able to heal. Aside from engaging directly in conversations about differences and similarities between professional and client and about unique interpersonal dynamics that exist in the therapy room, professionals who are aware of intersectionality are able to observe and identify when various identities are salient and/or when a disconnect exists between the professional and their client because of a disconnect between identities.

Points of Interaction

In this section, we discuss some areas in which identity interactions may occur between professionals and clients. This list is by no means exhaustive, but it may help professionals to begin to raise their awareness around therapy dynamics with gender-expansive clients.

Socioeconomic Status

A significant difference may exist between client and professional socioeconomic status and access to resources. Professionals may often have the benefit of a reliable and adequate income, typically in spaces that are safe and affirming of minority identities. According to national surveys, this sort of job security and stability is generally not experienced by the majority of gender-expansive individuals in the United States. On the contrary, gender-expansive people generally report being discriminated against at work, losing their jobs because of their identities, and/or experiencing difficulty finding a job in the first place.

Given the vocational issues and difficulty maintaining an income that clients may experience, professionals should raise their own awareness of the many privileges they may enjoy because of their income and should avoid projecting their own financial stability on clients. Activities such as driving to work, seeing a movie on the weekend, or sleeping in a comfortably air-conditioned home may be luxuries that are not available to some gender-expansive clients. When professionals attempt to make conversation by asking a client if they saw a popular movie or if they went out to eat at a popular restaurant, they may be inadvertently marginalizing their client. The financial cost of transition is very high, and for clients saving up for transition services, many relatively mundane recreational activities may be out of reach.

Sexual Orientation

Professionals need to be aware of the historical treatment of gender-expansive people by lesbian, gay, and bisexual (LGB) communities that we highlighted earlier in this chapter. Even though transgender individuals are included as the "T" in the abbreviation LGBTQ+, transgender people have been left behind and even marginalized by cisgender gay men and others. Thus, LGB people are not automatically perceived as safe for gender-expansive clients. If a professional discloses their sexual orientation in an effort to connect with a client, depending on the setting and context, they may do more to distance themself from the client and/or to raise concerns in the client. As we discuss elsewhere in this book, sexual orientation is very different from gender identity. Although gender-expansive clients may identify as sexual minority members, their identities may be far more complex than the oversimplified categories lesbian, gay, and bisexual.

Furthermore, professionals may benefit from exploring all of the different sexual orientations that individuals currently identify with. For example, individuals may identify as queer, questioning, demisexual, aromantic, asexual, pansexual, and so on. Even when a client identifies as a sexual minority, they may not feel safe in the larger LGBTQ+ community. Sexual orientation, just like gender identity, should be approached with humility and openness.

Race

We discussed, in earlier sections of this chapter, the lack of focus that has been placed on racial minority LGBTQ+ people. Although transgender women of color are credited with starting and maintaining the early movement for LGBTQ+ rights, gender-expansive people of color are often overlooked in research, scholarship, political movements, and media. Gender-expansive women of color are subjected to some of the highest rates of violence, and the number of gender-expansive women of color killed every year is staggering.

Historically and even currently, psychology and mental health professions have not been kind to people of color. More often than not, mental health services may be viewed as an extension of White culture that attempts to marginalize and pathologize the lives of minority communities. To be sure, some diagnoses, such as attention deficit hyperactivity disorder (ADHD) are more often rendered to men of color. In the US South, more children of color are diagnosed with learning disorders than White children are. The Minnesota Multiphasic Personality Inventory (MMPI) personality scale includes a measure of "paranoia," which psychologists may see as a pathology, but may in fact be a protective and healthy response for some people of color. A great deal has been written about the cultural bias in mental health.

Given the historical marginalization of both gender-expansive people and people of color, clients who identify as gender-expansive people of color may mistrust White, cisgender professionals. This lack of trust is well founded and may be difficult to navigate in therapy. However, if a strong bond can be formed, working across racial or ethnic differences can provide healing for gender-expansive people of color.

Social Support

Professionals may enjoy a great deal more social support than their clients. Gender-expansive people may be kicked out of their homes by their families and may lose their partners when and if they come out. Some gender-expansive clients may decide to "stay in the closet" or may choose not to disclose their identities for fear that they will lose significant others. Professionals may not assume that their clients are as supported as professionals are. At present, mental health therapy is a prestigious job and professionals may hold a great deal of power both inside and outside of their vocation. Professionals should be aware of this power and security, especially as it impacts gender-expansive clients.

When professionals enter the therapy room assuming that clients will want to connect with them or that clients will automatically feel safe with them, they may be ignorant of the risks involved in bonding with others. For people who have been cast out of their homes and who have lost family members for simply disclosing who they are, trusting another person can be hard. Professionals should be aware that building a therapeutic alliance can be a slow process with gender-expansive clients. When this bond is created, it is special and valuable. Professionals should do everything they can to be clear, direct, and open with clients in an effort to avoid betrayal or abandonment dynamics with gender-expansive clients.

Age

When it comes to terminology, gender theory, and identities, age can play a disproportionate role in the ways that professionals and clients think and feel. For example, some members of older generations of LGBTQ+ people have a strong reaction to the word "queer" because the term was used to hurt, marginalize, and shame them.

Younger professionals who are in touch with the most recent language and labels in the LGBTQ+ community may assume that such terms are acceptable for use with all clients. This is not the case, and using some terminology with clients of different ages may be off-putting for various clients.

However, some professionals may be unaware of current terminology and may use inappropriate terms like "transsexual." Though some individuals may identify as transsexual, others may be deeply offended by the use of this term.

Aside from language usage, age may impact the point at which some gender-expansive people were able to access transition services (e.g., hormone therapy, gender-affirming surgeries, etc.). Older generations of gender-expansive people may express frustration about or even resentment for younger generations of gender-expansive people who may be more supported and able to access transition services earlier in life. As you can see, age and generational affiliation can impact a multitude of interactions in therapy. Thus, professionals will benefit from awareness of the many unique ways that age impacts work with gender-expansive clients.

Summary and Recommendations

- Gender-expansive clients may hold a variety of marginalized experiences and identities.
- Focusing on individual identities misses the complexity of a person's experience.
- A client's gender identity is only part of their story, even when they are receiving treatment for gender-identity-related concerns.
- It is important to have identified and explored your own privileged and marginalized identities.
- Exploring your marginalized identities can build empathy and understanding.
- Professionals who maintain awareness of their privilege are able to provide more affirming services.

Reflection Questions

1. What is your most salient privileged identity and how does that identity shape your interpersonal interactions daily?
2. What privileges and advantages have contributed to success in your career?

3. How has privilege cultivated biases and unreasonable expectations in your work?
4. What is your most marginalized identity and how does that identity shape your interpersonal interactions daily?
5. How have you learned to deal with disadvantages in life?
6. How have marginalized identities or disadvantages cultivated biases or unreasonable expectations in your work?
7. What is your plan to incorporate intersectional awareness into your work regularly?

References and Suggested Readings

Budge, S. L., Thai, J. L., Tebbe, E. A., & Howard, K. A. (2016). The intersection of race, sexual orientation, socioeconomic status, trans identity, and mental health outcomes. *The Counseling Psychologist, 44*(7), 1025–1049.

Carpenter, C. S., Eppink, S. T., & Gonzales, G. (2020). Transgender status, gender identity, and socioeconomic outcomes in the United States. *ILR Review, 73*(3), 573–599.

Centers for Disease Control and Prevention. (2020). *Disability impacts all of us.* https://www.cdc.gov/ncbddd/disabilityandhealth/infographic-disability-impacts-all.html

Crenshaw, K. W. (1989). Demarginalizing the intersection of race and sex: A Black feminist critique of antidiscrimination doctrine, feminist theory, and antiracist politics. *University of Chicago Legal Forum, 1989*(1), 139–167.

de Vries, K. M. (2015). Transgender people of color at the center: Conceptualizing a new intersectional model. *Ethnicities, 15*(1), 3–27.

Jackson, J. M. (2021). Black feminisms, queer feminisms, trans feminisms: Meditating on Pauli Murray, Shirley Chisholm, and Marsha P. Johnson against the erasure of history. In J. Hobson (Ed.), *The Routledge companion to black women's cultural histories* (pp. 284–294). Routledge.

James, S. E., Herman, J. L., Rankin, S., Keisling, M., Mottet, L., & Anafi, M. (2016). *The report of the 2015 U.S. Transgender Survey.* National Center for Transgender Equality.

Johnson, M. (2014). The It Gets Better Project: A study in (and of) Whiteness—In LGBT youth and media cultures. In C. Pullen (Ed.), *Queer youth and media cultures* (pp. 278–291). Palgrave Macmillan.

Mulcahy, A., Streed, C. G., Jr., Wallisch, A. M., Batza, K., Kurth, N., Hall, J. P., McMaughan, D. J. (2022). Gender identity, disability, and unmet healthcare needs among disabled people living in the community in the United States. *International Journal of Environmental Research and Public Health, 19*, 2588. https://doi.org/10.3390/ijerph19052588

Shepard, B. (2013). From community organization to direct services: The Street Trans Action Revolutionaries to Sylvia Rivera Law Project. *Journal of Social Service Research, 39*(1), 95–114. https://doi.org/10.1080/01488376.2012.727669

Wesp, L. M., Malcoe, L. H., Elliott, A., & Poteat, T. (2019). Intersectionality research for transgender health justice: A theory-driven conceptual framework for structural analysis of transgender health inequities. *Transgender Health, 4*(1), 287–296. https://doi.org/10.1089/trgh.2019.0039

4

Gender Identity and Lifespan Development

There has been much in the news about transgender youth and their ability to access health care and transition, if medical transition is something they need/want. During each legislative session in states across the United States, legislators debate restrictions that impact gender-expansive people across the lifespan. Older people who identify as gender expansive may be faced with navigating how to tell their children and spouses about their identities, and whether their families will be open to calling them "Mom" when for 30+ years they have been called "Dad."

Both gender-expansive and cisgender people go through a process of discovering and hopefully accepting and ultimately affirming their gender identity. Unfortunately, this process can be more complex for gender-expansive people. Cisgender people are usually able to take their gender identity for granted, and, due to cisgender privilege, they are likely to have their gender identity recognized and affirmed from a young age. However, gender-expansive people have to decide whether to come out and how to navigate changes in relationships throughout their lives.

In this chapter, we provide readers with a context for understanding gender identity across the lifespan in order to provide tools that will help readers with combating assumptions and creating spaces that are safe for gender-expansive people of all ages. We will discuss unique concerns that may arise for gender-expansive individuals from early childhood through late adulthood, depending on when in life they come out as gender expansive. We will also discuss educational and vocational development for gender-expansive individuals. We begin by examining a few possible developmental pathways as they show up in the cases of Bill, Molly, and Rowan. It is important to note that what we present here does not capture all experiences.

Bill

Bill knew at about age three that something was different about him. He tended toward a gender expression that was not acceptable for little girls his age. For example, he was intensely physical in sports activities and wanted to play soccer and baseball with boys' rather than girls' teams, and he asked his parents if he could join Boy Scouts. One day at dinner, his mom asked him, "Why won't you just wear a dress like a good little girl?" Bill replied, without thinking, "Because I am a boy." His mother left the table in tears, but she later told him that she just wanted him to be happy, healthy, and safe. Bill's mother bought him toy trucks and allowed him to dress however he wanted. Bill's father did not entirely approve, but he did not intervene. Later in life, after leaving the army and entering college, Bill began socially transitioning. It was not easy for his parents, but they worked hard to use he/him pronouns and to refer to Bill as their son.

Molly

Molly did not realize until she was almost 30 years old that she was a woman. She always knew that her body felt wrong, and she had dreams of being a woman, but she suppressed what she called her "feminine side" in an effort to fit into her family and into her local community. Over her lifetime, she became more and more unhappy, eventually feeling as if she were living the life of an imposter. One day, she was watching the evening news. The news anchor panned to an interview with a transgender woman who was talking about her coming-out process. Suddenly, it clicked for Molly. She realized, "I am a woman." The realization washed over her and, for the first time in her life, she just felt right. It took her another five years to come out to her family and friends because she knew they would probably reject her. To her surprise, Molly's wife and daughter expressed love and understanding. They continue to support Molly even though they both live in different states now.

Rowan

Rowan came out to their parents a couple of times. When they were 12 years old, they sat their parents down and informed their parents that they were a transgender woman who was attracted to women.

Rowan's parents became frightened and frustrated and they placed Rowan in therapy with a Christian counselor with the hope that therapy would "fix" Rowan. After a year, Rowan refused to go back to therapy. They said that they had formed a community online and that they had discovered that it was possible to identify as gender fluid and pansexual. They expressed that those identities fit for them, and they announced that they were changing their name to Rowan. Rowan's parents agreed to call them Rowan at home if Rowan would promise not to come out at church or to the rest of the family. Rowan agreed not to disclose their identity to others. They began to rely heavily on their online community for emotional and social support.

Early Awareness

Many children are aware of their gender identity from a very young age, often as young as three or four years old (Adelson, 2012; Kohlberg, 1966), but there is some variability in the age at which that identity is crystalized. Early gender awareness is common among both cisgender and gender-expansive children. We also know that kids make important decisions about their lives based, in part, on how they understand their gender. For lots of children, gender influences both daily choices (like what clothes to wear) and more long-range decisions (such as what type of job they want when they grow up).

As reflected in some of the vignettes above, gender-expansive people have described knowing from a young age that they "were different" or that identifying as a boy or girl just "didn't quite fit." We have heard some people share that for many years they worried something was "wrong with them" because they wanted, for example, to wear women's clothing or makeup. Many of these same clients did not feel safe expressing their feelings to their families of origin and other people in their lives so they postponed transitioning until early, middle, or late adulthood. Some gender-expansive clients say that they did not have or know the words to describe themselves and, because of that, they were not able to fully realize and embrace their gender-expansive identity until later in life.

Gender Assumptions

In Western countries in particular, people are generally programmed to assume that sex and gender are aligned from the moment a person is born. When an ultrasound reveals that a fetus has a penis, we proclaim, "It's a boy!" We further reinforce assumptions with gender reveal parties and we buy blue baby clothes for baby showers. In other words, a child with a penis must be a boy and a child with a vagina must be a girl. If a child is born with ambiguous genitals, they are usually assigned female and their genitals are surgically altered. When genital surgery is performed on intersex persons, they are generally too young to consent to the process. Some medical professionals may claim that such surgeries are intended to reduce psychological damage by helping them conform to cisgender and heterosexual norms, but there is no evidence to support this claim (InterACT & Human Rights Watch, 2017).

Because of the culture we have built up around gender and sex, we typically will not challenge our assumptions unless someone directly invites us to do so. Take a moment to consider how you would respond if a friend refused to tell you the assigned gender of their child and instead said, "We are waiting for Slate to tell us their gender." Think about how you would make decisions about what clothes to buy. Reflect on what you would think of your friend for approaching their child's gender in this way. It is possible that, without any direction from your friend, you would take a hard look at the baby in an effort to figure out what gender to assign them.

Unfortunately, it is often not safe for gender-expansive children and adults to tell the people around them that their assigned sex and the gender that they were assumed to identify with by default are wrong. They may feel unable to express their true identities and to reshape the environments they grow up and live in. Strict expectations surrounding gender can be very stifling and harmful to anyone who has a gender identity or gender expression that does not conform to those expectations, regardless of whether they identity as cisgender or gender expansive.

Childhood and Adolescence

Childhood

We will only briefly cover them here, but a variety of models have been put forth to conceptualize how children develop their gender identity and how they learn which behaviors are labeled "appropriate" or "inappropriate" depending on how the world around them perceives their gender. Children may be reinforced or punished for certain behaviors based on their perceived gender (Perry et al., 2019). The cultural context in which a child grows up can also influence the beliefs and values that they have about gender (Ridgeway & Kricheli-Katz, 2013). As with most things, we know that gender identity results from a combination of biology and socialization.

Around the ages of three to four, a child who is gender expansive may start noticing that the way the world perceives their gender doesn't match the gender with which they identify. Depending on how supportive a gender-expansive child perceives their environment to be, they may or may not feel safe expressing this mismatch. Providing a safe environment where any child, and especially a gender-expansive child, can be their authentic self is extremely important for helping them accept and affirm their identity from a young age.

In this book, we often refer to a client's gender journey. That is because gender discovery and identification is a process. Some children may strongly identify with a certain gender identity early on, whereas others may possess a gender identity that is more fluid. Rowan's case vignette is an example of the way a child or adult may reevaluate and change the pronouns and terminology that they use to describe themselves at various points throughout their life (Knutson et al., 2019). This most likely will not be the case for many of the gender-expansive clients that you will work with, but it is important to provide a space (as appropriate given the professional services you are providing) that allows for clients to explore and try on new identities, names, pronouns, and terminology to describe themselves.

It is extremely important for a gender-expansive child to have access to the language that they need to describe themselves, access that will often be influenced by whether they live in a supportive environment. We find that, if a child is able to describe themselves as gender expansive and in the process find out that there are other people like them in the world, they are more likely to accept their gender identity and express it to those around them.

Adolescence

When a child or teenager comes out as gender expansive, the people around them such as family members, friends, teachers, or care providers may not believe them, may not want to believe them, or may dismiss their disclosure as "a phase." Responses from people in a gender-expansive person's life may be influenced by a variety of things, including a fear of the unknown or a fear that the gender-expansive person will "have a hard life." This can put pressure on gender-expansive children or adolescents to "prove" that their gender is authentic (Afrasiabi & Junbakhsh, 2019), something that cisgender individuals do not have to do because of cisgender privilege. In extreme cases, children may be forced into therapy that is supposed to change their gender identity. Identity change therapy (also known as conversion therapy or reparative therapy) is damaging, unsuccessful, and banned by many professional organizations (e.g., Ashley, 2020).

Gender-expansive adolescents generally live with and rely on their biological families for support and basic necessities. The dependence of adolescence places gender-expansive youth in a uniquely vulnerable situation when coming out compared to older age groups. Gender-expansive adolescents who come out to their family may be forced out of their homes if their family is not supportive. Rejection at such a young age could lead to fear of opening up to others, internalization of negative beliefs, and increased suicide risk.

Rejection from one's family of origin also puts gender-expansive youth at a disproportionately high risk for becoming homeless, compared to cisgender youth (Tierney & Ward, 2017). Because of this very real fear of becoming homeless, gender-expansive adolescents may not come out until after moving away from their parents' home. A gender-expansive adolescent who does not come out may be able to remain at home, but this will most likely be at the cost of increased distress because they will continue to be forced to live and express themselves in ways that are not aligned with their gender identity.

Puberty

Puberty brings many bodily changes that are somewhat irreversible or only partially reversible, such as development of primary and secondary sex characteristics. For a gender-expansive adolescent, undergoing a puberty aligned with their sex assigned at birth and not their gender identity can be very distressing. You might be able to imagine the distress and discomfort experienced, for example, by a young trans teen who identifies as male but who begins to menstruate. Family members and medical providers may support social transition steps (for example changing clothing, pronouns, or name), but because of the irreversible or only partially reversible aspects of many medical transition steps, families and physicians may be hesitant to support medical interventions (e.g., hormonal therapy, gender-affirming surgeries).

One safe way to reduce the likelihood of extreme distress and to ease concerns about providing irreversible medical interventions at a young age is to place a child on puberty blockers. It is crucial for parents, health professionals, and other practitioners to have these conversations early because puberty blockers are typically prescribed during Tanner developmental stages 2 and 3, meaning that blockers might be needed as early as age 11 or 12 to be most effective (Hembree et al., 2017). Puberty blockers are designed to put puberty-induced physical changes on pause. In the meantime, a gender-expansive teen can continue to socially transition and then, at a later date, be given the appropriate hormone therapy to affirm their gender.

The effects of puberty blockers are reversible because puberty will only be delayed and will continue with or without hormone therapy once the blockers are removed. Some adverse effects may be experienced while on puberty blockers (e.g., delayed or decreased height), but these are far overshadowed by the life-saving psychological benefits of preventing an unwanted puberty for a gender-expansive adolescent (Rew et al., 2021). The use of puberty blockers and other transition-related health care has become politicized recently, with some state legislators introducing legislation to deny health care to youth under 18 who identify as gender expansive.

It is important to know that early access to gender-affirming hormone therapy may result in infertility (Nahata et al., 2019). Because children may desire interventions to preserve their ability to have biological children later, counseling regarding available fertility preservation options should be provided (Nahata et al., 2017). A full overview of endocrinological considerations and treatments is beyond the scope of this book. We recommend consulting the Endocrine Society's Standards (Hembree et al., 2017) and WPATH *Standards of Care* (World Professional Association for Transgender Health [WPATH], 2011) for more information.

School

Identifying as gender expansive while in elementary, middle, or high school brings additional complexities and stressors. Many research findings indicate that K–12 school environments can be toxic for gender-expansive people and that youth typically report experiencing higher rates of victimization and bullying compared to their cisgender peers (Day et al., 2018; Kosciw et al., 2018; McGuire et al., 2010). Scholars have even found gender-expansive students typically experience higher victimization in schools that have less inclusive sex education efforts because this can create an environment where gender-expansive students are not recognized or respected (Proulx et al., 2019). Recently there has also been much discussion about all-gender restrooms and locker rooms in schools, and the ability of trans youth to participate in school athletics, with some states introducing legislation to limit access for trans youth. It's no surprise that an unaccepting school environment can increase the likelihood of distress and poor academic performance for a gender-expansive adolescent.

Early Adulthood

In early adulthood (ages in the 20s and 30s), people balance a variety of needs, goals, and desires. These may include trying to start a career, becoming established in a career, starting a family, or continuing school in higher education. A gender-expansive person may face unique challenges in these areas, regardless of whether they have transitioned personally, socially, and/or medically. For example, a transgender woman who has transitioned to living her life as a woman may encounter higher rates of violence and discrimination and may be at higher risk for unemployment. Experiences of exclusion, aggression, and discrimination can lead to depression, anxiety, or other mental health concerns and can also contribute to being increasingly more disconnected from the surrounding world.

Work

A gender-expansive person may choose or feel the need to come out at work. In the United States, people spend the majority or a large portion of their time working. Therefore, being open about gender identity at work is important for many gender-expansive people. For someone who is gender-expansive, this can be a complex and potentially distressing process, especially if they have been working for an employer for a long time before coming out. Federal workplace protections were granted for gender-expansive people in *Bostock v. Clayton County, Georgia* on June 15, 2020, but most states do not provide workplace protections based on gender identity. Therefore, a safe working environment is not guaranteed for gender-expansive people. Employers can still fire gender-expansive people based on gender identity and then claim they did so for other reasons.

Even if a gender-expansive person finds themselves in a supportive work environment, few places of employment have policies in place to guide managers and colleagues as they support gender-expansive employees through the transition process at work. A gender-expansive person may face a number of barriers to coming out at work as they navigate possible changes that might be visibly apparent, such as changes in clothing, appearance, pronouns, or name. For example, a person working at a supermarket may have to work with their company to have their name changed on their nametag. The company may have to decide if a legal name change is required before a nametag can be changed. Such decisions depend largely on the workplace and environment.

The lack of workplace protections and the high rates of workplace discrimination and unemployment that gender-expansive people experience can make coming out at work risky for a gender-expansive person. Coming out at work may involve a long, meticulous planning process. Other jobs may be sought out, or coming out at work may be delayed indefinitely. For example, one gender-expansive client privately came out to trusted coworkers over the course of nearly a year and drafted a carefully thought-out letter for upper management to explain their plans for gender transition before coming out to the company as whole. The process of coming out as gender expansive at work, just as coming out in other contexts, must often be a carefully crafted and well-thought-out process because of a justified fear of rejection and even of unemployment.

Middle to Late Adulthood

When thinking about gender-expansive issues, an emphasis is generally placed on the concerns and struggles of adolescents and young adults. Researchers and scholars tend to focus on concerns such as coming out to parents, coming out at school, puberty, hormone therapy, and coming out at work. People who transition later in adulthood may face similar concerns, but other factors may be more prominent or salient for someone who transitions in their 40s, 50s, 60s, 70s, or even later in life.

Clients who wait to come out until they are older may be forced to challenge entrenched ideas about their gender identity. They may have to come out to children, partners, and/or lifelong friends. Loved ones may express feeling betrayed by the client or may tearfully suggest that they never really knew the gender-expansive person. In addition to the losses and deaths that older adults experience, gender-expansive people may face other losses and painful separations.

Clients who delay coming out and/or transition may also experience a delayed or renewed adolescence. When a person finally feels congruent and seen, they may experience an exhilarating sense of liberation and excitement. Those positive feelings may lead to risky behaviors or uncharacteristic immaturity. Gender-affirming hormones may also contribute to new feelings of emotional lability and altered emotions. Transition, regardless of when it happens during a person's life, can lead to remarkable changes and unfamiliar experiences.

Gender-expansive people may also transition early in life, navigate the process of working and forming families, and may later retire. Older gender-expansive adults are grandmothers, grandfathers, grandparents, and happily single members of older adult communities. After living fulfilling lives in their affirmed genders, they may pass away peaceful and fulfilled. Lifespan development may pose a variety of challenges for gender-expansive people, but the journey can be deeply rewarding.

Summary and Recommendations

- Children generally start developing an awareness of their gender identity by the ages of three or four.
- Gender-expansive people will often go through a long and complex process of finding and affirming their gender identity.
- Gender discovery is unique to each individual and is influenced by sociocultural messages and expectations surrounding gender.
- Congruence between mind and body is critical for many gender-expansive people.
- Puberty blockers may be needed as early as age 11 or 12 to prevent a gender-expansive adolescent from experiencing a puberty that is not aligned with their gender identity.
- Gender-expansive people face unique and complex challenges in relation to school, the workplace, relationships, and starting or maintaining a family.
- It is especially important to consider the unique stressors that a gender-expansive client may be facing when figuring out their gender transition due to their age and stage in life.

Reflection Questions

1. When did you first learn about gender?
2. When did you first figure out what your gender is?
3. What sorts of messages did you hear from others about your gender?
4. How have your gender identity and/or expression changed over time?
5. What is your reaction to gender-affirming treatment for gender-expansive children?
6. At what age do you think a person is able to make decisions about gender-related care?
7. What is your role in preventing distress, discrimination, and violence against gender-expansive people?

References and Suggested Readings

Adelson, S. L. (2012). Practice parameter on gay, lesbian, or bisexual sexual orientation, gender nonconformity, and gender discordance in children and adolescents. *Journal of the American Academy of Child & Adolescent Psychiatry, 51*(9), 957–974.

Afrasiabi, H., & Junbakhsh, M. (2019). Meanings and experiences of being transgender: A qualitative study among transgender youth. *The Qualitative Report, 24*(8), 1866–1876.

Ashley, F. (2020). Homophobia, conversion therapy, and care models for trans youth: Defending the gender-affirmative approach. *Journal of LGBT Youth, 17*(4), 361–383. https://doi.org/10.1080/19361653.2019.1665610

Day, J. K., Perez-Brumer, A., & Russell, S. T. (2018). Safe schools? Transgender youth's school experiences and perceptions of school climate. *Journal of Youth and Adolescence,* 1–12.

Hembree, W. C., Cohen-Kettenis, P. T., Gooren, L., Hannema, S. E., Meyer, W. J., Murad, M. H., Rosenthal, S. M., Safer, J. D., Tangpricha, V., & T'Sjoen, G. G. (2017). Endocrine treatment of gender-dysphoric/gender-incongruent persons: An endocrine society clinical practice guideline. *Journal of Clinical Endocrinology & Metabolism, 102*(11), 3869–3903. https://doi.org/10.1210/jc.2017-01658

InterACT & Human Rights Watch. (2017). *"I want to be like nature made me": Medically unnecessary surgeries on intersex children in the US.* Human Rights Watch.

Knutson, D., Koch, J. M., & Goldbach, C. (2019). Recommended terminology, pronouns, and documentation for work with transgender and non-binary populations. *Practice Innovations, 4*(4), 214. https://doi.org/10.1037/pri0000098

Kohlberg, L. A. (1966). A cognitive-developmental analysis of children's sex role concepts and attitudes. *The Development of Sex Differences,* 82–173.

Kosciw, J. G., Greytak, E. A., Zongrone, A. D., Clark, C. M., & Truong, N. L. (2018). *The 2017 national school climate survey: The experiences of lesbian, gay, bisexual, transgender, and queer youth in our nation's schools.* Gay, Lesbian and Straight Education Network (GLSEN).

McGuire, J. K., Anderson, C. R., Toomey, R. B., & Russell, S. T. (2010). School climate for transgender youth: A mixed method investigation of student experiences and school responses. *Journal of Youth and Adolescence, 39*(10), 1175–1188.

Nahata, L., Chen, D., Moravek, M. B., Quinn, G. P., Sutter, M. E., Taylor, J., Tishelman, A. C., & Gomez-Lobo, V. (2019). Understudied and under-reported: Fertility issues in transgender youth—a narrative review. *Journal of Pediatrics, 205*, 265–271. https://doi.org/10.1016/j.jpeds.2018.09.009

Nahata, L., Tishelman, A. C., Caltabellotta, N. M., & Quinn, G. P. (2017). Low fertility preservation utilization among transgender youth. *Journal of Adolescent Health, 61*(1), 40–44. https://doi.org/10.1016/j.jadohealth.2016.12.012

Perry, D. G., Pauletti, R. E., & Cooper, P. J. (2019). Gender identity in childhood: A review of the literature. *International Journal of Behavioral Development, 43*(4), 289–304. https://doi.org/10.1177/0165025418811129

Proulx, C. N., Coulter, R. W., Egan, J. E., Matthews, D. D., & Mair, C. (2019). Associations of lesbian, gay, bisexual, transgender, and questioning-inclusive sex education with mental health outcomes and school-based victimization in US high school students. *Journal of Adolescent Health, 64*(5), 608–614. https://doi.org/10.1016/j.jadohealth.2018.11.012

Rew, L., Young, C. C., Monge, M., & Bogucka, R. (2021). Puberty blockers for transgender and gender diverse youth—A critical review of the literature. *Child and Adolescent Mental Health, 26*(1), 3–14. https://doi.org/10.1111/camh.12437

Ridgeway, C. L., & Kricheli-Katz, T. (2013). Intersecting cultural beliefs in social relations: Gender, race, and class binds and freedoms. *Gender & Society, 27*(3), 294–318.

Tierney, W. G., & Ward, J. D. (2017). Coming out and leaving home: A policy and research agenda for LGBT homeless students. *Educational Researcher, 46*(9), 498–507.

World Professional Association for Transgender Health. (2011). Standards of care for the health of transsexual, transgender, and gender-nonconforming people (7th ed.). *International Journal of Transgenderism, 13*(4), 165–232. https://doi.org/10.1080/15532739.2011.700873

5

Gender Identity and Geographic Location

I t may seem funny or even odd that we would devote an entire chapter to geographic location. Given all of the factors that impact mental wellness (e.g., abuse, discrimination, interpersonal relationships), focusing specifically on location may seem trivial. However, a client's location has a sizable and sometimes direct impact on many aspects of the client's wellness. For example, the very type, duration, quality, and characteristics of a client's interpersonal relationships are shaped by where the client lives. Location also impacts access to support groups and organizations, quality of mental and physical health care, exposure to discrimination, and a number of other factors and resources. As we further explore the experiences of Bill, Molly, and Rowan, we will emphasize how location impacts their unique experiences.

Bill

Bill loves living in Boston, Massachusetts. He grew up in a big city on the west coast, Los Angeles, and he has always enjoyed the big-city feel. After leaving the army, Bill attended Boston University for his information technology degree and then he stayed. He feels privileged to live in a city with so many LGBTQ+ services. When he decided to begin his medical transition, he had access to great surgeons and other providers without having to travel very far. His main complaint is that it was hard for him to make friends. If he hadn't started attending college when he moved to Boston, he isn't sure how he would have made friends. Now that he has friends, he finds it easy to live in a "queer bubble," and he sometimes forgets that an oppressive world exists outside of his friend group and affirming work environment.

Molly

At times, Molly loves living in rural North Dakota. The countryside around her is beautiful, and, as an introvert, she finds solitude energizing. However, finding human service and health providers who are competent with affirmative care is a nightmare. Molly tells a number of horror stories about visits to local providers who have asked her invasive, inappropriate questions and who have made outlandish recommendations. She now drives four and a half hours, one way (nine-hour round trip) to Fargo whenever she needs affirming services. The cost of gas places a considerable drain on her fixed income and she fears encountering violence and harassment if she uses the bathroom on the way to Fargo. She has suffered from several urinary tract infections due to lack of access to a safe bathroom. Last-minute provider cancelations and rising gas prices take a considerable toll on Molly. She is not seeing a mental health provider at present because she feels her physical health is more important. Scheduling two providers on the same day and/or traveling to Fargo twice a week is cost and resource prohibitive.

Rowan

Rowan finds living just outside of Los Angeles (LA) very frustrating. They know that a wide variety of LGBTQ+ affirming services are available in LA, but the services are just out of reach. Thousand Oaks is often associated with the LA metro area, but Rowan experiences people in Thousand Oaks to be much more conservative than people in LA. Rowan does not have a car and they rely on their parents to drive them to human service professional appointments. As a result, they end up going to professionals who are unaccustomed to working with gender-fluid, pansexual clients. Rowan tries not to complain too much about where they live, though. They realize things could be worse. Professionals in their area still see more queer clients than professionals in rural areas, and Rowan feels somewhat close to queer social spaces. Sometimes their friends drive out to meet them for lunch or for a movie.

Cultural Nuance

In this chapter, we split our content into urban and nonurban or rural sections, with a brief discussion of semi-rural/semi-urban settings. First, however, it is important to note that definitions of *urban* and *rural* abound, and it is often difficult to draw discrete lines between geographic experiences based on population densities. To be sure, the experience of a person in rural southern Illinois will be rather different than that of a person in remote Florida. Mental health concerns, comorbidities, and family dynamics may vary widely from place to place.

For one thing, laws and policies that impact gender-expansive people are in constant flux and the legal landscape can vary a great deal between countries and geographic regions (e.g., states, provinces, municipalities). It is not possible to provide a comprehensive overview of the anti–gender-expansive laws that have been passed in the United States and around the world because new laws are constantly being proposed, rejected, passed, challenged in courts, and struck down by judges. Legislators continue to write and introduce bills intended to restrict bathroom access, participation in sports, access to medical care, and transition-related services for adolescents.

Given the great deal of variance across geographic locations, it is important for professionals to know their area. Using local vernacular, knowing local truisms, and being familiar with common family dynamics are not only central to building rapport; they are key parts of providing effective services. We will focus on large rural and urban differences, but we won't be able to cover all of the nuanced ways that people in your area may live. This is particularly important to consider when you are an urban provider reaching rural populations or when you are a rural provider treating a new urban transplant. In these and other cases, you and your client may have some adjustments to make.

Teletherapy

The onset of the COVID-19 pandemic increased the demand for and necessity of providing remote electronic human services. There are now more remote platforms, technologies, and service providers than ever before. If you are an affirming provider, regardless of where you are located, we recommend considering ways to broaden your reach to meet the needs of gender-expansive clients across the country. The more specialized your focus, the higher the demand is likely to be for your services. Of course, professionals must remain mindful of licensing jurisdictions, scope of practice limitations, and ethics codes. Whenever possible, though, we recommend looking for ways to reach and support gender-expansive clients wherever possible. For example, if you are close to a state line, it may be possible for you to become licensed in the neighboring state, thereby expanding your reach into another large service area.

Urban Areas

When one considers urban areas, major, high-profile cities such as New York, Detroit, and Los Angeles may come to mind. According to the 2010 US Census, the United States is home to 486 different urbanized areas and at least 80% of the US population is located in urban locations (Ratcliffe et al., 2016). Definitions for *urban* vary, but the US Census Bureau defines *urbanized areas* as locations in which there is a concentration of at least 50,000 people. Thus, these locations are characterized by higher concentrations of people.

With higher concentrations of people come higher concentrations of resources such as medical centers, LGBTQ+ resource centers, nursing homes, mental health consortia, and other health support networks. Where more agencies exist, higher concentrations of therapists, doctors, health specialists, and social networks are sure to be found. Thus, residents of urban areas are more likely to have ready access to medical and mental health care, as well as to social support.

Scholars suggest that providers in these urban areas are also more likely to be competent to address transgender health concerns when compared to their rural counterparts, although this has not born out in the research (Eliason & Hughes, 2004). These scholars suggest that urban providers have access to more LGBTQ+ affirmative training, more contact with LGBTQ+ resource centers, and more interaction with transgender people themselves. Whether or not providers are more competent in urban areas, there are certainly more of them concentrated in urban spaces. This means that urban transgender people share greater proximity to specialists and to a higher volume of providers in general. One downside for clients, however, may be longer wait times or a less personal interaction than in rural areas.

If you are a therapist in an urban area who wishes to improve your services for transgender people, you will need to acquaint yourself with available resources. This will include other providers, comprehensive medical centers that provide transition services, and LGBTQ+ resource centers. It may feel reassuring to be in a space where your clients have so many options, but location privilege may also preclude you from taking into account some very important considerations.

Some general guidelines or suggestions for your work with urban transgender populations follow.

Transportation

It may be true that more resources are available, but travel to those places is not guaranteed. Your transgender clients may rely on public transportation in order to see you for therapy. If a client is not out or if they are unable to pass as their affirmed gender, public transportation may be particularly dangerous for them. They may be late to appointments and/or may cancel appointments during different transportation traffic hours, outages, and upgrades.

Violence and Safety

Gender-expansive people, especially transgender women of color, experience disproportionately high rates of discrimination and violence. For example, transgender women of color who engage in sex work are among the most at-risk populations in the United States. Your client may have had experiences of feeling threatened, afraid, or have even been assaulted. Numerous negative experiences (e.g., misgendering, deadnaming, physical violence) can quickly create an unsafe and exclusionary environment for gender-expansive individuals. Furthermore, they can experience violence, discrimination, and other risks to their safety in both urban and rural areas, but the frequency and severity of such experiences will likely be uniquely affected by where they live and whether they hold other marginalized identities (e.g., transgender person of color, transgender person living with a disability). Clients may benefit when you think about where your office is located, what hours you are open, and when you are prepared to address issues of trauma and safety.

Fees for Service

The cost of living is high in urban areas, and transgender people may struggle, more than others, to pay the bills. As an urban provider, you may charge higher rates for your services than those in less populated areas. For transgender people who may be forced into lower-paying jobs or who are not protected from being fired because of their identities, your fee may place an unmanageable burden on your client's finances. When forced to choose between you and buying groceries, clients may decide not to see you.

Discretion

In urban areas, individuals may be subject to greater exposure. High-profile businesspeople who have yet to come out, for example, may express concern about being seen entering a facility known to provide services to transgender people. They may also express worry about a partner or significant other discovering that they are meeting with you. Therefore, clients may ask you to use less typical forms of communication for cancelations and appointment reminders such as Skype, texting, WhatsApp, Facebook Messenger, and other platforms. Although therapists might express concerns about the security and/or appropriateness of such platforms for therapeutic communication, a growing body of research indicates that electronic platforms may be used to deliver effective therapeutic interventions (e.g., Griffiths & Christensen, 2007).

Family, Partners, and Friends

An important part of a transgender client's work may be focused on interpersonal growth. Given that clients may have strong and broad social networks in their urban location, they may ask to bring family members, friends, or partners to therapy in order to get help with communication or to give their significant other more perspective into their life. Clinicians may benefit from being prepared to address these requests; this may include appropriate paperwork or other therapeutic tools. Transgender clients may benefit from concurrent participation in individual therapy and group therapy, both of which may be readily available in urban areas.

Urban areas may contain more resources for gender-expansive clients, but they may also expose gender-expansive clients to more scrutiny and visibility. Queer communities in urban areas can become close or even enmeshed. When community members use the same clinic, therapist, or other provider, it may be hard for clients to maintain anonymity. Professionals in urban areas may consider ways to maintain client confidentiality, especially when a client's access to services could expose them to social risk or could make them the focus of gossip.

Positive Aspects of Rural Areas

The US Census Bureau defines rural areas as any areas that are not urban (Ratcliffe et al., 2016). Around 20% of the US population is located in rural areas, but the proportion of gender-expansive people in these areas may be greater than expected. In other words, although urban areas are more densely populated, rural areas may include disproportionately large populations of gender-expansive people. Given that no comprehensive, nationwide data on gender-expansive population characteristics are available, such population characteristics are not possible to determine.

Given the many benefits that urban areas provide, it may be easy for urban providers to wonder why an individual would choose to live in a rural, lower-resourced area. In fact, anyone who has not lived in a rural town may wonder about the benefits of residing in such a location. It may be true that rural spaces have their drawbacks and we will discuss them, but it is important to note that rural locations have myriad benefits as well. Throughout this section, we draw from some previous work (Koch & Knutson, 2016), and we encourage you to read that article for a more in-depth exploration of transgender clients in rural and small towns.

Proximity to Family

In rural locations, individuals may grow up very close to home, may help out with the family trade, and may be expected to carry on the family business. For example, farm families may rely on children heavily, and living in the family cluster of homes may be a core value for gender-expansive people in rural areas. The fact that clients are relied upon to check on their grandparents, feed their parents' cattle, or teach Sunday School at the family church are all sources of pride and belonging.

Faith, Friends, and Church

In rural areas, social support networks may be close knit and highly active. For example, when a client falls ill, they may expect to be inundated by food (e.g., casseroles, prepared meals) and offers of support. In rural areas where faith and religious traditions may hold a stronger and more central position in the community, clients may enjoy participating in weekly services, sharing in faith-based conversations, and participating in faith-based social outreach. Simply walking into a store and being known by name may be reassuring, familiar, and affirming.

The Beauty of Nature

Rural clients may love and benefit from the beauty of their surroundings. Living in a home on the side of a mountain or in a lush valley carries with it all of the positive aspects of exposure to nature. Some clients may thoroughly enjoy their surroundings and may balk at any suggestion that living in a more urban area would be a beneficial alternative. Gender-expansive clients in rural areas may live in historic family homes or surrounded by a lifetime of memories that make their location truly special and irreplaceable.

Access to Services

Although rural location may mean fewer providers with LGBTQ+ expertise, it may mean being able to see the family doctor whom a client has seen and had a strong relationship with for 20 or more years. For example, Julie once had a client who was over 60 whose rural longtime family practitioner was one of the first people they came out to, and it was a lovely, supportive experience. In our experience, rural-located service providers often do not have the harried schedules that urban providers have, so it may be easier to schedule appointments, with less wait time, and office staff, nurses, and providers may know clients by name.

Limiting Aspects of Rural Areas

Regardless, scholars indicate that levels of distress reported by gender-expansive people in rural areas may be higher relative to individuals in urban settings. All of the causes of this increased distress are unknown, but several rural characteristics have been implicated. We briefly describe each one, although other resources are available that may provide a more in-depth understanding of rural factors. You may notice that, in rural areas, many of the strengths of the location may also be sources of distress.

Proximity to Family

Gender-expansive people who live close to family may be more reluctant to transition and/or may fear being cast out of the family network if they come out. Just as connection to the family business and/or family traditions can be highly reassuring, being separated from family support systems (or even the threat of being separated) can be both painful and deeply distressing.

Faith, Friends, and Church

In a place where people know each other's names and business, the coming-out process may be particularly fraught. News may travel fast in rural locations, and rural clients can expect that, when one person knows about their identity, everyone knows. This reality is incredibly stressful for some, given that the client won't be able to go anywhere in town without fearing that they have been outed and that they are being judged. Because the church often plays a central role in rural communities and religious communities have not tended to take a positive view of gender diversity, rural residents may tend toward more negative views about gender-expansive individuals.

Seclusion

Beautiful, natural areas may be secluded and sparsely populated. This means that gender-expansive people in rural areas may have fewer in-person connections with fellow community members. In research studies, we've been told by participants that they value the rare opportunities to interact with other gender-expansive people in a physical space.

Internet Access and Remote Connections

Given the lack of in-person contact with other gender-expansive people or communities, rural clients may turn to electronic forms of communication such as phones, social media, and online applications. In rural areas, access to the internet, texting, and even cellular connections may be unreliable and expensive.

Travel and Resource Access

In rural areas, gender-expansive clients may be forced to travel long distances to obtain affirmative therapy from trained professionals. Given that clients may require multiple medical services (e.g., surgeries, hormone therapy, psychiatry, etc.), clients may be forced to make several trips into town. If trips to town or the closest urban area require many hours of driving and if clients are not able to schedule their appointments all in one day, they may be forced to ask for substantial amounts of time off from work.

Access to Competent Providers

Medical providers and mental health therapists in rural areas may be less prepared to provide services for gender-expansive people in rural areas. This may be because the providers have less contact with gender-expansive individuals and/or were not trained to provide affirming services. As we have conducted research, we have heard disheartening stories from participants who were subjected to transphobic behaviors and treatment at rural hospitals and during interactions with therapists. If you are a competent provider in a rural area, your name may be shared through social networks, and you may notice an increase in gender-expansive clients seeking services from you over time. If you connect with gender-expansive communities outside of work and/or identify as a gender-expansive person yourself, you may encounter your clients in social spaces and may have to navigate dual relationships. It can be helpful to address this possibility with clients at intake and to set a plan with them regarding the possibility of future interactions outside of your professional work with them.

Semi-Rural and Semi-Urban Areas

As one might expect, some areas of the United States are neither completely urban nor fully rural. These spaces exist on the outskirts of cities and/or within large towns. Semi-urban areas are areas such as suburbs or housing districts that surround larger metropolitan cities. Semi-rural areas are small towns and residential areas that collect around state universities. As would be expected, these areas feature many of the shortcomings and benefits of both rural and urban locations. In some ways, semi-urban and semi-rural areas may be the most varied and difficult to classify of all the geographic areas we've discussed so far. Although it is impossible to provide a full analysis of these in-between locations, there are some unique issues that should be considered.

For one thing, the quality of life in semi-urban areas may vary widely. Some areas may be very costly to live in while others may be neglected spaces to which people of lower socioeconomic status are pushed through gentrification. Regardless, these areas feature a less favorable ratio between cost of living and availability of services. In low socioeconomic areas, resources may be stretched very thin; these areas are often faced with poverty, dwindling social services, and economic oppression. However, some extra-urban areas may feature a very high cost of living, without the attenuating closeness of resources and density of health-care and social support facilities.

Additionally, like rural areas, semi-urban locations and semi-rural areas may be very spread out and may not have access to mass transit services. Maintaining a car in these areas may be very expensive and the dangers of long commutes in somewhat densely populated areas cannot be understated. These areas may get less attention during inclement weather (e.g., snow, ice, torrential rain) and residents may feel a greater impact from natural disasters.

People Who Immigrate

Although our book focuses on services provided in the United States, it is important to recognize that immigration status may impact the people you work with. There is a growing body of evidence that recent immigration to the United States has a profound impact on a person's experience, perspective, and sources of social support. We urge providers to consider country of origin and ethnic heritage while providing services. Books and websites on international LGBTQ+ issues may serve as helpful guides.

General Guidelines

Regardless of location, there are some general guidelines that may aid providers in their work with gender-expansive individuals from across the United States and even around the world. We offer them here to guide evaluation, assessment, and work with transgender clients from a variety of geographic areas. These items may serve as an inventory of sorts.

Explore the Geographic Culture of Origin

Geographic locations have their own unique cultures, expectations, codes, and lexicons. Knowing about your client's unique culture of origin will assist you with tailoring interventions that are culturally appropriate. Given that assumptions about, biases toward, and stereotypes surrounding gender identity are culturally based, it will be very important for you to understand the client's cultural context before interacting with them to challenge and process negative experiences.

Assess Distance and Physical Access to Resources

As an affirmative counselor, you will be responsible for more than just the client's mental well-being because mental health is about much more than just talk therapy. At times, you may find that you serve as a case manager. Scholars and researchers strongly recommend that professionals compile a resource list that brings together services in their immediate area. The resource list should include both online and in-person resources.

Explore Spatial Connections to Community and Religion

In both urban and rural regions, a client's relationship to religion and to faith communities may be varied, complex, and a source of both joy and pain. The individual's source of community may be associated with their religious beliefs. Clients may also draw community from local LGBTQ+ centers or from online groups. Understanding a client's ties to community will give you an understanding of their level of social support and will help you to understand ways to further grow the support base they already have.

Address Family Businesses, Ties, and Expectations

In any location, a child may be expected to carry on the family name, business, and/or trade. The type of trade and/or the ties to family businesses may be very location based and may be shaped by a long family history. Migration from one or more other geographic location may underlie shared family myths, memories, and memorabilia. Knowing the geographic connections, ties, and expectations held in a family will give you an idea of how clients interact with their families, especially through any coming-out process.

Explore the Impact of Local Laws and Policies

It is important to be aware of any laws and policies in your area (e.g., state, municipality, province) that restrict access for gender-expansive people. Even proposed anti–gender-expansive laws and the media attention they receive can have a negative emotional impact on gender-expansive clients. It may be important to help clients plan for and navigate issues with access to medical care, facilities, and other resources.

Assess Availability, Longevity, and Commitment

Given the long commute distances, limited financial resources, and tenuous connection to work that gender-expansive clients may face, it is important to understand how clients will pay for your services, how they prefer to communicate with you, and what risks surround their continued access to therapy with you. As you assess for these dimensions, it will be important that you be prepared to respond appropriately.

Summary and Recommendations

- Client experiences and needs will vary, based on location and resource access.
- There are both positive and negative aspects of living in rural, urban, and suburban areas.
- Clients have good reasons for living where they live.
- Social interactions and connections are impacted by location and proximity.
- Professionals who use technology to reach clients are likely to be more accessible and to see a broader range of clients in different areas with different concerns.
- It is important to learn the cultures and climates that surround the gender-expansive people you serve.
- Maintaining a resource list is one of the most effective ways to support gender-expansive clients, regardless of location.

Reflection Questions

1. What biases (if any) do you hold against rural areas?
2. What biases (if any) do you hold against urban areas?
3. What are your assumptions and/or biases when it comes to other countries and cultures?
4. How might your biases and assumptions negatively impact your work with gender-expansive clients?
5. What is at least one step you could take to improve care for gender-expansive clients in rural areas?
6. What is at least one step you could take to improve care for gender-expansive clients in urban areas?

References and Suggested Readings

Eliason, M. J., & Hughes, T. (2004). Treatment counselor's attitudes about lesbian, gay, bisexual, and transgendered clients: Urban vs. rural settings. *Substance Use and Misuse, 39*(4), 625–644. https://doi.org/10.1081/ja-120030063

Griffiths, K. M., & Christensen, H. (2007). Internet-based mental health programs: A powerful tool in the rural medical kit. *Australian Journal of Rural Health, 15*(2), 81–87. https://doi.org/10.1111/j.1440-1584.2007.00859.x

Koch, J. M., & Knutson, D. (2016). Transgender clients in rural areas and small towns. *Journal of Rural Mental Health, 40*(3–4), 154–163. https://doi.org/10.1037/rmh0000056

Movement Advancement Project. (2019). *Where we call home: Transgender people in rural America.* https://www.lgbtmap.org/file/Rural-Trans-Report-Nov2019.pdf

Movement Advancement Project. (2022). *Mapping transgender equality in the United States.* https://www.lgbtmap.org/mapping-trans-equality

Ratcliffe, M., Burd, C., Holder, C., Fields, A. (2016). *Defining rural at the U.S. Census Bureau: American Community Survey and Geography Brief* (US Census Bureau Report No. ACSGEO-1). US Census Bureau. https://www.census.gov/content/dam/Census/library/publications/2016/acs/acsgeo-1.pdf

SECTION II

Elements of Affirmative Practice

6

Relationship Building

In any human service profession, building a strong, positive, healthy relationship with clients is important. Rapport is the keystone of work with gender-diverse clients, who may feel particularly vulnerable and may be looking for someone who understands gender diversity. In this chapter, we will talk you through building positive relationships, beginning with messages that you communicate before you even meet with the client. We discuss the importance of the initial contact with the client, developing trust in the early stages of counseling, and strengthening the therapeutic alliance across the relationship. Finally, we conclude with a discussion of termination and post-termination with clients.

Bill

Bill was hesitant about accessing mental health support services at the Veterans Affairs (VA) medical facility for the first time. He experienced the general apprehension that many veterans report related to help-seeking. On top of those worries, Bill was concerned that VA staff would not know how to handle a transgender patient. Some of Bill's anxiety was fueled by an awareness that different federal administrations have had varying agendas related to LGBTQ+ people in the military and veterans' services. Policy around inclusion of transgender people in the military has gone through many changes in recent years.

Bill was pleasantly surprised to discover that many of the helping professionals he encountered worked hard to be affirming. Even though his providers lacked specific training in gender-expansive care, they provided Bill with the services he needed. He discovered that the VA had a program that provided packers, binders, and other important resources for veterans. Bill became involved in a LGBTQ+ group that allowed him to build friendships with other gender-expansive veterans.

Molly

When Molly started searching for a mental health therapist, it took her more than a year to find one with whom she could work. She started by searching for providers in her area, because her commute to the near-est large city was both time and cost prohibitive. When she arrived at her first therapist's office, she immediately noticed how many crosses were on the wall. One of them was emblazoned with the message, "Sin is a choice, redemption is a gift." Molly worried that her thera-pist would be displeased about her gender identity, and it turned out that he was. When she came out to him, he offered to transfer her to another therapist.

Molly continued to call therapists within a 60-mile radius, but many did not take her insurance. She found a therapist with a sliding scale fee that she could afford, but she discontinued services after the ther-apist suggested he knew she was transgender because her index and middle fingers were the same length. Frustrated and distressed, Molly finally posted about her experiences in a social media group. Several members of the group referred her to a teletherapist who specialized in gender-expansive care. Molly did not love the idea of meeting with her therapist remotely, but she knew she could not wait much longer with-out getting help. She hit it off with her therapist right away, and, after a while, she adjusted to the teletherapy environment.

Rowan

When Rowan was experiencing a great deal of confusion about what major they should pursue, they decided to talk to the academic affairs coordinator. They knew that the coordinator was trained to help with enrollment and course selection and that some coordinators were also great at academic coaching. At their first visit, Rowan sat in the wait-ing room feeling apprehensive. Their worries were calmed, though, when the coordinator came to the waiting room, introduced herself, and shared her pronouns. When she took Rowan back to her office, Rowan noticed a transgender pride flag displayed on the coordinator's desk. Rowan felt confident that the coordinator cared about their iden-tity and well-being.

Instead of launching into the standard academic advising spiel, the coordinator took time to get to know Rowan as a person. Rowan felt comfortable coming out to the coordinator as gender fluid. The coordi-nator expressed appreciation for Rowan's trust; she asked Rowan if it was okay to document their identity. Rowan asked that the coordinator keep the information just between the two of them. Over time, Rowan's interactions with the coordinator helped them feel safer and more connected with others on campus. They were excited when they decided to pursue pre-veterinary science, but they were sad to leave academic advisement. They still visit the coordinator to check in and to share about their academic progress.

Prior to Meeting a Client

Many gender-expansive clients share Molly's experience trying to find an affirming professional. Clients may cycle through professionals, discontinuing services after they discover the professional they are working with is biased or is operating on outdated assumptions. Switching service providers disrupts treatment, intervention, and record keeping. It is also a distressing and disappointing process, especially considering the emotional energy it can take to find, reach out to, and open up to a professional. The good news is that you can reduce distress and increase resilience for a gender-expansive person even before they walk through your door or meet with you remotely.

For example, you can (re)consider the ways you advertise and publicize your services (see Koch & Knutson, 2016). You can advertise on sites and platforms such as websites, Facebook, Instagram, or chat rooms that support gender-expansive communities. You can include gender-expansive symbols such as the transgender pride flag or the nonbinary pride flag on your websites and media. Also consider listing your ability to provide gender-expansive services in national or local directories (e.g., Psychology Today, LinkedIn) that are likely to be frequented by gender-expansive people looking for support or even on social media profiles (e.g., Instagram, Twitter). Do not be surprised if you discover that gender-expansive clients have "Googled you" or conducted an informal, internet-based background check on you before contacting you to request services. Your ratings and feedback on Google, Health Grades, and other sites are likely to factor into a client's decision about whether to reach out to you.

You can also make sure to use gender-inclusive language and images in your advertisement materials, such as using language that acknowledges nonbinary people instead of only mentioning men and women. In addition to using inclusive language, be sure to use imagery that represents the diversity of gender-expansive identities, such as multiple pride flags (e.g., transgender, nonbinary, genderqueer) or images of individuals with a range of gender, race, and other identities. Even subtle attempts at inclusion and affirmation are likely to be noticed by gender-expansive prospective clients. Conversely, it is important to think about any embedded messages that may communicate exclusion, such as heavily featured religious symbols or political messaging. Of course, some gender-expansive clients may be strongly religious and/or politically aligned with you, but others will avoid using your services because they fear your religious or political views hint at negative opinions about gender-expansive people.

Not only is it important to be intentional about how you frame your services in advertisements; you should also consider adding your contact information to resource lists maintained by other affirming providers. Many local gender-expansive communities, LGBTQ+ centers, and human service professionals maintain informal lists of affirming and recommended providers. If you provide affirming services and you earn the trust of your local gender-expansive community members, you are more likely to be sought out by other members of the community. You should also maintain your own list of recommended or affirming providers (e.g., surgeons, voice specialists, cosmetologists, endocrinologists, and so on) so that you will be able to help your clients find the services they need without having to go through the extended process of vetting other providers.

The staff who work in your office are another early point of contact with clients that you should think about. Even if you are the most affirming human service professional in the world, you may lose clients because your support staff lack training to appropriately engage with gender-expansive people. For example, the person who calls a client to remind them of their appointment may say "ma'am" or "sir" based on assumptions they form about a person's voice. Similarly, a front desk person may announce in the waiting room, "Timothy, please come to the front desk to pick up your paperwork," and then say, "You're not Timothy" when someone approaches the desk who presents as a woman. Misgendering and deadnaming like this could prompt a gender-expansive client to leave your waiting room without ever seeing you for services. Training staff in gender-affirming care is an essential part of being an affirmative provider.

Also consider the physical or virtual space out of which you operate. It can help to put yourself in your gender-expansive client's shoes and to think about how you would feel entering your own work-space. For example, think about what it would be like if you did not have a restroom you could feel comfortable using. Reflect on how you would feel sitting in the waiting room as a gender-expansive person. If you are a gynecologist, for example, would a transgender man feel conspicuous sitting in your waiting room before being called to the back for an exam? Likewise, would a nonbinary person have access to a gender-inclusive bathroom, or would they be forced to choose between gendered bathrooms? Consider the literature in your waiting room, the artwork, and other aspects that make your environment a comfortable and welcoming space.

First Appointment

The first appointment or contact with a gender-expansive client sets the tone for any future relationship with them. Assuming that your support staff interacted with the client appropriately, it is now your turn to begin building rapport with the client. In many cases, the first appointment is focused on information-gathering. The amount of information needed will vary between human service professionals. For example, a barber will need to know how the client's hair has been cut in the past and/or what they want their haircut to look like, whereas a primary care provider will need to know about health history, current medications, and so on.

Some professionals collect the information they need verbally, some use paperwork, and some professionals use a mix of both methods. Regardless of how you collect client information, we recommend considering a few important tips for making your data collection process affirming. First, look over your process and ask yourself if your questions and forms are inclusive of gender-expansive people. For example, it is possible that you ask about gender and have an option for "Other, please specify: _____" and a blank line that allows clients to fill in their gender identity (if they do not iden-tify as cisgender male or cisgender female). Please be aware that the word "other" is othering and that it may leave gender-expansive clients feeling unwelcome or like an afterthought. We recommend using something like, "Please self-identify: _____" or similar wording instead.

Then, ask yourself if the questions you ask clients are necessary. Think through your data-collection protocol and reflect on what purpose each question you are asking serves. Consider whether you need the information at all. For example, if you are a speech therapist, is it necessary for you to know about all of the gender-affirming surgeries a client has had? Knowing about vocal feminization surgery may be important, but other gender-affirming surgeries are likely unnecessary to ask about in the context of speech therapy work. If you are providing sexual health services at a state health agency, do you need to know if the client is on gender-affirming hormones? Asking invasive questions that are not completely necessary is a sure way to turn a visit into a nightmare for a gender-expansive client.

However, if a client walks away from the first appointment or point of contact feeling affirmed, they are likely to return and to share about their positive experience with other gender-expansive clients. If you become well-known in your state, province, area, or country for providing excellent affirming services, you may eventually experience a surge in referrals and new clients. Unfortunately, affirming services are still sparse and there are not enough affirming providers to meet the increasing demand for gender-affirming services. The lack of service providers further highlights the importance of your work to create an affirming environment for gender-expansive clients in your own practice.

Early Stages of the Relationship

As we discuss the early stages of rapport-building with gender-expansive clients, we will assume you have read Section I, especially Chapter 2 on exploring your gender identity and Chapter 3 on intersectionality. If you have not read those chapters, we strongly recommend that you do so before continuing this chapter. Relationship-building with gender-expansive clients is based on self-awareness and on clarity about your own identities. It requires that you remain open and transparent about your level of competence and expertise, as well as display humility so as not to create invalidating and harmful interactions. It is unlikely that you will be prepared for such deep and thoughtful conversations if you have not yet explored your own biases, expectations, and who you are as an intersectional person.

Knowing who you are will also help you to make space for the client to tell their own story. Most human service jobs rely heavily on interpersonal skills and communication. Massage therapists, optometrists, chiropractors, nurses, and so on are likely to ask for and to hear about what a client did over the weekend or about what a client does for a living. As those stories unfold, clients provide (or withhold) important details about their lives. For example, a client who identifies as a man may disclose that they just got back from a vacation with his husband. How a professional responds to that information will either further solidify or fracture the closeness of the relationship that they enjoy with their client.

One important component of these early interactions is letting the client tell their own story. That is easier said than done because making space for client narratives is about more than just staying silent so that a client can talk. Stories are sources of important information such as the degree to which gender is part of the client's presenting concern, which pronouns the client uses, how the client describes their gender identity, and so on. Listening closely, with minimal bias, allows professionals to engage with clients on their own terms. We recommend, whenever possible, waiting for a client to explain their identities and experiences. Guessing at pronouns, identities, labels, and physical attributes can cause serious relational ruptures.

While forming an early professional/client relationship, we caution providers against assuming that gender is involved in a client's presenting concerns. Overemphasizing gender during treatment is referred to, by some, as the "trans broken arm" phenomenon (see Knutson et al., 2017). This phrase refers to the fact that a transgender person with a broken arm simply needs treatment for a broken arm, but they may be asked all sorts of questions about the hormones they are on or what surgeries they have undergone. Sometimes it is hard for professionals to see past a person's identity when it is a largely irrelevant factor in service provision. Conversely, professionals are cautioned not to overlook gender identity when it is an essential component of providing an effective intervention. Individuals who have explored their own identities and biases may be more likely to strike the appropriate balance.

Strengthening the Relationship

Over time, professionals and their clients will likely fall into a regular pattern of interacting, relating, and modifying services as needed. We hope that, as you work with more and more gender-expansive clients, your comfort with affirming behaviors such as sharing your pronouns or avoiding gender assumptions will grow. We caution professionals, though, against falling into a rut with individual gender-expansive clients or with gender-affirming care in general. For example, a client's pronouns and/or name may change over the course of their work with you. Likewise, terminology used by gender-expansive clients may develop and change over time. It is important for affirming providers to check in with clients to make sure they are receiving the care they need. It is also necessary for providers to stay connected to gender-expansive communities through watching YouTube videos, volunteering at community centers, or following gender-expansive social media accounts. Staying up to date with scholarly articles may help, but scientific papers may not be as current as other sources of information and community engagement. When referencing scholarly work, it is also important to assess whether the voices of gender-expansive individuals were actually centered in the research, or if predominately cisgender researchers have forwarded assumptions about gender-expansive people that may or may not be accurate.

During the course of working with gender-expansive clients, it is likely that you will experience therapeutic ruptures or a client discontinuing services with you. The way you handle ruptures and unplanned terminations is a vital part of affirming care. When people make mistakes (e.g., when they misgender or deadname a person) in the world outside of your workplace, they are generally unrepentant, awkwardly apologetic, defensive, or downright cruel. As a professional, you have the opportunity to provide your client with a healing, corrective experience. In other words, you have the chance to behave differently in a way that counters past experiences and that provides your client with an opportunity to heal, even if they decide to terminate services anyway.

When you make a mistake, we recommend acknowledging your mistake, saying you are sorry, correcting your mistake, and then moving on. For example, imagine you are working with a client, who uses they/them pronouns, to help them identify the insurance policy that works best for them. With the client sitting in front of you, you call a colleague into your office for a second opinion. Gesturing to your client, you say, "He was thinking that he would sign up for—" Suddenly you realize your mistake. You quickly say, "I'm sorry, they were thinking that they would sign up for—" You may feel compelled to start apologizing and trying to explain your mistake, but that just puts the client on the spot, makes them feel like they need to take care of you, and leaves them in the position of feeling awkward.

The same principle applies when a colleague makes a mistake. For example, if you are at the front desk of your place of business and the front desk assistant says, "Wren is out front. She is here to see you." You can simply interject, "This client uses he/him pronouns," and then move on. As you become more comfortable working in gender-diverse spaces, you may find that correcting yourself and others becomes easier. Mistakes are part of being human and they are bound to happen. Sometimes, it is what we do after a mistake that determines the power of its impact.

Occasionally providers make bigger mistakes than just using the wrong pronouns. We do not have space here to fully describe all of the errors that may occur in the work of human service professionals, but most mistakes can be handled in similar ways. Beyond apologizing and correcting yourself, it may be important for you to acknowledge your mistake and to open space for the client to talk about how they were impacted. Please remember that your mistake should not require the client forgiving you or saying, "that's okay." It is not the client's job to take care of you if you get upset or feel guilty about slipping up. If your client accepts your apology and chooses to keep working with you, it is your responsibility to work on any biases or expectations that led to your error. It is not okay to keep making the same mistakes.

Ruptures may also occur in the therapeutic relationship when clients request services that are inconsistent with best practices and/or when they ask for resources that cannot be provided right away. For example, clients may be eager to obtain a letter that they need in order to access some transition services and they may want you to write one for them at their first session. Clients may also be under the misguided impression that they can receive therapy to change their gender identity, or they may request an intervention that is inconsistent with current research and scholarship. It is important to work with clients to build rapport and increase safety, even when the service the client is requesting cannot be provided or must be delayed.

Termination and Beyond

If you have worked for several months or years with a gender-expansive client, it is likely that you have experienced difficult ruptures and emotional reconciliations, listened to moving stories, and heard about painful experiences. Regardless of the services you are providing for your client, it is likely that you will have to say goodbye at some point. You may find yourself feeling attached to your client and you may even be reluctant to let your client go. Likewise, your client may be very sad to discontinue their working relationship with you.

There are a variety of reasons that clients discontinue services. Their financial situation may change, they may move, they may get well or resolve their issues, their body may heal, their insurance may change, and so on. It can be incredibly frustrating or even disappointing when you can see that the client still needs your help or support but chooses or is forced to discontinue services. However, it is important to remember that gender-expansive people are incredibly resilient and that you are not the only professional who is able to make a positive impact on their lives. In fact, another professional may be able to provide services with a different focus, expertise, or benefit for the client.

Goodbyes are hard and it is possible that gender-expansive clients have said a lot of them. Some gender-expansive youth are kicked out of their homes and some gender-expansive adults are estranged from their friends and family when they come out. Navigating goodbyes may be difficult, and healthy goodbyes may be uncharted territory for any client, especially gender-expansive people. It is important to keep this in mind when terminating services. To the furthest extent possible (and within ethical limits), we recommend being supportive and transparent throughout the termination process. Be prepared for clients to give you gifts (e.g., a plant to symbolize their growth, a painting to express gratitude) that mark the importance of the relationship you have built.

Not all terminations will be emotional, though. Some clients may be eager to move to the next step of their transition process, for example. Clients may obtain their desired electrolysis results, voice coaching, or a letter of support for gender-affirming surgery. When they obtain those milestones, they may be ready to move on with their lives. Those goodbyes, too, can be celebrated. It is important to remember that a gender-expansive client's progress and needs are not about you.

Please be aware that, if you provide effective services and if you become close to your clients, they may contact you after termination. Some clients will want to update you on their progress or will want to share about major life events. Other clients will ask for letters of recommendation for hormones or surgery, for an emotional support animal, or for other documentation (for example, a letter for a student in college who dropped out mid-semester and hopes to get a tuition refund). It may be important for you to consider policies such as how long after providing services you wait before accepting social media friend/follow requests, if at all. You may also want to consider how to respond if you are contacted by a present or past client on a social media platform, via text message, or via email. Those policies should be communicated to clients prior to termination or even during your first meeting with them.

Summary and Recommendations

* Affirming practice starts before you actually meet a client.
* Training of office staff is crucial.
* Gender-expansive clients notice affirming and invalidating messages in advertisements, websites, and flyers.
* Your office layout and the facilities you provide are important.
* Paperwork and documentation can be "othering" or inclusive.
* If you make a mistake, apologize, correct yourself, and move on.
* Mistakes can be opportunities for healing and corrective experiences.
* Client pronouns, names, and identities may change over the course of your work with them.
* Termination can be hard, but it can also be something to celebrate.

Reflection Questions

1. What is at least one addition you could make to your advertisements that would make them more affirming and inviting for gender-expansive people?
2. What is at least one way you could make your office/workspace more affirming?
3. What is at least one modification you could make to your paperwork to make it more affirming?
4. What is at least one alteration you could make to your information-gathering procedures to make them more appropriate for gender-expansive people?
5. What is your policy regarding communication with current clients via social media or other internet-based platforms?
6. What is your policy regarding communication with past clients via social media or other internet-based platforms?
7. What is your policy regarding friending/following former clients?
8. How can you make your termination process more affirming and healing for gender-expansive clients?

References and Suggested Readings

Knutson, D., & Koch, J. M. (2018). Person-centered therapy as applied to work with transgender and gender diverse clients. *Journal of Humanistic Psychology, 62*(1), 1–19. https://doi.org/10.1177%2F0022167818791082

Knutson, D., & Koch, J. M. (2021). A cotherapy supervision approach using person-centered theory with a gender fluid client. *Clinical Case Studies, 20*(5), 368–384. https://doi.org/10.1177%2F15346501211003157

Knutson, D., Koch, J. M., Arthur, T., Mitchell, T. A., & Martyr, M. A. (2017). "Trans broken arm": Health care stories from transgender people in rural areas. *Journal of Research on Women and Gender, 7*(1), 30–46. https://digital.library.txstate.edu/handle/10877/12890

Knutson, D., Koch, J. M., & Goldbach, C. (2019). Recommended terminology, pronouns, and documentation for work with transgender and non-binary populations. *Practice Innovations, 4*, 214–224. https://doi.org/10.1037/pri0000098

Koch, J. M., & Knutson, D. (2016). Transgender clients in rural areas and small towns. *Journal of Rural Mental Health, 40*(3–4), 154–163. https://doi.org/10.1037/rmh0000056

7

Assessment and Diagnosis Frameworks

The history of assessment and diagnosis for gender-expansive people has been long, varied, and often marked by troubling assumptions. Treatment, theory, and diagnosis for gender-expansive people in the Western world (and more specifically in the United States) are relatively new (Drescher, 2015). Hirschfeld (1923) was credited as the first person to differentiate gender-expansive individuals from those with minority sexual orientations. Over the intervening years, researchers and specialists have continued to develop assessment and diagnostic frameworks that support treatment for gender-expansive people. We understand that not all human service professionals will formally assess or diagnose gender-expansive clients, but we maintain that it is important to be familiar with this information as you strive to understand and affirm your clients' experiences. We begin the chapter by reviewing cases and providing historical background before offering an overview of assessment techniques, diagnostic considerations, and common errors. This chapter is, by no means, comprehensive, and it should be used as a starting point for discussion and further reading. More detailed discussions of assessment with clients who present with neurodiverse diagnoses, report severe trauma histories, hold multiple marginalized identities on which assessment instruments have not been normed, and/or are younger than 18 years old are provided elsewhere (e.g., Knutson & Koch, 2021).

Bill

Bill experienced a spike in distress when he entered puberty and began to develop breast tissue. He began restricting his food consumption in an effort to keep his hips and breasts from developing. Later, Bill enlisted in the military, in part, as a way to escape his distress. The discipline and structure of the army environment dovetailed nicely with his desire to control his body and its development. Bill also liked the more masculine clothing he was able to wear in the field.

When Bill saw his first therapist at the VA following his honorable discharge, he got lucky. He disclosed his history of disordered eating and his gender-expansive identity. He worried that his therapist would dive right into interventions focused on increasing his caloric intake, but, instead, the therapist conceptualized Bill's disordered eating as an effort to maintain gender congruence. Following the therapist's recommendation, Bill worked with a dietician while the therapist worked to increase Bill's access to affirmative interventions to increase Bill's gender congruence. After Bill started gender-affirming hormone therapy and received top surgery (to remove breast tissue), he began to eat more regularly.

Molly

Molly struggled to find professionals who were willing to assess her readiness for gender-affirming surgery. Many professionals told her that they lacked the education and training necessary to conduct such an assessment. Molly found that incredibly frustrating because she knew that WPATH, the Endocrine Society, and other groups provided clear guidelines for assessment and diagnosis. She also knew that her surgeon, Dr. Smith, listed the information he required on his website. It felt to Molly that the professionals she contacted just did not want to help her. It seemed to her that those providers could, with appropriate supervision and consultation, provide the basic services she needed in order to access gender-affirming surgery.

Molly finally found a couple of providers who were willing to help. However, in order to receive their services, she had to drive to the states in which they were licensed. One of the providers charged $800 for a full assessment and that was on top of Molly's travel and lodging costs. She had been saving plenty of money to pay her surgeon, but by the time she paid for all of the documentation she needed, she had to start saving again. Her depression deepened as she realized that she would have to wait four more years to afford the surgeries she needed. She worried about her letters "expiring" and having to pay for them again closer to her scheduled surgery appointments.

Rowan

Rowan began accessing gender-affirming hormones from their local Planned Parenthood. They were very worried at their first appointment because they had heard from other gender-fluid people that professionals are hesitant to prescribe hormones for clients who "are not transgender enough." In other words, professionals sometimes refused to provide hormones for gender-expansive people who did not profess to identify as men or women. Rowan understood those providers feared their clients would later "change their minds" and "regret" their decision to take hormones.

When Rowan talked to their nurse at Planned Parenthood, they were prepared to exaggerate their transition goals, suggesting that they wanted to present as binary. They were relieved, though, when the nurse and other professionals used an informed consent model. Instead of grilling Rowan about the legitimacy of their gender-expansive identity, the professionals provided Rowan information about what to expect from hormone therapy. They emphasized that the outcomes of therapy might not be the ones Rowan hoped for and then they gave Rowan the opportunity to consent for treatment. Rowan walked away from the visit having received exactly the care and clarity they needed, and they felt great.

A Brief History of Mental Health Diagnostic Categories

One early researcher of transgender treatment was John Money (Money et al., 1957). Money's work informed early versions of the *Diagnostic and Statistical Manual for Mental Disorders* (*DSM*; American Psychiatric Association [APA], 2013). In *DSM I* and *II*, transgender individuals were diagnosed with "transvestitism" under the umbrella of sexual deviation (APA, 1952; APA, 1968). With the *DSM III* update, a category of gender identity disorders was created (APA, 1980). Finally, in *DSM 5*, the diagnosis for transgender people was further revised to *Gender Dysphoria* (APA, 2013). We discuss the concept of gender dysphoria in Chapter 9. It is important to note that gender-expansive people's personal experiences of gender dysphoria can be much more expansive than what is presented in the *DSM-5* diagnosis. To account for this, we will use gender dysphoria (not capitalized) to refer to the personal experiences of distress and Gender Dysphoria (capitalized) to refer specifically to the *DSM-5* diagnosis.

Not all transgender individuals experience gender dysphoria, and individuals who do receive a gender dysphoria diagnosis may report varying levels and degrees of associated symptoms (Schulz, 2018; Winters, 2006). At present, gender-expansive individuals and allies are divided over the continued inclusion of gender dysphoria diagnoses in leading medical manuals (see Vance et al., 2017). For some, what amounts to a *transgender diagnosis* in diagnostic manuals contributes to stigma and an illness model that presents transgender identities as pathological. For others, a diagnosis provides access to life-saving treatments by providing a structure for diagnosis, insurance billing, and medical treatment. For many professionals, scholars, and clients, the benefits of a diagnosis outweigh the drawbacks, but it is important to recognize that those negative aspects exist.

Please note that the *International Classification of Diseases (ICD) 10*, which is used by insurance companies for billing purposes in the United States, still uses the diagnosis "Gender Disorder." Therapists who work with clients who are reliant on insurance may feel uncomfortable with providing an *ICD 10* diagnosis of gender disorder, but may feel forced to do so in order for their clients to get the health care they need from surgeons or endocrinologists. The *ICD 11* will move this diagnosis out of the medical condition section (World Health Organization [WHO], 2018). In the *ICD-11*, gender identity disorder will be replaced with gender incongruence. Gender incongruence will be moved to the section on conditions related to sexual health. As a result, at least internationally, gender disorder will no longer be considered a psychological disturbance. However, the medical establishment in the United States must adopt *ICD 11* revisions and they are generally slow to do so. Additionally, the *DSM 5* remains an influential diagnostic text in the United States, especially for mental health providers. This chapter is written on *ICD 10* and *DSM 5* guidelines because those are the ones still used/employed in US medicine and mental health.

Assessment

Assessing transgender identity may seem difficult for professionals who are unfamiliar with the process. The *DSM 5* and *ICD 10* provide guidelines for diagnosis, but they offer little guidance for documentation and/or measurement of gender dysphoria. For example, existing professional manuals do not provide diagnostic tools that aid professionals charged with providing supportive documentation of the necessity of gender-affirming transition. The World Professional Association for Transgender Health (WPATH) *Standards of Care (SOC)* 7th edition (WPATH, 2011) serve as a guide for medical professionals and mental health providers, but they are nonbinding. In other words, professionals may consult the *Standards of Care 7* for recommended practice with gender-expansive clients, but they are not bound to behave in keeping with the WPATH standards. The *SOC* 8th edition is supposed to be released soon, but will continue to be advisory and nonbinding.

Given that professionals are often asked to write letters of support for gender-affirming medical interventions (e.g., affirming hormone therapy, affirming surgeries), they may feel responsible for fully understanding and endorsing gender-expansive peoples' identities. In other words, they may feel charged to confirm, beyond a doubt, that gender dysphoria is present. There are a variety of ways to approach evaluations of gender dysphoria and the necessity of transition. We include a brief review of formal measures, informal approaches, and intake or information-gathering procedures.

As you read about different approaches, we recommend that you reflect on your own beliefs and expectations around the process of assessment. You may notice in this chapter a tension between a strong recommendation that you increase access to affirming care by stepping outside of your comfort zone and providing services to gender-expansive people and an admonishment that you only provide services you are competent to provide. We would suggest, though, that it is possible to reconcile the tension between those two imperatives by obtaining training and engaging in the self-reflection necessary both to provide new services and to achieve the competence to do so. We hope this chapter will start you down that path, if you are not on it already.

Formal Measures

Researchers have constructed a number of scales to facilitate measurement of gender dysphoria. To date, no single measure has risen to the top as the best or most widely used. Among the most cited are the Utrecht Gender Dysphoria Scale (Cohen-Kettenis & Van Goozen, 1997) and the Gender Identity/Gender Dysphoria Questionnaire for

Adolescents and Adults (Deogracias et al., 2007). These measures are criticized for focusing on binary transgender identities or for leaving out nonbinary folks, and for narrow or limited interpretations of gender dysphoria (Galupo & Pulice-Farrow, 2020). Researchers are working to expand and/or supplement current gender dysphoria scales and approaches to measurement (Goldbach & Knutson, 2021).

Other measures used to assess gender are the Bem Sex Role Inventory (Bem, 1974) and the Cross-Gender Questionnaire (Docter & Fleming, 1993), but they are not widely used because of considerable limitations. For example, the Bem Sex Role Inventory does not directly measure gender dysphoria. The Cross-Gender Questionnaire focuses only on transgender women and is, therefore, rarely used by either researchers or health-care providers.

A more recent addition, the Gender Preoccupation and Stability Questionnaire (Hakeem et al., 2016), is more inclusive of nonbinary people, although the measure was normed on binary transgender populations. Underlying this measure is the assumption that gender dysphoria is an internal, individual problem. Although the quality of measures of gender dysphoria is increasing, no single measure is adequate to establish medically significant levels of distress when used in isolation.

Although it was not designed to be a diagnostic tool for gender dysphoria, the Gender Congruence and Life Satisfaction Scale (Jones et al., 2019) is another recent tool designed to assess distress on factors related to experiences of gender dysphoria (e.g., body dissatisfaction, psychological functioning). Importantly, this measure was designed to be inclusive of both binary and nonbinary gender-expansive individuals and the final items were created following feedback directly from gender-expansive community members.

We offer a few notes of caution about the use of gender dysphoria measures. For one thing, some of the items in these questionnaires are outdated and may come across as offensive to transgender clients (see Galupo & Pulice-Farrow, 2020). In research studies we have conducted, participants have reported experiencing frustration or discomfort when asked to complete some of the early gender dysphoria measures. Given the imperfect and limited way that these questionnaires measure gender dysphoria, summary scores may be marginally helpful. If anything, the individual items in some of the measures may serve as guides for dialogue about gender dysphoria and distress experienced by transgender people. These individual items may guide informal or interview-based assessment.

Informal or Interview-Based Assessment

Given the broad range and diversity of transgender and nonbinary identities, interview-based assessments of gender dysphoria and distress may be more useful than standardized measures and questionnaires. Open-ended questions provide the sort of rich and contextualized data that more broadly describe the interpersonal difficulties, discrimination, minority stress, resource limitations, resilience, coping skills, and other life experiences endorsed by gender-expansive people.

When asking questions about a transgender person's lived experience, it is important to be appropriately curious. We have conducted research in which clients have told us traumatic stories about being treated as novelties or medical anomalies by providers. As discussed elsewhere in this book, medical providers may overemphasize an individual's transgender identity in their treatment or may not recognize ways that a person's identity is salient (e.g., transgender broken arm phenomenon). One useful rule of thumb is to reflect on whether it would be appropriate to ask a cisgender friend the question you intend to ask a gender-expansive individual. If you must ask an invasive question, you may want to ask yourself, "Why do I need to know this and how will the information aid me in addressing the presenting concern I am being asked to treat?"

Many of the same questions that are used to assess other distress are useful for evaluating gender dysphoria. For example, duration, intensity, age of onset, presentation, and impact on relationships and daily activities may be important to know. Please note that gender dysphoria may fluctuate throughout a person's lifespan and/or even throughout their day. A comprehensive assessment may include understanding the unique ways a given individual experiences dysphoria within their own context and how a particular pattern may relate to experiences, setting, relationships, vocation, and so on.

Intake Protocols

If it is a factor in a person's life, gender dysphoria may impact each person somewhat differently. This means it may take time to fully understand each client's experience and their needs related to transition and affirmative interventions. One way to maximize this process is to conduct a transgender affirmative, inclusive intake. Intake forms that include questions about pronouns, gender identity, and gender expression may provide a great deal of important preliminary information about gender-expansive clients and may provide a starting point for further assessment.

Additionally, it may be important to discuss presenting concerns, goals for treatment, and desired medical interventions at a very early stage. This will allow providers to be upfront about the services they are willing and/or able to provide without leading clients on. If you are collecting information for a specific purpose (e.g., for a surgeon, endocrinologist), make sure you familiarize yourself with the information that provider requires. Different providers will require different information, and many provide a list of required information on their websites. Consider calling and chatting with the provider about their approach to care and gathering information about the quality of their work. Doing so will increase your ability to make confident referrals and will expand your knowledge as well. It will also help you to formulate even more appropriate and useful questions for your intake and assessment processes.

Diagnosis

Given the extensive description of gender dysphoria in the *DSM 5*, we will not spend a great deal of time discussing diagnostic criteria. We will, however, discuss many issues, considerations, and pitfalls that go into the assignment of a diagnosis or diagnoses. Of course, assessment is the cornerstone of assigning a proper diagnosis, but there are many things to consider that surround the diagnosis itself.

Default Diagnosis

Gender-expansive people may present with a wide variety of typical issues that are important to document. As does any other person, gender-expansive individuals present with generalized anxiety, adjustment issues, interpersonal distress, and mild depression. These disorders and difficulties may interact with dysphoria, hormone levels, and minority stress. Sometimes helping a client to lower their gender dysphoria can reduce other distress levels (see Knutson & Koch, 2021). However, some co-occurring disorders may need separate or specific treatments. For example, if a client loses a loved one, they will require grief counseling, not treatment for gender dysphoria. A Gender Dysphoria diagnosis may be required for the client to access gender-affirming care, but it does not have to be the only diagnosis and/or focus of treatment.

Differential Diagnoses

Gender Dysphoria may be difficult to diagnose and may be a catalyst behind other disorders and maladaptive coping behaviors (see Knutson & Koch, 2021). For example, clients may present with what appear to be eating disorders, body dysmorphic disorder, difficulties in interpersonal relationships, severe depression, paranoia, and persistent anxiety. To the degree that these disorders stem from gender dysphoria, minority stress, or physiological factors, they may be due to gender dysphoria. For example, when Bill was entering puberty, he limited his food intake in an effort to avoid developing breasts and hips. Although his food restriction qualified as disordered eating, the cause behind his behaviors was much more complex and later alleviated by gender-affirming interventions.

Stabilization

One early argument in gender dysphoria treatment was that clients needed to be "stabilized" before they could undergo gender affirmative medical interventions. The idea was that depression, anxiety, and other disorders needed to be in remission before treatment could commence. Although gender-affirming medical interventions do not magically fix all of a person's difficulties, it is now widely accepted that gender-affirming medical and mental health interventions are a first step in treatment, not a last step. In fact, after treatment, individuals may experience a reduction in general distress, especially when that distress is related directly to gender dysphoria, minority distress, and discrimination.

Diagnoses as Permission or Endorsement for Treatment

Gender-expansive clients may seek a diagnosis and/or "gender therapy" in an effort to obtain a letter of support for gender-affirming treatment. Some professionals may feel reticent to render a diagnosis because they are concerned that if the client changes their mind about gender-affirming surgeries after they have been performed, the professional will be the target of litigation. This fear may inspire strict adherence to the WPATH *Standards of Care 7* or to other structured procedures to evaluate when a client is "transgender enough" to require medical interventions. Of course, adherence to current standards is important, but guidelines and recommendations should not be used as an excuse to do nothing or to deny care when it is needed.

The fear that gender-expansive individuals will "change their minds" is overblown and based on a misunderstanding of gender-expansive identities. Although some people may "detransition," or revert to identifying with their sex and gender assigned at birth, current research suggests that a small percentage of individuals detransition. Furthermore, research suggests that the vast majority of those who do detransition likely do so in response to external influences (e.g., pervasive discrimination, social stigma, pressure from unsupportive family) and not because they changed their mind or realized that they are not gender expansive (Turban et al., 2021). The current system for transition sets up medical providers and professionals as gatekeepers who are able to deny much needed care without justification.

We advocate for a more person-centered, client-focused approach to letter writing and evaluation that takes each individual at face value. Clients who are oriented and competent to give consent and ask for what they need should be empowered to do so. This includes a shift from focusing on the provider as the evaluator to viewing the individual as the expert on their own identity. Of course, there is ongoing research around the provision of surgical interventions for clients who are diagnosed with severe emotional and neurocognitive disorders, but in many cases provider resistance to gender-affirming interventions may be based in biases that such interventions are dangerous, irreversible, or fundamentally wrong in some way. As individuals continue to recognize the curative power of gender-affirmative interventions, we hope that many of the existing barriers and roadblocks will be removed. For more information about letter writing and maintaining records, see Chapter 10.

Ethics and Diagnoses

A major delemma professionals may face is "to diagnose or not to diagnose." Given the violence that has been done to gender-expansive people in society, professionals may worry that they are perpetuating stereotypes and prejudice when they render a gender dysphoria diagnosis. It is important to be open with clients about the implications of a given diagnosis and about the rationale behind rendering it. Given that a diagnosis of gender dysphoria may enable individuals to seek life-saving care, it would be unethical to withhold such a diagnosis only on the grounds that the professional is uncomfortable rendering it.

Some professionals may not feel competent to render a diagnosis. A professional's discomfort is, again, not an adequate argument against providing vital care. We recognize that not all professionals receive specific training in gender-affirming care. In fact, very few providers do. Thus, it is even more important to build competence in this area if possible. Simply passing a client on to another professional is unlikely to result in the client receiving quality care. We encourage professionals to read current literature and to consult with other providers as needed.

Individuals at clinics may find their own desire to treat gender-expansive clients at odds with guidance from their site or administrators. Individual professionals within restrictive organizations may be eager to provide supportive services, to write letters, and to support individuals in their transitions. Although this may not be possible at a given site, we encourage professionals to advocate, both locally and globally, for gender-expansive rights and access to services.

Common Pitfalls

There are a number of traps that professionals can fall into when assessing and diagnosing gender-expansive clients. We list a few here, but this list is not comprehensive. Many of the common pitfalls are more easily avoided when professionals have adequately explored their biases and have challenged their inaccurate assumptions about gender-expansive people.

Refusing to Write a Letter

Sometimes professionals will agree to see clients without being upfront about the limits of their competence and about the services they provide. For example, we have heard stories from people in which they have seen a professional for six months, assuming that they will receive a letter of support for gender-affirming surgery. However, after several months, these clients have been informed that letter writing is not a service their professional is willing to provide. Given the limited resources gender-expansive clients may have, such experiences are particularly cruel and hurtful.

Ignoring Gender-Expansive Identities and Intersections

Although being gender expansive may not be the focus of therapy, it is an important element in interpersonal relationships, in the therapeutic relationship, and in other domains. In research on race, scholars talk about the colorblind phenomenon or the tendency of (often White) individuals to claim that they are so unbiased that they do not respond to or recognize skin tone, or they "see all people the same." Likewise, professionals may try to become so open or unbiased that they claim not to see or respond to gender. While this may fulfill a theoretical ideal of gender equity, it is not consistent with reality. Gender-expansive identities and experiences do not have to be overemphasized but should be appropriately included in assessment, diagnosis, and treatment. Providers should also consider how a client's other identities and environmental variables may inform the client's understanding of their gender identity and other stressors that may or may not be connected to gender identity.

Homogenizing the Population

Just as with any other population, gender-expansive people are not all alike. There is incredible diversity in the gender-expansive community. Our chapters and recommendations serve as general guides, but the processes of diagnosis and assessment are not detailed in legal codes. As discussed elsewhere, gender-expansive individuals, paths to transition, resilience, and experiences of discrimination are very diverse and contextual. Diagnostic and assessment frameworks should be sufficiently flexible to encompass and consider a wide range of identities, experiences, and goals.

Being Unprepared to Provide Affirming Services

Competent providers are rare, and word about competent providers spreads fast. If you provide competent gender-expansive affirmative care, you may experience an influx of gender-expansive clients seeking your services. In fact, some gender-expansive community members maintain lists of providers and local referrals. If you plan to expand your services to encompass gender-expansive populations, doing so may take planning and intentionality. For example, you may wish to consider what continuing education you pursue, where you advertise your services, and whether you provide supervision and/or consultation to other professionals who want to increase their competence with gender-expansive populations.

Summary and Recommendations

* Gender dysphoria, as a diagnosis, is still developing and being reconceptualized.
* Assessment tools (e.g., questionnaires, inventories) have specific limitations that professionals should be aware of.

- The assessment process begins at intake.
- Assessment interviews should include questions about duration, intensity, age of onset, presentation, and impact on relationships and daily activities.
- Different medical providers will want different information and it is important to consider who will read and/or use the assessment information you collect.
- It may be important to talk through the pros and cons of providing a diagnosis of gender dysphoria with a client.
- It is very important to think about how gender dysphoria may interact with other diagnoses that the client qualifies for.

Reflection Questions

1. How do you feel about rendering a gender dysphoria diagnosis, given the history and implications of diagnoses for gender-expansive people?
2. What assessment questions could you add to your intake forms?
3. What questions do you feel it is important to ask when assessing gender-expansive people?
4. What are your biases when it comes to recommending gender-expansive people who do not identify with binary man/woman identities for gender-affirming hormone therapy?
5. What are your biases about recommending gender-expansive people who do not identify with binary man/woman identities for other medical transition interventions such as gender-affirming surgeries?
6. How can you work to challenge biases against gender-affirming hormone and surgery referrals?
7. What is one specific way you could work to move from a gatekeeping model to an informed consent model of care?

References and Suggested Readings

American Psychiatric Association. (1952). *Diagnostic and statistical manual of mental disorders*. American Psychiatric Press.

American Psychiatric Association. (1968). *Diagnostic and statistical manual of mental disorders* (2nd ed.). American Psychiatric Press.

American Psychiatric Association. (1980). *Diagnostic and statistical manual of mental disorders* (3rd ed.). American Psychiatric Press.

American Psychiatric Association. (2013). *Diagnostic and statistical manual of mental disorders* (5th ed.). American Psychiatric Press.

Bem, S. L. (1974). The measurement of psychological androgyny. *Journal of Consulting and Clinical Psychology, 42*(2), 155–162.

Cohen-Kettenis, P. T., & Van Goozen, S. H. (1997). Sex reassignment of adolescent transsexuals: A follow-up study. *Journal of the American Academy of Child & Adolescent Psychiatry, 36*(2), 263–271.

Deogracias, J. J., Johnson, L. L., Meyer-Bahlburg, H. F., Kessler, S. J., Schober, J. M., & Zucker, K. J. (2007). The gender identity/gender dysphoria questionnaire for adolescents and adults. *Journal of Sex Research, 44*(4), 370–379.

Docter, R. F., & Fleming, J. S. (1993). Dimensions of transvestism and transsexualism: The validation and factorial structure of the Cross-Gender Questionnaire. *Journal of Psychology & Human Sexuality, 5*(4), 15–38.

Drescher, J. (2015). Queer diagnoses revisited: The past and future of homosexuality and gender diagnoses in *DSM* and *ICD. International Review of Psychiatry, 27*(5), 386–395. https://doi.org/10.3109/09540261.2015.1053847

Galupo, M. P., & Pulice-Farrow, L. (2020). Subjective ratings of gender dysphoria scales by transgender individuals. *Archives of Sexual Behavior, 49*(2), 479–488. https://doi.org/10.1007/s10508-019-01556-2

Goldbach, C., & Knutson, D. (2021). Development and initial validation of the socio-cultural gender dysphoria scale (SGDS). *Psychology of Sexual Orientation and Gender Diversity.* https://doi.org/10.1037/sgd0000548

Hakeem, A., Črnčec, R., Asghari-Fard, M., Harte, F., & Eapen, V. (2016). Develop-ment and validation of a measure for assessing gender dysphoria in adults: The Gender Preoccupation and Stability Questionnaire. *International Journal of Trans-genderism, 17*(3–4), 131–140. https://doi.org/10.1080/15532739.2016.1217812

Hirschfeld, M. (1923). Die intersexuelle constitution. *Jarbuch Fur Sexuelle Zwischen-stufen, 23,* 3–27.

Jones, B. A., Bouman, W. P., Haycraft, E., & Arcelus, J. (2019). The Gender Congru-ence and Life Satisfaction Scale (GCLS): Development and validation of a scale to measure outcomes from transgender health services. *International Journal of Transgenderism, 20*(1), 63–80.

Knutson, D., & Koch, J. M. (2021). A cotherapy supervision approach using per-son-centered theory with a gender fluid client. *Clinical Case Studies, 20*(5), 368–384. https://doi.org/10.1177%2F15346501211003157

Money, J., Hampson, J. G., & Hampson, J. L. (1957). Imprinting and the establish-ment of gender role. *AMA Archives of Neurology & Psychiatry, 77*(3), 333–336.

Schulz, S. L. (2018). The informed consent model of transgender care: An alternative to the diagnosis of gender dysphoria. *Journal of Humanistic Psychology, 58*(1), 72–92. https://doi.org/10.1177/0022167817745217

Turban, J. L., Loo, S. S., Almazan, A. N., & Keuroghlian, A. S. (2021). Factors lead-ing to "detransition" among transgender and gender diverse people in the United States: A mixed-methods analysis. *LGBT Health, 8*(4), 273–280. https://www.apa .org/about/policy/sexual-orientation

Winters, K. (2006). Gender dissonance: Diagnostic reform of gender identity disorder for adults. *Journal of Psychology & Human Sexuality, 17*(3–4), 71–89. https://doi .org/10.1300/J056v17n03_04

Vance, S. R., Jr., Deutsch, M. B., Rosenthal, S. M., & Buckelew, S. M. (2017). Enhanc-ing pediatric trainees' and students' knowledge in providing care to transgender youth. *Journal of Adolescent Health, 60*(4), 425–430. https://doi.org/10.1016/j .jadohealth.2016.11.020

World Health Organization. (2018). *ICD-11: Classifying disease to map the way we live and die.* http://www.who.int/health-topics/international-classification-of-diseases

World Professional Association for Transgender Health. (2011). Standards of care for the health of transsexual, transgender, and gender-nonconforming people (7th ed.). *International Journal of Transgenderism, 13*(4), 165–232. https://doi.org/10.1080 /15532739.2011.700873

8

Ethics and Professional Standards

E thical practice is foundational to providing professional services for all clients. Professional organizations such as the American Psychological Association (APA), American Counseling Association (ACA), American Association for Marriage and Family Therapy (AAMFT), and National Association of Social Workers (NASW) provide codes of ethics to guide practice with general populations (APA, 2017; ACA, 2014; AAMFT, 2015; NASW, 2021), and professionals are generally trained in the ethical codes of their field. These are a great start, but they are very broad, so some organizations have produced additional ethics codes and guidelines specifically for work with gender-expansive people, such as the *American Psychological Association Guidelines for Psychological Practice with Transgender and Gender Nonconforming People* (APA, 2015).

Here, we build on existing guidelines, specifically by addressing gender-expansive ethics from four perspectives: positive ethics, ethical and legal issues, ethics and practice concerns, and ethics of multicultural and social justice practice. We begin by grounding those models in the cases we refer to throughout this book. Ethics impact every bit of the work we do as professionals, and, therefore, this chapter covers a lot of topics. It may be a good idea to grab a highlighter and note the portions of this chapter that you want to revisit in the future. We used headings throughout the chapter to facilitate indexing and future access to chapter content.

Bill

The therapist Bill saw at the VA came across to Bill as highly ethical and professional. Bill Googled the therapist prior to seeing her and came across pictures of his therapist at gender-expansive rights rallies. In one of the photos, the therapist was wearing a "Protect Trans Kids"

T-shirt. At Bill's first session, his therapist brought up the possibility that Bill might see her at rallies. She also mentioned that she provided treatment for several gender-expansive veterans. Bill and his therapist discussed ways they would maintain boundaries, despite their shared community involvement.

Bill's therapist also actively worked to avoid doing harm to Bill. She, of course, worked to ensure that Bill was not at risk for suicide or self-harm, but she also tried hard to remain aware of other ways that the VA system could expose Bill to harm. For example, when she had to ask for Bill's former legal name in the intake session, she began by explaining why the system required that name. She acknowledged that providing it could be harmful, and she offered to have Bill write the name down instead of saying it out loud. Instead of feeling distressed, Bill felt affirmed and cared for because of his therapist's beneficent behavior.

Molly

Molly experienced general difficulty finding affirming providers in her area, but she did locate a massage therapist she really liked. She started seeing him because she was experiencing sciatic nerve pain. After a few visits, the pain went away, but she kept seeing her massage therapist monthly because he was a great listener and he affirmed her experiences. She found that she could talk to him about anything while he was working on her. She shared him as a resource in a transgender support group. Thereafter, several people in her local community who were not out as gender expansive started seeing her massage therapist.

As the massage therapist started picking up more and more gender-expansive clients, he realized that there was a possibility his clients could be harmed. He worried clients would see each other in his waiting room or that they would fear being outed because they were seeing "the trans massage therapist." He walked through an ethical decision-making model and the ethical dilemma questions below to identify steps he could take to protect his clients. For example, he talked to new and existing clients about the fact that he provided treatment for a variety of people with diverse gender identities, and he reaffirmed his commitment to confidentiality. He also made sure to intentionally schedule his clients on different days and at different times of the day so that clients would not pass each other in the waiting room.

Rowan

As noted in an earlier vignette, Rowan's interaction with their academic adviser was an essential part of Rowan finding a degree program they wanted to pursue. Rowan kept in touch with their adviser, consulting as needed about important academic decisions. After establishing a working relationship with their academic adviser, they noticed that the adviser also attended an online gender-expansive support group that Rowan joined. A few months later, the intermural soccer team on which Rowan played lost a few members and was merged with another team on which Rowan's adviser played.

After the teams merged, Rowan stopped by to visit their adviser in the adviser's office. The adviser brought up their dual relationships and asked if Rowan would prefer to be transferred to another academic adviser. Rowan thanked their adviser for asking, but Rowan stated that they actually felt more comfortable receiving services from the adviser. They expressed trust that the adviser would hold appropriate boundaries and would continue to provide appropriate academic advice. Rowan laughingly said, "I feel like you understand my struggles and it isn't like you're going to give me bad advice just because I scored a goal on you."

Positive Ethics

Positive ethics differ from an "ethical dilemma" approach (Corey et al., 2019). Positive ethics help professionals to think ahead or to fireproof interactions with clients as opposed to simply helping professionals put out fires after they have started. This approach is aspirational in nature and rooted in ways that professionals can best serve the client. Rather than a focus on the codified ethical standards that make up the majority of professional ethics codes, a positive ethics approach is more linked to general ethical principles such as justice, fidelity, autonomy, nonmaleficence, beneficence, and veracity (ACA, 2014). The positive ethics model asks professionals to "walk the walk" of ethical practice in both personal and professional lives.

We take this approach as a counternarrative to the idea that ethical practice with gender-expansive clients is entirely based on addressing and/or resolving dilemmas such as treating dysphoria, trying to stay out of legal trouble, and so on. This is important to do, given that the history of diagnosis and treatment for gender-expansive

individuals is filled with misunderstanding and a tendency to pathologize gender-expansive identities themselves (see Chapter 7). Of course,
resolution of ethical issues is an essential skill for practitioners, but
approaching ethics solely from this prevention standpoint may not
best support diverse gender-expansive clients and may perpetuate the
medical/illness model that has historically been applied to members
of this population. Furthermore, positive approaches are congruent
with the content and goals of gender-expansive affirmative therapy,
a model that focuses on celebrating gender diversity and empowering
gender-expansive persons (Knutson & Koch, 2018).

Taking a Positive Ethics Approach

Approaching ethics from a positive perspective may require clinicians to engage in self-exploration related to their understandings
and beliefs surrounding gender identity and gender diversity. Such an
active approach, undertaken prior to and during work with gender-
expansive clients, will help practitioners to speak with *veracity*, or
truthfulness, about their own understanding of gender identity, and
will likely help cisgender practitioners to understand the influence of
cisgender privilege on their own development as individuals and as
practitioners (see Chapter 2).

Positive ethics encourage professionals to act in ways that support client well-being, both within and outside of the therapeutic
relationship. For example, professionals working from this perspective understand that numerous legal and social issues create
undue stress and harm for gender-expansive people. A professional
oriented toward positive ethics may view such policies and laws as
being directly harmful to clients with whom they are either working
currently or will work in the future and, with that knowledge, advocate to change them.

Professionals working from a positive ethics framework realize
that they may encounter their clients at a protest gathering, that clients may be aware of their broader activism activities, and that the
provider may end up treating the friends of their clients or other community members who know each other. This is because the professional works from the ethical perspective that it is most helpful to
gender-expansive clients to proactively support their well-being by
advocating for fair and just policies. Positive ethics goes beyond the
most basic ethical imperative to do no harm and emphasizes the need
to do good for clients.

Positive Ethics and Decision Making

Using a decision-making framework can also help professionals as they work with gender-expansive clients. In fact, some professional codes of ethics (e.g., APA, ACA, American School Counseling Association [ASCA]) strongly suggest that ethical decision-making frameworks or models should be used when encountering ethical dilemmas. The Canadian Counseling and Psychotherapy Association (CCPA, 2015) suggests that as ethical dilemmas occur practitioners should ask themselves questions such as:

* What emotions and intuition am I aware of as I consider this ethical dilemma, and what are they telling me to do?
* How can my values best show caring for the client in this situation?
* How will my decision affect other relevant individuals in this ethical dilemma?
* What decision would I feel best about publicizing?
* Have I made any decisions I would feel uncomfortable publicizing?
* What decision would best define who I am as a person?

We recommend applying these questions to the dilemmas presented in the case studies at the beginning of this chapter. As you do so, we hope you will discover that such decision-making frameworks are very helpful in helping professionals to think through the potential issues that come up when faced with ethical situations in work with gender-expansive clients. In particular, the question about publicizing your decision helps you to consider how others would view and respond to your behaviors. It helps you explore what others might do in your shoes.

With most dilemmas, there is not a clear "right" and "wrong" answer. The answer usually lies in a gray area. The goal is to select a course of action that has the most benefits for the client and that poses the fewest drawbacks. It may help to list each possible course of action and then to list pros and cons below each option. Before you act, it is also helpful to consult with other professionals who specialize in gender-expansive work. That is because the most ethical and affirming course of action may not be the most socially acceptable one. In other words, you may experience disapproval if you publicize your course of action, but that does not mean it is the wrong one.

Nonmaleficence and Positive Ethics

A primary ethical principle for professionals is to avoid doing harm. In fact, Stanley (2017) suggests that when working with LGBTQ+

clients, there is a need to focus directly on aspirational principles, beginning with the primary ethical obligation to "do no harm." Professionals often focus on the very real, very obvious forms of harm that can come to clients and try to avoid those situations. However, harm is not limited to commonly considered forms of violence such as suicide and self-harm.

Without understanding one's own gender identity and gender journey, there is tremendous capacity to do harm. For example, professionals should think about the potential impact of misgendering gender-expansive clients, both in person and in paperwork. To provide competent services, a mandate based on ethics codes, we must consider what harm looks like in a gender-expansive world. We think about harm broadly: harm can occur when professional and client meet face to face but can also occur outside of sessions. Bill's therapist in the vignette above provided a great example of working to avoid harm.

Ethics and Legal Issues

Perhaps more than is the case in clinical work with other populations, work with gender-expansive clients is collaborative. Depending on their area or region, professionals can best support their gender-expansive clients by having a network of resources that may include physicians, professionals, specialists such as endocrinologists, voice therapy coaches, aestheticians, and the list goes on. An ideal is that mental health professionals work as part of a collaborative gender team, but that is often only possible in large cities with a wealth of resources and integrated care facilities. Of course, collaboration brings up important ethical considerations such as confidentiality, releases of information, and, most importantly, discussions with gender-expansive clients about their own preferences for how their providers are allowed to collaborate.

The number of legal issues that some gender-expansive individuals face might surprise clinicians who are just beginning to work with gender-expansive communities. From varied state laws related to employment and housing protections to the ability to serve as an openly trans person in the military, to the legal right to change names and gender markers on important documentation, laws may create hurdles and challenges for gender-expansive clients. Due to the consistency of these challenges, it is essential for clinicians to be able to support gender-expansive clients in both navigating and processing these situations.

It is also important for professionals to remain aware of any changes or updates to the laws and regulations that apply to their area. Here is an example: in Molly's state, people may not change their gender markers on their driver's licenses without proof of gender affirmation/sex reassignment surgery. This can cause problems for gender-expansive people traveling via air; their appearance may not match the sex on their ID. However, it is possible for people to change the gender marker on their US-issued passport, and that is an appropriate identification to offer to TSA in the United States for flights.

Conversion Therapy

Conversion therapy refers to the unethical and harmful practice of forcing lesbian, gay, bisexual, or other queer-identified individuals to adopt a heterosexual sexual orientation (APA, 2009) and/or forcing transgender individuals to accept the wrong gender identity or the gender that is culturally expected based on their sex assigned at birth (American Academy of Child & Adolescent Psychiatry [AACAP], 2018). Conversion therapy is also sometimes called reparative therapy or deliverance therapy. Conversion therapy is not only ineffective; it is also extremely harmful (AACAP, 2018; APA, 2021). The practice is denounced by the vast majority of psychological and mental health organizations and providers, and legislation has gradually followed suit, with Minnesota being the 21st state to ban conversion therapy for minors as of July 15, 2021. Treatment should always be focused on affirming an individual's gender identity and/or sexual orientation; therefore, conversion therapy should never be conducted for transgender or queer individuals.

Julie sometimes shares a painful example of a client who had a strict religious upbringing. The client self-referred for depression related to a romantic relationship, but around the third session shared that they "believed they were" transgender and asked her if she could "fix" them because they were in so much distress. They wanted to have a "normal" life with a "normal" partner, children, and so on. Julie realized they wanted to know if Julie would do conversion therapy. Although Julie empathized with the client's pain and distress, she had to explain that this was something she could not do. She provided data and literature showing that conversion therapy (a) did not work and (b) could actually harm the client. The client terminated, and likely looked for a different therapist; conversion therapy was not banned in that state and was frequently practiced in that part of the country.

Ethics and Practice Concerns

Literature on ethical practice with gender-expansive clients commonly discusses the idea of multiple relationships (Kessler & Waehler, 2005; Schank et al., 2010). Ethical codes highlight the potential risks of entering into harmful multiple relationships with clients. We encourage you to note that professionals are not banned from all dual relationships, but that they are forbidden from entering harmful ones. For any professional working with gender-expansive clients, avoiding all multiple relationships could have a severe and deleterious impact. As noted above, professionals providing care for Bill and Molly are engaged with the community and they are likely to interact with family members, friends, or even partners of their clients. It is the responsibility of those providers to ensure that their dual/multiple relationships do not cause their clients harm.

Multiple Relationships with a Single Client

Community membership and/or participation may be important for professionals working with gender-expansive clients. Engagement and advocacy within the community may inevitably lead to multiple relationships with current clients. For example, let's go back to Rowan and their academic adviser. Rowan actually felt more cared for because of the dual/multiple relationships they had with their academic adviser. In fact, Rowan felt safe and they trusted that the adviser would continue to act appropriately. Their dual relationship was not harmful. In fact, transferring Rowan to another professional might have disrupted Rowan's progress by forcing them to establish trust and a working relationship with an entirely new professional.

Relationships with Client Families

Sometimes engaging collaboratively with the family members of gender-expansive clients presents another type of multiple relationship. Some people discuss gender-affirming actions, including social and medical transitions, as family issues. It may be important for providers to integrate family members into work with gender-expansive clients and may be necessary for clients under 18. Of course, it is essential for providers to understand the dynamics of the gender-expansive clients' family relationships to assess for potential harm that might come from families who are rejecting of their gender-expansive family member. For a more thorough discussion of family dynamics, see Chapter 12.

Rural Considerations

For professionals in rural settings and/or remote areas, avoiding multiple relationships may be even less of an option. If a given professional is the only service provider or the only affirming provider in their area, they may be the go-to person for everyone seeking affirming services. If that person identifies as gender expansive or with a minoritized sexual orientation (e.g., lesbian, gay, bisexual), they may be part of the community they are providing services for. We discuss managing multiple relationships in rural communities in Chapter 5.

Informed Consent

Informed consent is an ethical imperative, commonly required prior to professionals providing services. Given all of the ethical issues that can arise while providing affirming services, we recommend including any possible ethical issues into your consent form. If you do not use a consent form because your profession does not require one (e.g., life coaching), it may still be important to have a discussion with your gender-diverse clients early in your professional relationship. Please remember that it is important to be proactive. If you start providing effective gender-affirming services, you may experience an influx of clients, and, as you do, you will encounter new ethical dilemmas that you will need to plan for.

Competence

The American Counseling Association *Code of Ethics* states that professionals "practice only within the boundaries of their competence, based on their education, training, supervised experience, state and national professional credentials, and appropriate professional experience" (ACA 2014). While this general ethical standard applies to all professionals, the World Professional Association of Transgender Health (WPATH) offers further insight into competence for mental health professionals working with gender-expansive clients. We are unable to provide a full summary of all of the competencies required by different organizations, but it is a good idea to be aware of them. Many organizations also provide webinars and trainings on affirming therapy that professionals may use to further increase and demonstrate competence.

Many academic training programs do not provide sufficient training in work with gender-expansive clients for someone to be considered competent. Rather, it may fall on the student or professional to seek additional training specific to working with gender-expansive people, relevant to their area of focus. In addition to trainings, professionals may benefit from reading the ever-increasing body of scientific literature about gender-expansive people. Professionals may also consider seeking supervision and engaging in regular consultation with others who focus on affirming work with gender-expansive people. These days, there are few excuses for a lack of knowledge and awareness of gender-expansive communities.

Multicultural and Social Justice Practice

Understanding clients' experiences is a multilayered process. For many gender-expansive clients, the lens of gender identity may be a primary one through which to view the world, but it is not the only lens. Guidelines on working with gender-expansive and gender-nonconforming clients (e.g., Burnes et al., 2010) and multicultural guidelines (e.g., APA, 2015) highlight the importance of an intersectional perspective in order to best understand clients.

People are complex and multilayered; identity development is concurrent (see Chapter 3). It is consistent with ethical practice to understand a client as a complex individual in whom traditionally static identities such as race, gender, ethnicity, sexual orientation, and religion intersect with identities that are potentially more fluid such as age, socioeconomic status, and ability status. Of course, each of these identity domains fits within a corresponding system of privilege and oppression. Historically, guidelines that address multicultural competence and practice in counseling have outlined some essential domains: awareness, knowledge, skills, and action. Those domains demonstrate that it is not enough to just know about a population. It is also important to have self-awareness, obtain skills, and act in support of gender-expansive people and other marginalized communities.

Summary and Recommendations

- Ethical therapists know themselves and explore their gender identities.
- Ethical therapists plan for ethical dilemmas that may arise when working with gender-diverse clients.
- Ethical therapists think through possible sources of harm and work to mitigate them.
- Ethical therapists use decision-making models and think critically about decisions they make when providing care for gender-diverse people.
- Consultation is a cornerstone of ethical work with gender-diverse clients.
- Multicultural awareness and practice are essential parts of ethical work.
- Ethical practice often includes collaboration and lifelong learning.

Reflection Questions

1. How will you navigate seeing a gender-expansive client at a political rally or other community event? Or at the grocery store or other public place?
2. Do you think it is okay to share your pro-gender-expansive policy views with your clients?
3. How will you navigate dual roles/relationships with gender-expansive clients?
4. How can you work with family members of a gender-expansive client?
5. What information should you consider adding to your informed consent forms?
6. What trainings or resources could you engage with over the next six months to increase your competence working with gender-expansive clients?

References and Suggested Readings

American Academy of Child & Adolescent Psychiatry. (2018). *Conversion therapy.* https://www.aacap.org/AACAP/Policy_Statements/2018/Conversion_Therapy .aspx

American Association for Marriage and Family Therapy. (2015). *AAMFT code of ethics.* https://www.aamft.org/Legal_Ethics/Code_of_Ethics.aspx

American Counseling Association. (2014). *2014 ACA code of ethics.* https://www .counseling.org/resources/aca-code-of-ethics.pdf

American Psychological Association. (2009). *Resolution on appropriate affirmative responses to sexual orientation distress and change efforts.* https://www.apa.org/about/policy/sexual-orientation

American Psychological Association. (2015). Guidelines for psychological practice with transgender and gender nonconforming people. *American Psychologist, 70*(9), 832–864. https://doi.org/10.1037/a0039906

American Psychological Association. (2017). *Ethical principles of psychologists and code of conduct.* https://www.apa.org/ethics/code/

American Psychological Association. (2021). *APA resolution on sexual orientation change efforts.* https://www.apa.org/about/policy/resolution-sexual-orientation -change-efforts.pdf

Burnes, T. R., Singh, A. A., Harper, A. J., Harper, B., Maxon-Kann, W., Pickering, D. L., Moundas, S., Scofield, T. R., Roan, A., Hosea, J., & ALGBTIC Transgender Committee. (2010). American Counseling Association: Competencies for counseling with transgender clients. *Journal of LGBT Issues in Counseling, 4*(3–4), 135–159.

Canadian Counseling and Psychotherapy Association. (2015). *Standards of practice* (5th ed.). https://www.ccpa-accp.ca/wp-content/uploads/2015/07/StandardsOf Practice_en_June2015.pdf

Corey, G., Corey, M. S., & Corey, C. (2019). *Issues and ethics in the helping professions* (10th ed.). CENGAGE Learning Custom Publishing.

Kessler, L. E., & Waehler, C. A. (2005). Addressing multiple relationships between clients and therapists in lesbian, gay, bisexual, and transgender communities. *Professional Psychology: Research and Practice, 36*(1), 66.

Knutson, D., & Koch, J. M. (2018). Person-centered therapy as applied to work with transgender and gender diverse clients. *Journal of Humanistic Psychology, 62*(1), 1–19. https://doi.org/10.1177%2F0022167818791082

National Association of Social Workers. (2021). *National Association of Social Workers code of ethics.* https://www.socialworkers.org/About/Ethics/Code-of-Ethics /Code-of-Ethics-English

Schank, J. A., Helbok, C. M., Haldeman, D. C., & Gallardo, M. E. (2010). Challenges and benefits of ethical small-community practice. *Professional Psychology: Research and Practice, 41*(6), 502. https://doi.org/10.1037/a0021689

Stanley, J. L. (2017). Teaching ethics in relation to LGBTQ issues in psychology. In T. R. Burnes & J. L. Stanley (Eds.), *Teaching LGBTQ psychology: Queering innovative pedagogy and practice* (pp. 61–84). American Psychological Association. https://doi.org/10.1037/0000015-004

Transitions, Care Teams, and Clinical Processes

A number of the chapters in this section may have felt somewhat unrelated to the work that some human service professionals do. It is important to have a working understanding of diagnosis, the letters that are available, and some treatment approaches, but many of our readers may not actually diagnose and treat. If you have been speed reading the last few chapters, we ask that you attend more closely to this one. We will discuss the options for transition, collaboration between professionals, and ways that multiple professionals may contribute to treatment. Please note that we use the plural form of transition, or transitions, to signify that there are many unique ways to transition, as demonstrated in the vignettes below.

Bill

As part of his advocacy work at the LGBTQ+ center in his area, Bill started a gender-expansive care collaborative. He was inspired by a person in his gender-expansive support group who said, "My therapist is amazing and all, but she can't give me everything I need. Lately, she has been working on makeup tips with me, but that takes away from our ability to focus on other stuff." Bill realized that he could do something to help centralize services for gender-expansive people in his community. Forming the collaborative took time, but now the team meets weekly for an hour to discuss referrals, ways to be more effective, and current needs in the community.

For example, at the collaborative's last meeting, a therapist in the mental health offices at the LGBTQ+ center (after obtaining the client's permission) shared with the group that she recently did an intake with a trans masculine client who just came out. Bill recommended that the client be given information about the local support group. Before the meeting adjourned, the therapist had a handful of flyers and a variety of resources to share with her client. Later in the meeting, the collaborative discussed ways to work together to reduce assault rates against gender-expansive people, which appeared to be increasing in their local community.

Molly

Molly always says that the first person she came out to was herself. She always knew she was different. She had dreams in which she was a woman and she feared, for many years, that she was gay. She was deeply attracted to her wife, but Molly did not feel the ability to connect with her wife fully. Strangely, she felt left out of her closest relationships. It was not until she discovered people like Laverne Cox and other visible advocates for gender-expansive rights that she finally allowed herself to ask, "Am I a woman?" She struggled with doubts about her identities as a woman and as a transgender person, asking herself things like "Am I actually transgender?" and "Am I 'trans enough' to transition?" It took time, but she eventually gained the self-confidence to begin her transition.

Molly began her transition process by socially transitioning. She began by telling a friend she had met online in a gender-expansive group that she was a trans woman. Over the following year, her friend helped her prepare and plan to tell her wife and children. Even though her wife asked for a divorce, Molly's wife continued to live with Molly for several years until Molly was able to move out of their shared home to live on her own. Eventually, Molly also pursued medical transition steps.

Rowan

Rowan's coming-out process is ongoing and has been rather complex. They legally changed their name to Rowan after they turned 18, shortly after they discontinued therapy with their Christian counselor and reached an agreement with their parents that they would not come out at church. An online gender-expansive group was a lifesaver for them. The group accepted Rowan's identity and gave them a space in which they felt affirmed. With the help of the online support group, Rowan was able to realize that there is no one way to express their gender as someone who identifies beyond the gender binary. They eventually started finding comfort in presenting more androgynously, wearing hoop earrings, stylish glasses, trousers, and collared shirts.

Rowan decided not to undergo top or bottom surgery because they found that they were ambivalent about their secondary sex characteristics. They did, however, continue the low dose of estrogen that they started with Planned Parenthood because they liked the way that the hormones softened their features and deemphasized their muscles. Rowan continued to follow their parents' wishes by "keeping their identity to themselves" in church and at school, but they enjoyed it when people seemed confused about what pronouns to use for them. In those moments, it felt that they were achieving their true self even if they still felt unable to be open about who they were with everyone around them.

Transitions

Gender transition broadly refers to the process of taking steps to socially and publicly identify as a gender other than the gender a person is assigned at birth, based on sex (Hendricks & Testa, 2012). As noted earlier, we use the plural form of transition, or "transitions," to signify that different gender-expansive people will approach transition in different ways and that some gender-expansive people will not transition at all. For many gender-expansive people, gender transition broadly involves a process or series of steps that include finding the gender role and gender expression that are most comfortable and affirming for them based on their current gender identity. Gender transition steps can be divided into two main categories: social transition and medical transition. The social and/or medical transition steps that a gender-expansive person takes often serve to reduce feelings of gender dysphoria and/or increase feelings of gender euphoria. The process is not necessarily linear, and there is no "right" way to transition.

Social and medical transition steps/processes could occur simultaneously, alternately, or one before the other. It is important to reiterate that some gender-expansive people do not experience gender dysphoria, some experience gender euphoria, and others experience a mix of both. (Refer to Chapter 7 for a more in-depth discussion on gender dysphoria.) Here, we will provide an overview of common social and medical transition processes. Then we will discuss how experiences of both gender dysphoria and gender euphoria, in addition to the concept of passing and process of coming out, can factor into transitions for gender-expansive people.

Social Transition

Social transitions include any social (i.e., nonmedical) changes that a gender-expansive person makes to live in a way that matches/affirms their internal gender identity (Huang & Davila, 2021). Some common social transition steps include using a new name and/or pronouns different from those assigned at birth, changing gender expression (e.g., clothing, makeup, jewelry, hairstyle) to be more representative of how the individual wants to outwardly convey their gender identity, using bathrooms aligned with their gender identity, and legally changing name and/or sex/gender on official documents (e.g., passport, birth certificate, driver's license). The specific goals that a gender-expansive person establishes for their social transition are unique to the individual. The goals are based on what they feel they need in order to have their gender identity affirmed by themselves and by others (Huang & Davila, 2021). In other words, there are infinite ways that people can socially transition, and gender-expansive people may pursue one, some, all, or none of the social transition steps previously listed.

Another step (or rather series of steps) that is often part of social transitions is coming out. Coming out is almost entirely a social process and is not a one-time event; gender-expansive people may "come out" in different ways on a daily, weekly, or other basis. However, as a person pursues other social and/or medical transition steps, it may be harder and harder for them to avoid coming out. Some people who do not wish to come out may complete their transition process in seclusion and then relocate to a new place where they can start out in their affirmed gender. Other people may come out in some spaces (e.g., to romantic partners, family, and friends), but may chose not to come out in other spaces (e.g., at work, at church, or elsewhere). It is important to understand whether a client wants to "be out" as a gender-expansive person in certain spaces before outing them to others. A client may trust you with information that they do not wish to be shared with others.

Furthermore, it is important to note that the social transition steps that gender-expansive people decide to take and are able to access can be influenced by age, cultural background, socioeconomic status, and other identity variables (Huang & Davila, 2021). Social transition steps may occur prior to medical transition, and early social transition steps can serve as a way for an individual to explore gender identities and expressions before pursuing medical interventions.

Medical Transition

Medical transitions involve any medical procedures (e.g., hormone therapy, gender-affirming surgeries) that are designed to physically change an individual's body to better match their affirmed gender identity (Rachlin, 2018). Within the context of gender transition, hormone therapy involves taking medication such as estrogen, testosterone, or androgen blockers through oral, subcutaneous, and/or injectable means. Hormone replacement therapy (HRT) or affirming hormone therapy is intended to change a gender-expansive person's secondary sex characteristics such as body fat distribution, hair growth, breast growth, or voice changes to be more aligned with how they wish to outwardly express their gender.

Gender-expansive people assigned male at birth (e.g., transgender women, trans feminine nonbinary individuals) may pursue surgeries intended to "feminize" their bodies, such as vaginoplasty, breast augmentation, orchiectomy, facial feminization surgeries, or feminizing body contouring (Boskey & Klein, 2021). Gender-expansive people assigned female at birth (e.g., transgender men, trans masculine nonbinary individuals) may pursue surgeries intended to "masculinize" their bodies such as phalloplasty, metoidioplasty, hysterectomy, mastectomy, or breast reduction (Boskey, 2021a, 2021b). Some nonbinary people may also pursue different types of surgery, although those surgeries may not necessarily be part of a "transition."

Gender Dysphoria

As we mentioned earlier, gender-expansive people typically pursue social and medical transition steps with the intent of decreasing their experiences of gender dysphoria and/or increasing their experiences of gender euphoria. Gender dysphoria has been categorized as body dysphoria and social dysphoria (Davidson, 2016). Body dysphoria involves distress that results from discomfort with one's sex characteristics or other physical attributes, such as genitals, breasts, or body hair, because these physical characteristics are not aligned with how an individual sees themselves in relation to their gender identity (Davidson, 2016). Social dysphoria focuses on distress resulting from social interactions that do not affirm one's gender identity, such as being perceived as the incorrect gender (Davidson, 2016). For example, being called "ma'am" in a grocery store or restaurant can be quite distressing to someone who identifies as a man or as nonbinary.

Medical and mental health providers often focus primarily or solely on body dysphoria, but this paints a very narrow picture of how gender dysphoria impacts gender-expansive individuals because it can lead to ignoring the possible role of invalidating social contexts (Galupo et al., 2020). We believe that systemic factors, such as public policy, political climate, and access to and availability of gender-expansive-affirmative resources, and factors related to social dysphoria, also contribute to gender dysphoria and need to be taken into account when working with gender-expansive clients.

Diagnosis and Access to Care

The diagnosis of gender dysphoria is controversial. In many cases, a diagnosis of gender dysphoria or even gender identity disorder is required to access affirming care and receive insurance coverage (see also Chapter 7). This is problematic because gender-expansive individuals who are deemed to have low or nonexistent levels of gender dysphoria may be denied gender-affirming care. To increase access to care and reduce the negative impacts of gatekeeping, we recommend an informed consent model for individuals who wish to pursue gender-expansive affirmative medical treatments (Schulz, 2018).

Affirming treatments for gender dysphoria generally affirm the gender identities of gender-expansive individuals (see Austin & Craig, 2015). Mental health providers write extensively about gender-expansive affirmative therapies that adapt leading treatment approaches to gender-expansive populations. Medical interventions are also commonly referred to as gender affirming. Again, access to these treatments generally requires a diagnosis of gender dysphoria.

However, gender-expansive individuals don't necessarily show up to therapy to process identity. The assumption that gender-expansive people are different and that gender-expansive identity saturates all aspects of a gender-expansive person's presentation is, as mentioned earlier, called the trans broken arm phenomenon. If a gender-expansive person presents in therapy to process a death or to explore possible careers, identity may be rarely discussed and only as much as it relates to the presenting concern.

Gender Euphoria

Experiencing a gender identity that is different from the gender and sex assigned at birth is not always associated with distress (i.e., gender dysphoria). For those who do have gender dysphoria, the dysphoria may come from a variety of sources and may impact the individual with varying levels of severity. Assuming that all gender-expansive individuals have dysphoria not only invalidates how some individuals experience their gender, it also contributes to further medicalization and stigmatization of gender-expansive individuals. It is problematic to assume that distress or a dysfunction needs to be present in order for someone to be gender expansive.

Many gender-expansive people also experience gender euphoria, a concept defined by Ashley and Ells (2018) as "a distinct enjoyment or satisfaction caused by the correspondence between the person's gender identity and gendered features associated with a gender other than the one assigned at birth" (p. 24). Gender euphoria is sometimes viewed as the "opposite" of gender dysphoria (Rachlin, 2018). Gender-expansive people are likely to experience greater and greater levels of gender euphoria as they experience higher congruence between their body, their environment, and their gender identity.

Passing

The gender euphoria and/or gender dysphoria that a gender-expansive person experiences may be influenced by their desire and ability to "pass." Within the context of gender transition and gender-expansive populations, the concept of passing refers to whether a gender-expansive individual is viewed by others as being cisgender (Bockting et al., 2013; Grzanka et al., 2018). For a gender-expansive individual who passes as cisgender, other people may not know that they are gender expansive until they come out as gender expansive to them. Passing can allow a gender-expansive individual to blend in more easily in a cisnormative society. Gender-expansive clients who desire to pass as cisgender may also discuss a desire to be "stealth," which refers to a gender-expansive person concealing their identity/status as a gender-expansive person from others.

It is extremely important to know that not all gender-expansive people have a desire to pass. It is therefore important to not assume that one of the goals that a gender-expansive client has for the gender transition is being able to eventually pass as cisgender. Some gender-expansive individuals desire to blend in and some do not want to or even care about blending in. A gender-expansive individual may change their outward appearance through clothing, makeup, hairstyling, medical procedures, or other interventions in order to be viewed as "passable" if passing is something that is important to them. The steps that a gender-expansive individual takes in their gender transition may reflect whether passing is something that is important to them.

Passing can also directly impact the interactions that a gender-expansive individual has with others and the resources that they are able to access. This is again because cisnormative society is more accepting and accommodating of individuals who neatly "fit in" to expectations and norms surrounding gender (Grzanka et al., 2018). The concept of passing and its importance to some individuals are influenced by a complex interplay of cisnormativity, lack of acceptance of gender-expansive individuals on a systemic level, a desire for physical safety, social dysphoria, and body dysphoria, among other factors. Please note that some clients react negatively to the idea of passing, given its cisnormative origins and implications.

Diverse Pathways

Not all gender-expansive individuals take the same steps to affirm their gender identity during the process of transition. Some individuals may only take steps related to socially transitioning, some may pursue a combination of steps related to socially and medically transitioning, and some may pursue steps to affirm their gender that were not discussed above. Some individuals may also desire medical transition steps without socially transitioning (Rachlin, 2018). Regardless, it is of vital importance to fit treatment to the specific needs and desires of each individual. Everyone conceptualizes and affirms their gender identity in different ways, and gender-expansive individuals have varying levels of gender dysphoria and gender euphoria. Therefore, there is no one-size-fits-all model for supporting gender transition. The mental health practitioner should create individualized treatment plans focused on meeting the transition-related goals of each client, while remembering that not everyone will want to transition, and that every transition will be different.

When it comes to transitions, most of the research and discussion focuses on mental and medical health providers, but many professionals play a role in gender-expansive care. As demonstrated in Rowan's case, many of the gender-affirming steps they took were cosmetic or social in nature. The way they styled their hair, the clothes they selected, and the communities they engaged with were essential parts of their transition processes. That is why we wrote this book to include all human service professionals. We believe it is important for all helping professionals who work with clients to be prepared to create affirming spaces for gender-expansive people.

Care Teams

Some hospitals, clinics, and continuum of care facilities organize care teams that meet regularly. For example, the first author worked in a continuum of care retirement facility as a chaplain early in his career. He met regularly with nurses, doctors, coordinators, and other facility staff to discuss ways to improve care for residents. The team would discuss interventions that might improve the mental, physical, spiritual, and emotional health of clients who were recovering from recent surgeries or who were terminally ill.

As demonstrated in Bill's case vignette, we believe it is important for professionals from a wide variety of disciplines to come together to address ways to improve gender-expansive care. In other chapters, we note that it is important to maintain referral lists for gender-expansive clients and we encourage our readers to be prepared to serve as case managers or resource connectors for their clients. If maintaining a resource list is all that you can do right now, you are making a difference. However, the more discussion and dialogue that takes place among professionals, the greater the difference we can make. If you have the chance in your present location, please consider organizing a discussion group to tackle ways to serve gender-expansive communities.

One great way to start the discussion is to invite a gender-expansive community member, researcher, or scholar to speak at your site. Getting together for training and information allows everyone to establish a shared language and approach to affirmative care. It also demonstrates to everyone that your group or business cares about gender-expansive health. If bringing in a speaker is not possible, there are excellent recordings and resources available on the internet that you can stream. You can even use this book to support discussion around ways to improve gender-expansive care through cooperation and collaboration.

Clinical Processes

Because this book is for a wide range of human service professionals, we will not continue to delve into medical and/or mental health clinical interventions. We do think, though, that is important to highlight that you do not have to be a physician, surgeon, psychologist, counselor, or other licensed health provider in order to improve health in gender-expansive communities. As we illustrated above, the goal is to help gender-expansive people feel safe, congruent, and like their true selves. This goal is accomplished, in part, by creating a more affirming world.

When you give a gender-affirming makeup lesson, offer gender-affirming haircuts, make gender-affirming space in your gynecology clinic, learn affirming terminology as a front desk staff person in an office, and so on, you are making a huge difference. As individual providers, we can only make a limited difference. When gender-expansive clients leave our offices or places of business, they enter a world that can be hurtful and violent. The more we work together to create a caring environment across the services we provide, the more we can create lasting change and healing for gender-expansive people everywhere.

Summary and Recommendations

- The process of transition can look different for every gender-expansive person.
- Gender transition can involve social and/or medical transition steps.
- Not all gender-expansive people transition.
- Not all gender-expansive people experience gender dysphoria.
- Gender-expansive people may experience a mix of gender dysphoria and gender euphoria.
- Passing may be important for some gender-expansive people, but some gender-expansive people may not desire or care to pass.
- Care teams or collaboratives are an excellent way to maximize service provision.
- Individual affirming providers in isolation may be less effective than communities of providers who work toward consistent, environmental change.
- Professionals do not have to be medical or mental health professionals in order to make a huge clinical difference for gender-expansive clients.

Reflection Questions

1. What is at least one resource (e.g., scholar, video, community member) you could contact/use to provide a gender-affirming training at your place of business?

2. Who is at least one other gender-affirming professional that you could partner or collaborate with?
3. What is at least one way you could be actively involved in reducing dysphoria for gender-expansive clients?
4. What is at least one way you could be actively involved in increasing gender euphoria for gender-expansive clients?
5. What is at least one tool you could provide clients to assist with social transition?
6. What is at least one tool you could provide clients to assist with medical transition?

References and Suggested Readings

Ashley, F., & Ells, C. (2018). In favor of covering ethically important cosmetic surgeries: Facial feminization surgery for transgender people. *American Journal of Bioethics, 18*(12), 23–25. https://doi.org/10.1080/15265161.2018.1531162

Austin, A., & Craig, S. L. (2015). Transgender affirmative cognitive behavioral therapy: Clinical considerations and applications. *Professional Psychology: Research and Practice, 46*(1), 21. https://doi.org/10.1037/a0038642

Bockting, W. O., Miner, M. H., Swinburne Romine, R. E., Hamilton, A., & Coleman, E. (2013). Stigma, mental health, and resilience in an online sample of the US transgender population. *American Journal of Public Health, 103*(5), 943–951.

Boskey, E. (2021a). Gender-affirming surgeries: Men, bottom. In A. Goldberg & G. Beemyn (Eds.), *The SAGE encyclopedia of trans studies* (Vol. 1, pp. 330–332). SAGE Publications, Inc. https://www.doi.org/10.4135/9781544393858.n116

Boskey, E. (2021b). Gender-affirming surgeries: Men, top. In A. Goldberg & G. Beemyn (Eds.), *The SAGE encyclopedia of trans studies* (Vol. 1, pp. 333–335). SAGE Publications, Inc. https://www.doi.org/10.4135/9781544393858.n117

Boskey, E., & Klein, P. (2021). Gender-affirming surgeries: Women. In A. Goldberg & G. Beemyn (Eds.), *The SAGE encyclopedia of trans studies* (Vol. 1, pp. 336–338). SAGE Publications, Inc. https://www.doi.org/10.4135/9781544393858.n118

Davidson, S. (2016). Gender inequality: Nonbinary transgender people in the workplace. *Cogent Social Sciences, 2*(1), 1–12. https://doi.org/10.1080/23311886.2016.1236511

Galupo, M. P., Pulice-Farrow, L., & Lindley, L. (2020). "Every time I get gendered male, I feel a pain in my chest": Understanding the social context for gender dysphoria. *Stigma and Health, 5*(2), 199–208. https://doi.org/10.1037/sah0000189

Grzanka, P. R., DeVore, E., Gonzalez, K. A., Pulice-Farrow, L., & Tierney, D. (2018). The biopolitics of passing and the possibility of radically inclusive transgender health care. *American Journal of Bioethics, 18*(12), 17–19.

Hendricks, M. L., & Testa, R. J. (2012). A conceptual framework for clinical work with transgender and gender nonconforming clients: An adaptation of the Minority Stress Model. *Professional Psychology: Research and Practice, 43*(5), 460–467. https://doi.org/10.1037/a0029597

Huang, H., & Davila, J. (2021). Social transition. In A. Goldberg & G. Beemyn (Eds.), *The SAHE encyclopedia of trans studies* (Vol. 2, pp. 791–795). SAGE Publications, Inc. https://www.doi.org/10.4135/9781544393858.n264

Rachlin, K. (2018). Medical transition without social transition: Expanding options for privately gendered bodies. *Transgender Studies Quarterly, 5*(2), 228–244. https://doi.org/10.1215/23289252-4348660

Schulz, S. L. (2018). The informed consent model of transgender care: An alternative to the diagnosis of gender dysphoria. *Journal of Humanistic Psychology, 58*(1), 72–92. https://doi.org/10.1177/0022167817745217

World Professional Association for Transgender Health. (2011). Standards of care for the health of transsexual, transgender, and gender-nonconforming people (7th ed.). *International Journal of Transgenderism, 13*(4), 165–232. https://doi.org/10.1080/15532739.2011.700873

Resources and Letter Writing

In this chapter, we provide you with some practical and useful tools for your practice. Many of the templates and resources we reference can be found in the appendixes toward the end of this book. Please use these tools with caution! They are intended to be used with full consent and disclosure, by people competent to provide gender-affirming care, and under supervision, as appropriate. Also, please note that our resources are based on care practices in the United States. If you are using one of these templates for the first time, please seek out a mentor to guide you through the process. Before jumping into our resources, we will provide examples of ways they could be used with Bill, Molly, and Rowan. Then we discuss letters, worksheets, and other resources.

Bill

Bill always knew that he would want bottom surgery (a radial forearm flap phalloplasty) as part of his transition. He started saving up money for the surgery before he left the military. As he got closer to being able to afford the surgery, he informed his therapist at the VA that he would need a surgery referral letter. The therapist had a background in gender-expansive care and she knew what basic information she needed for a letter that conformed to WPATH standards. Bill also provided her with the contact information and additional requirements that Bill's surgeon had listed on her website as needing to be included in a referral letter for surgery at her clinic.

Bill's therapist reviewed the information Bill provided and she identified that, in the course of her work with Bill, she had not collected some essential information that needed to be included in the letter. She scheduled a 30-minute session with Bill to collect the information she needed and to confirm the data she already had was still accurate.

Then she drafted the letter and shared it with Bill so that he could check it for accuracy. Bill made small recommendations for changes. After finalizing the letter, and having Bill fill out a release form, Bill's therapist sent it to Bill's surgeon. Bill's therapist made sure the letter included her most recent contact information so that Bill's surgeon could contact her to consult as needed.

Molly

As discussed in an earlier vignette, Molly has to travel long distances to access affirmative care in a large city. She rarely stops to use restrooms along the way, but when she does, she is terrified that the gas station attendant will harass her or will call the police if they see Molly use the women's bathroom. Molly requested a carry letter from her physician. She knows it is not legally binding, but she finds it comforting to have a document to present to the police if she ever needs it.

Rowan

Rowan read about transition timelines online. They are a talented artist and they decided to draw an artful depiction of their future transition goals. They painted a picture of a rocky path to symbolize the bumpy transition road ahead. They also included bends and curves in the road to show that the path through transition will not be a direct one. Instead of writing their transition steps on the roadmap, they used sticky notes to affix their transition steps to the path. They are a bit of a perfectionist, and did not want to mess up their painting when they had to delay a step or when they had to move a step earlier in their transition. They experienced mixed feelings as they constructed their roadmap. It felt good to have a plan, but they were disappointed that they could not take all of their steps at once.

Resources

The WPATH (2011) *Standards of Care* note that affirming health care for gender-expansive people encompasses a wide range of disciplines and human service providers. For example, gender-expansive people benefit from attending support groups, access to resources such as binders, packers, breast forms, voice therapy, cosmetology, legal support, and so on. Some clinics and businesses maintain case workers who are trained to coordinate services for clients, but in gender-affirmative care, we suggest that everyone who provides affirming services should be prepared to serve as a case manager. In other words, it is up to all of us to maintain directories of affirming services and referral lists of people we trust.

We have found that it is helpful for human service professionals to maintain a list of gender-expansive-friendly services that is updated and modified regularly. Appendix A includes a template you are welcome to use. There are a multitude of ways to identify providers. We regularly find and network with providers at Pride events and booths, by contacting LGBTQ+ community centers, from our gender-expansive clients themselves, and even through word of mouth. For example, one of the authors learned that a new boutique lingerie store was opening in her town of Stillwater, Oklahoma. She learned that it was owned by the friend of a friend, and through word of mouth she was told that the owner was very trans friendly and discreet. She recommended the store to a couple of transitioning clients, who went and reported wonderful, positive, "freeing" experiences.

Letters

As discussed in Chapter 4, not all gender-expansive people will choose to transition, and mental health providers should be familiar with the fact that hormone replacement therapy and surgery may be medically necessary to reduce gender dysphoria for some people (WPATH, 2011). Transition will look different for every person. Some nonbinary folks may want surgeries but may not consider this "transition" (and in fact may face more resistance from health-care providers than those going through a binary transition). For gender-expansive persons who desire to transition, the role of the mental health provider as a letter writer can have a huge impact on how smoothly this process goes. It is important for mental health providers to be aware of the potential "gatekeeping" role that they play and the power that they have to support or be a barrier to their client's transition.

There are generally three types of letters that a provider might write to support a gender-expansive person. These are a letter of recommendation (also referred to as a referral letter) for affirming hormone therapy (HT), a letter of recommendation for surgery, and a "carry letter." WPATH recommends one referral letter for hormone replacement therapy, one referral letter for breast/chest surgery (some people refer to this as "top surgery"), and two referral letters for genital surgery (also called "bottom surgery")—one from a mental health professional and another from a person "who has had only an evaluative role with the patient" (WPATH, 2011, p. 27). Julie recently had a client whose surgeon required three letters, two from mental health providers and one from another physician. Please see Appendixes B, C, and D for sample letters for a hypothetical client.

Affirming Hormone Therapy

In discussing affirming hormone therapy, clients may use the terminology hormone replacement therapy or HRT. Some clients may use the term "T" to refer to testosterone. Letters for affirming hormone therapy used to be required by endocrinologists and other providers, but some providers no longer require them. If you are asked to provide a letter of support for hormone therapy, you should be aware that WPATH (2011, p. 26) recommends including the following elements in your letter (although different providers may have different requirements):

* The client's general identifying characteristics
* Results of the client's psychosocial assessment, including any diagnoses
* The duration of the referring health professional's relationship with the client, including the type of evaluation and therapy to date
* An explanation that the criteria for hormone therapy have been met and a brief description of the clinical rationale for supporting the client's request for hormone therapy
* A statement about the fact that informed consent has been obtained from the client
* A statement that the referring health professional is available for coordination of care and welcomes a phone call to establish this

The letter in Appendix B includes all of the required elements.

Affirming Surgeries

Clients may refer to surgeries as "top surgery" or "bottom surgery." Top surgery generally refers to breast/chest surgery—either breast implants or mastectomy. Bottom surgery generally refers to genital surgery, sometimes referred to as sexual reassignment surgery (SRS) or gender affirmation surgery (GAS). Clients will generally (but not always) prefer to use these terms rather than specific terms such as orchiectomy, but it is important for you to use the correct name for a given procedure in your letter. It is also extremely important to not make assumptions about what kind of surgeries clients may want or not want. Clients may also desire other gender-affirming surgeries that fall outside of "top surgery" and "bottom surgery," such as facial feminization surgery (FFS), facial masculinization, and body contouring.

The WPATH *SOC 7* (2011) mention that mental health providers may help clients to be both psychologically prepared and practically prepared prior to seeking hormone replacement therapy or surgery. It is important for mental health providers to note that a mental health screening/assessment is needed for referrals, but psychotherapy is not a requirement. A letter of recommendation for surgery may be similar in content to a letter for affirming hormones. Also, some providers may not require a letter for breast removal and/or augmentation. According to WPATH (2011, pp. 27–28), the surgery letter of recommendation should contain the following (but surgeons may have their own requirements):

- The client's general identifying characteristics
- Results of the client's psychosocial assessment, including any diagnoses
- The duration of the referring health professional's relationship with the client, including the type of evaluation and therapy to date
- An explanation that the criteria for surgery have been met and a brief description of the clinical rationale for supporting the client's request for surgery
- A statement about the fact that informed consent has been obtained from the client
- A statement that the referring health professional is available for coordination of care and welcomes a phone call to establish this

The letter template in Appendix C incorporates all of the information above. Please note that some standards may change with WPATH *SOC 8*, but the templates in this chapter are likely to remain helpful as foundational guides and examples.

In providing letters of recommendation or referral for medical treatment, it is extremely important to have a good understanding of the expectations and policies of the physician, surgeon, or endocrinologist. While the WPATH *SOC* attempt to provide some standards, these are flexible in nature and are interpreted differently by different physicians. For example, the current standards state that psychotherapy "although highly recommended—is not a requirement" (WPATH, 2011, p. 28). However, in our experience, some physicians will explicitly state that they will not make an appointment without documentation of, for example, at least six months of psychotherapy.

Likewise, insurance companies may have specific requirements different from the WPATH recommendations. At the time of this writing, for example, the federal Blue Cross Blue Shield insurance company requires at least 12 consecutive months of psychotherapy to cover any transition-related surgery. Further, different states in the United States may have legal policies or ethical standards for mental health providers that are not in alignment with the WPATH *SOC*. We recommend that all providers familiarize themselves both with regional insurance practices and any legislation that would govern providing referrals or recommendation for HRT or surgeries.

Sometimes, clients in the United States or Canada may travel internationally for surgeries or other health care. The doctors in these different countries also may have different expectations. We highly recommend, if a gender-expansive client is seeking a letter of recommendation for a procedure and they have a physician in mind, that mental health professionals (a) obtain release consent to have a phone conversation with the physician's office to collaborate on care, (b) ask the client to provide information about the physician's website, or (c) ask the client to provide any email communication or details of the physician's written policies so that they may gain a thorough understanding of what the physician is looking for in a letter.

Carry Letters

Clients sometimes request "carry letters." An example of a carry letter is included in Appendix D. These letters have no legal bearing, but some clients might like to have one for personal safety reasons. A carry letter may be provided, for example, to law officers or to TSA agents to help explain why a client's outward appearance may not match personal identification. An example of this might be if a client is pulled over for speeding on the highway—she may have a very different appearance in person (long hair, makeup, dress) from what is reflected on her driver's license card (male gender marker, short hair). A carry letter may help address some initial confusion on the part of the law officer. Again, it is important to communicate to your clients that how a law officer may actually respond to this information may vary and could in fact place them at more risk.

Other Resources

Throughout this book, we have encouraged you to consider ways to improve your service delivery to gender-expansive clients. At the end of each chapter, we included questions designed to help you consider ways to update consent forms, intake paperwork, and so on. In an effort to support that work, we included Appendix E, a planning worksheet designed to help you identify, implement, and delegate (if applicable) various service improvement tasks. You may have noticed that we mentioned the worksheet in the introduction. If you were referred to this section before reading the other chapters, please go back and start from the beginning. If you are just reaching this section of the book after reading the rest of the content, we encourage you to track and document the ways in which you wish to implement change in your own practice. The template in Appendix E contains a couple of examples, but please feel free to disregard them if they are unhelpful. The point is for you to tailor the changes and updates to your own human service profession.

Competence-Building Resources

As mentioned in Chapter 8, it is important for clinicians to gauge their own competence in working with gender-expansive clients. Reading this book is a start! We also recommend that all human service providers read, at a minimum, the WPATH *Standards of Care*, available at https://www.wpath.org. Other important resources to reference include:

- The American Psychological Association Guidelines: https://www.apa .org/practice/guidelines/transgender.pdf
- The American Counseling Association Guidelines: https://www.counsel ing.org/docs/default-source/competencies/algbtic_competencies.pdf ?sfvrsn=d8d3732f_12

Transition Care Resources

In our work with gender-expansive clients, we find that it is sometimes helpful to help clients construct a transition timeline (see Knutson & Koch, 2021). Some clients get excited about the activity, and they end up drawing visually engaging graphics such as roads that curve into the distance with distance markers along the way that document each transition step in the order that the client plans to complete the step. Other clients simply list their transition timeline similar to this example below:

- In the next six months
    - Begin saving up to move out of Mom and Dad's house
    - Search for roommate to help split the cost of rent
- In the next year
    - Move out of Mom and Dad's house with roommate
    - Begin saving for surgery
- In the next year and six months
    - Complete legal name change
    - Change name on all academic, work, and legal documents
- In the next two years
    - Locate a surgeon for top surgery
    - Obtain letters to support top surgery

The list above is only the beginning of what could end up being a very long timeline with a large number of intermediate steps. As clients begin planning out their transition, they may discover that it is more involved than they had guessed. As they discuss the list with you, they may discover things they left out or they may come to the realization that a step will take longer than they expected.

It is important to be prepared to help clients deal with disappointment and frustration over how long it may take them to complete their timeline. As they continue to work with you, they may share sadness over the fact that a planned activity remains out of reach and must be pushed back. However, it is also possible that clients will discover that they are able to reach a goal sooner than expected. We recommend explaining to clients, up front, that timelines are only guides. They will have to be revised and rewritten multiple times. However, they are a very helpful way to assist clients as they begin to reason through and conceptualize their eventual transition process.

Web-Based Resources

One of our favorite websites is https://www.transgendermap.com by Andrea James. It is full of wonderful resources for gender-expansive clients. For example, it provides a sample transition timeline and offers a wealth of topics for transitioning clients to consider. Some topics include financing, insurance, workplace, legal issues, name choice, name change, driver's license, birth certificate, passport, marriage, will, and other documents. Other resources are available online, but make sure you pull them from a reputable source. It goes without saying that not everything you find through a search engine is useful or appropriate for use with gender-expansive clients.

Summary and Recommendations

- If you have never written a hormone or surgery letter, seek supervision or mentorship before writing your first one.
- Double-check and confirm your competence to use the resources in this chapter.
- Create and revise a resource list that you can provide to your clients. Make sure you vet the sources you recommend.
- Familiarize yourself with the resources in the Appendixes of this book so that you will be prepared to use them as needed.
- A transition timeline/roadmap can be a helpful way to assist clients with planning their futures.
- Carry letters are not legally binding, but they may help reduce a client's anxiety and distress.

Reflection Questions

1. What is your comfort level with writing a referral letter for surgery?
2. Try identifying one person who could mentor you as you write your first referral letter or identify one person you could mentor as they write their first referral letter.
3. What is one objective that you could add to your service improvement worksheet?
4. What is one transition step, not listed in the timeline above, that you imagine a gender-expansive client might want to take?
5. What is one resource or contact you could add to your resource list right away?
6. What is one other reputable online resource, not listed above, that you could consult?
7. When do you plan to read the WPATH *Standards of Care* (2011) if you have not already done so?
8. What is the next fact sheet or care guideline document (e.g., AMA, ACA, APA) that you plan to read and when do you plan to read it?

References and Suggested Readings

American Psychological Association. (2015). Guidelines for psychological practice with transgender and gender nonconforming people. *American Psychologist, 70*(9), 832–864. https://doi.org/10.1037/a0039906

Burnes, T. R., Singh, A. A., Harper, A. J., Harper, B., Maxon-Kann, W., Pickering, D. L., Moundas, S., Scofield, T. R., Roan, A., Hosea, J., & ALGBTIC Transgender Committee. (2010). American Counseling Association: Competencies for counseling with transgender clients. *Journal of LGBT Issues in Counseling, 4*(3–4), 135–159.

Knutson, D., & Koch, J. M. (2021). A cotherapy supervision approach using person-centered theory with a gender fluid client. *Clinical Case Studies, 20*(5), 368–384. https://doi.org/10.1177%2F15346501211003157

World Professional Association for Transgender Health. (2011). Standards of care for the health of transsexual, transgender, and gender nonconforming people (7th ed.). *International Journal of Transgenderism, 13*(4), 165–232. https://www.tandfonline.com/doi/abs/10.1080/15532739.2011.700873

SECTION III

Affirmative Care in Context

Affirmative Work in Various Settings

It goes without saying that human service professionals work in a variety of settings and provide a broad range of services. For the most part, this book is focused on generalist practice. We try to highlight common dynamics and considerations that are shared between human service settings. However, each workplace and specialization is different and the ways that professionals practice affirmative care is unique. We will not be able to cover all trades, services, and specializations. Instead, this chapter is focused on helping professionals identify the unique aspects of their jobs as well as ways that their approaches to care can be modified to make them more affirming of gender-expansive people. Such interdisciplinary differences are first highlighted in the cases of Bill, Molly, and Rowan and then are further examined throughout the rest of the chapter.

Bill

When he is not working his full-time job, leading support groups, and volunteering at the LGBTQ+ center, Bill sometimes gives presentations on gender-affirming care to local businesses and organizations. He loves being able to answer questions like "What is the big deal about pronouns? I don't care if people get mine wrong." He also welcomes the opportunity to push back against statements like "Gender-fluid people just sound like they can't make up their mind." Bill enjoys presenting because it seems to him that most people want to be gender affirming and they will be if they are given the chance to sort out their biases and to learn skills. He is always surprised by how much people grow when their places of employment are willing to take a risk and open dialogue about gender diversity. He has seen, firsthand, how much of a difference it can make when leaders in any business take a visible stand in favor of affirming care.

Molly

Molly loves driving into the small town 15 miles from her home to get her hair done every month. Molly's stylist is very affirming, and Molly always feels safe with her. The other stylists are friendly too. Getting her hair done is the highlight of Molly's month because she rarely gets out of the house and there are few places in town where she feels safe. Last month, Molly needed to move her appointment, so she called the salon and a new receptionist answered the phone. When the receptionist answered the phone, Molly gave her name and requested a different day for her appointment. The receptionist replied, "Sir, I don't think there is any availability that day." Molly was shocked and she fell silent on the phone. After a brief moment, the receptionist said, "Oh, I'm sorry. Your voice was deep and I thought you had to be a guy. There is an open appointment that day after all. I put you down for 10:00 a.m."

Rowan

Rowan started to consider coming out at school and at church. They started getting very worried about how people would react, especially their parents, who had warned them not to disclose their gender identity outside of their home. As Rowan's distress continued to increase, they realized they needed help getting their anxiety back under control. They finally broke down and scheduled an appointment with a college counselor at their school. On the phone, the counselor explained to Rowan that therapy services had to be billed to Rowan's school account, but they said the center had things set up so that the bill would show up as "general student services." The counselor also explained that he would log Rowan's affirmed name in the student records, but that the name would not appear in records that were accessible to Rowan's parents. Rowan felt much safer knowing that they would be able to access services without being outed to their parents or others.

Imagine that you have been referred an 18-year-old client, Jennifer. She identifies as a Black trans woman. How might your work with Jennifer differ if you were seeing her as a school counselor in a high school setting? Or as a college counselor in a counseling center? Or as a career counselor? Or as a group counselor in a community mental health setting? Or in private practice? Our approaches to work with gender-expansive clients will vary depending on the settings in which we work. In this chapter, we help readers understand the nuances of gender-affirming work in different settings, and the different structural strengths and limitations of these settings.

General Considerations

Later in the chapter, we will talk about specific settings (e.g., mental health clinics, retail outlets, medical facilities, schools, and so on) in which professionals may take somewhat nuanced approaches to affirming care. First, though, we focus on general ways that services can foster gender-affirming environments for both employees and clients. If you are interested in ways to implement affirming care using an ecological approach, see also the Knutson and colleagues 2021 article about a systemic approach to gender-affirming care in universities and the importance of thinking about leaders, support staff, and broader systems.

Leadership

When leaders in an organization value gender inclusivity, they increase the likelihood that meaningful change will occur. People at the top make decisions about allocating resources, building décor, expansion and design of spaces, and so on. If you are a current or future leader in your field, you are probably aware of how much employees and colleagues look up to you and value your opinion. You hold a lot of power, and you have the opportunity to use that power to create positive change for your employees and for the clients they serve.

If gender inclusion is one of your values, we recommend considering how your daily decisions impact people of all genders. Once you start asking yourself regularly, "What does _____ [fill in the blank] decision mean for gender inclusivity," you will be amazed how even the smallest decision can impact gender-expansive people. For example, your employees may be encouraged to greet clients who walk into your retail space by saying, "Hello, sir/ma'am." On the surface it seems like a nice thing to encourage, but gendering clients can lead to errors and major mistakes. Instead, consider recommending that your employees simply say "Hello" and drop any gender-based honorifics (such as sir, ma'am, or miss) from their vocabulary when interacting with clients. Your employees will quickly find that referring to a client's gender is unnecessary and adds nothing to an encounter that cannot be replaced with a smile and a respectful, warm demeanor. Being present and thinking inclusively can trickle down even into the ways your employees engage with and create space for clients.

Likewise, thinking about inclusion can impact the space you occupy. Consider walking through your physical space with "gender-inclusive glasses" on. As you tour your space, you may notice that your bathrooms are inclusive, but they communicate that inclusivity by displaying two genders on the bathroom sign, so they are not really gender-neutral or inclusive of nonbinary or agender folk. In retail settings, you may also discover that your product is partitioned in a way that communicates that some products are only for boys/men and others are only for girls/women. When you think through a gender-inclusive lens, you can become aware of how, for example, a gender-fluid person might feel shopping in your store.

You may not have the power to change everything in your space, and you may not need to. You do have the opportunity, though, to give the gift of inclusivity wherever possible. Some leaders may fear backlash from their employees, but it is our experience that inclusivity makes a better work environment for everyone. Most employees get into human service professional jobs because they want to help other people. By making your business more gender inclusive, you empower the people around you to fulfill that mission.

Support Staff

Regardless of the setting in which you work, it is imperative that any staff who might come into contact with clients receive training in gender-affirmative customer service. As demonstrated in Molly's case at the beginning of this chapter, it is not enough to be gender affirming yourself. Clients may feel very safe with you, and they may look forward to working with you regularly, but they may not always deal with you directly. Providing affirming services is about making sure that everyone at your location is prepared to work with gender-expansive clients from the initial point of contact.

Clients often already feel nervous and worried about how they will be treated in a given setting, so their experiences with staff who serve as an initial point of contact between clients and your business are particularly important. If a gender-expansive client has a negative experience during their first interaction with you, they are unlikely to use your services, no matter how affirming your setting is. If the gender-expansive client is connected to other community members, they may also share their negative experience and encourage other gender-expansive people to avoid your services.

Training for people who answer phones is particularly important because they are not able to interact with clients face to face. It is important for staff to know that the pitch of a person's voice is not the same as their gender. By default, staff people should avoid honorifics (e.g., ma'am, sir) and binary gender pronouns (e.g., she, he) unless they know what pronouns a client uses. As a general rule, calling a person by their name throughout the call is a better approach to ensuring that the person is referred to appropriately and remains engaged throughout the call.

People who run reception desks will also benefit from training and awareness building. Some reception desk workers may react skeptically or dismissively to a client's appearance or name. For example, a client's current gender expression may not match the gender expression in their driver's license photo. Staff members should be able to appropriately navigate these encounters. They should also be aware of the rationale behind any paperwork they hand to a client. Some clients may ask if they have to provide their legal name, or they may question why they are being asked to list their pronouns. Well-trained reception staff know how to navigate inquiries and to explain important contextual nuance.

If your service has a reputation for gender inclusivity and affirmative care, you may attract employees who are eager to serve gender-expansive populations. That is why we encourage professionals to take a broader gender-affirming approach to leadership, training, and the overall system of their settings. When the culture, environment, and design of a service is inclusive, the expectations around inclusive behaviors are obvious to employees and clients alike.

For example, think of attending an important phone interview for a job or a promotion you really want. Even though you will be talking on the phone with your prospective employer or current boss, you will probably wear business attire, sit at a desk, and set your notes in front of you. That is because your environment shapes your mindset. Wearing sweatpants and lying in bed will probably make for a less successful interview. Likewise, gender-exclusive environments communicate that gender inclusion is not important and the mindsets of the people in that setting will probably reflect that.

Operating Systems

Human service professionals use a variety of operating systems such as computer software, online advertising, text messaging, and so on to interact with clients and to complete the tasks they are assigned. We have talked about inclusive space, but we also encourage you to consider creating inclusive systems. For example, your website is a nonphysical space that also communicates your commitment to gender inclusion. Just as you might hang a gender-expansive pride flag in your space, you can increase visibility and inclusion with logos and images in your online store. You can also organize products so that they are searchable by people of any gender, and you can feature gender-expansive models.

Your online forms and your on-site client tracking systems should be gender inclusive and should facilitate accurate identification of your clients. For example, a staff person at a front desk is more likely to use the correct name for a client if the client's affirmed name is foregrounded, rather than included in a side note. You might be surprised how many prospective clients you lose when those clients, for example, are forced to choose between Mr. or Ms. as a prefix to their name. Gender inclusivity is not only a vital part of making a better, more affirming world. It is also, quite frankly, good for business.

Location Specifics

We already acknowledged that we do not have the space to provide a comprehensive overview of unique ways that different human service professionals practice gender affirmation. Instead, we started by offering general principles that may apply across settings. Now we provide examples of different settings in an effort to get you thinking about the uniqueness of your own site. You may work in one of the settings we list below, but if you do not we encourage you to think about ways that the recommendations below connect with and/or inform the work that you do. In the sections that follow, we focus on three types of providers who may interact with gender-expansive people as they progress from childhood, through the educational system or systems, and into middle and late adulthood.

Schools

The issue of youth and young adults identifying as transgender or gender expansive, and working toward transition in some cases, is a topic that has gained much national attention in recent years (e.g., Knutson et al., 2021). The American School Counselor Association (ASCA) *National Model* offers a framework for school counselors that is data informed, systematic, and developmentally appropriate; it aims to improve student achievement and attendance (ASCA, 2012). School counselors largely work with a whole-school, preventive approach when possible. In this case, the first course of action would be to engage in whole-school, preventive psychoeducation for all students and faculty/staff around gender, differences between gender identity and gender expression, differences between gender and sex, what it means to be gender expansive, and so on. In some states and school districts, however, this kind of curriculum is disallowed, which creates an ethical dilemma for the licensed/certified school counselor who is bound to follow ASCA ethical codes as well as state/school district mandates (ASCA, 2016).

Imagine that you are a school counselor working with Jennifer, the gender-expansive high school senior we mentioned earlier in this chapter. Using the ASCA *Ethical Standards for School Counselors* and the ASCA *National Model*, you would be compelled to consider your responsibility to Jennifer, your responsibility to other students, your responsibility to Jennifer's parents, your responsibility to the school (as a whole, faculty, staff, administration), and your responsibility to yourself (ASCA, 2012; ASCA, 2016). In our experience, school counselors and people who work with youth particularly struggle with balancing their responsibility to a young person with their responsibility to the young person's parents. It can be hard to balance the child's confidentiality and privacy with the parents' rights.

Considering all of your levels of responsibility helps you to think through the process of establishing collaborative relationships and partnerships to promote the development and safety of gender-expansive young people. We encourage you not to forget that your responsibility reaches beyond the individual or individuals you are working with. Gender-inclusive advocates also work with leadership to develop systemic change in their schools and communities. Developing gender-expansive cultural competence in schools is inherently collaborative, complex, and a vital part of cultivating health for future generations.

College or University Counseling Centers

Similar to school settings, many university or college counseling centers (UCCs) work from a preventive model in which the larger student population needs are addressed through psychoeducation, with group or individual counseling available to those who have more needs. Professionals working in UCCs typically collaborate with other student services offices on campuses, such as diversity offices or offices that serve LGBTQ+ students. They may also partner with student organizations for LGBTQ+ students.

At the systems level, counselors who work in UCCs may engage in university/college-level advocacy, psychoeducation, and outreach. For example, professionals may advocate for options for pronouns or different names to be used in assigned university email addresses, in learning management systems (such as Canvas or Blackboard), or across university systems (for financial aid offices, the registrar's office, the bursar, the library, etc.). Counselors in UCCs may assist with efforts to develop clothing closets and clothing exchange programs for use by gender-expansive students. They may develop, contribute to, or participate in trainings for incoming students, faculty, and staff such as Safe Zone trainings. They may engage in other activities such as tabling for special events (Transgender Day of Remembrance; National Coming Out Day; National Day of Silence; International Day against Homophobia, Transphobia and Biphobia [IDAHOT]; Pride Month).

Smaller-group–level activities might include guest lectures in courses for students or group counseling offerings. When offering group counseling, it will also be important to keep in mind whether you would want to offer a group for all gender-expansive students, or special groups for trans men, trans women, or nonbinary folks. See also Chapter 13 on group counseling.

At the individual level, activities are both preventive and responsive. Individual work with gender-expansive students might include psychoeducation like, for example, how to talk to a professor about what name the client uses and what their pronouns are. In some fields such as humanities, instructors may be more open to these conversations than in other fields, but, in general, gender-expansive students may need to role-play or discuss their options to increase their confidence in interactions with instructors. One special consideration might be letter writing. For example, even if a UCC professional is licensed and competent to write letters of recommendation for hormones or surgery, the university may disallow it due to concerns about liability issues. It is important for professionals in these settings to understand university/college policies and to advocate for change and inclusion, when possible.

Private Practitioners

Many human service professionals go into private practice or shared group practice. For example, psychologists may operate out of a single office in an office building that caters to a wide range of professionals, or a barber may rent a chair in a salon. Some private practice spaces handle billing, manage scheduling, and provide other services for a commission. Private practice may entitle a practitioner or human service professional a great deal of freedom, or it may restrict a professional's ability to fully control their environment. For example, a private practitioner may not be able to give constructive feedback to a front desk staff person without working with the firm that provides the support staff that the practitioner uses.

If you are an intermediary who provides services for private practitioners, you have the opportunity to shape, to some degree, the quality of services that the practitioners provide. By hiring and training support staff, you can ensure that gender-expansive clients are affirmed as they seek out and engage with services provided through your firm. However, we encourage you to be mindful of the private practitioners you agree to work with. Your gender-affirming services may clash with or even contradict biased and/or discriminatory services provided by some people in your network. You can advocate for gender-affirming clients by ensuring that you work with and support affirming practitioners.

If you are a private practitioner, you also have the opportunity to shape the landscape of affirming care. For example, you can rent office space from gender-expansive lessor and/or you can purchase products and services from gender-expansive entrepreneurs. At the very least, you can ensure that the subcontractors who receive your money value gender affirmation as much as you do. The way we spend our money and the partnerships we form are powerful. You have the ability to do a lot of good by thinking gender affirmatively as you make business decisions.

Corporate and Large Companies

Large companies seem increasingly invested in demonstrating an openness to gender diversity as evidenced by clothing, cosmetics, credit card, search engine, and other commercials featuring gender inclusivity. Many corporations seem ready to consider social justice–oriented feedback and accountability from employees and clients/customers. We do not discuss large businesses in depth here, but we want to highlight the fact that gender-affirmative change across various settings is not limited to your workspace or company. When we band together to demand change from companies and providers locally and globally, we hold the power to make a difference. Therefore, we recommend considering your personal spending habits as well as the ways you engage with (or refuse to engage with) systems (e.g., social media, apps, media content providers, and so on).

Conclusion

As you finish this chapter, we hope you feel equipped with countless ways you can change your workspace, the systems with which you engage, and the world around you. It may feel overwhelming to consider all of the ways you can make a difference, but please remember that you do not have to fix everything overnight and that you do not have to take responsibility for all of the gender discrimination in the world. Making small changes over time can add up to a huge shift. Every action you take to support gender inclusivity is a precious gift.

Summary and Recommendations

* It is important to ensure that staff are properly trained to interact with clients in gender-affirming ways.
* Inclusive climates and spaces inspire gender-inclusive behaviors.
* Both spaces and systems can be either gender inclusive or gender exclusive.
* It can be hard to maintain appropriate boundaries around your responsibilities to a gender-expansive youth and your responsibilities to their parents when the values and goals of the two differ.
* It is vital to provide training for people at all levels of a given setting, business, or organization.
* Gender inclusion in education is an important part of ensuring the mental and emotional health of future generations.
* Directing your money to goods and services that are provided by gender-affirming or gender-expansive people is a great way to expand your gender affirmative footprint.

Reflection Questions

1. What is one alteration that you could make to your physical or online workspace that would make it more gender inclusive (e.g., changing bathroom signage, hiring gender-expansive models, changing forms to be more inclusive of a range of gender identities and pronouns)?
2. What is one training that you could provide to your employees or that you could recommend to your company leadership? What should be included in such a training?
3. How could you better promote cultural competence to create an inclusive school environment?
4. How could you more effectively monitor and ensure your own competence working with gender-expansive students?
5. What is one good or service that you could source from gender-affirming or gender-expansive businesses or subcontractors?
6. What is one way you could advocate for greater gender inclusivity in your immediate work surroundings (e.g., on your floor, your department, or at your workstation)?

References and Suggested Readings

American School Counselor Association (2012). *ASCA National Model: A framework for school counseling programs* (3rd ed). American School Counselor Association.

American School Counselor Association (2016). *ASCA ethical standards for school counselors.* https://www.schoolcounselor.org/getmedia/f041cbd0-7004-47a5-ba01-3a5d657c6743/Ethical-Standards.pdf

Gay, Lesbian and Straight Education Network (GLSEN). https://www.glsen.org

Knutson, D., Matsuno, E., Goldbach, C., Hashtpari, H., & Smith, N. G. (2021). Advocating for transgender and nonbinary affirmative spaces in graduate education. *Higher Education, 83,* 461–479. https://doi.org/10.1007/s10734-020-00673-5

Society for Human Resource Management. (2022). *Employing transgender workers.* https://www.shrm.org/resourcesandtools/tools-andsamples/toolkits/pages/employingtransgenderworkers.aspx

Trans Employment Program. https://www.sfcenter.org/transgender-employment-program-tep/

Transgender Law Center. https://transgenderlawcenter.org/

12

Partners and Families

Working with couples, people in polyamorous relationships, and families is generally a complex process. Each time you bring someone new into the mix, you're introducing new opinions, experiences, and biases. Because of biases, fears, and sometimes outright ignorance, things get even more complicated when partners and family members are brought into discussions involving gender identity and gender transition. People who come out as gender expansive are someone else's partners, children, parents, and so on, and the coming out process impacts not only the gender-expansive individual but also those closest to them.

Bill

Bill identifies as polyamorous and he is currently in a romantic relationship with three other gender-expansive people. Bill lives with two of his partners in the Boston area and the third partner is currently living in California. Bill's parents were very supportive when he came out as a trans man, but they struggle with accepting Bill's relationships. When Bill came out to his mother as a trans man, she was able to reimagine Bill's future as a man who was attracted to women. She got excited about having a daughter-in-law and she looked forward to the day when she would be able to go shopping and have girls' nights again. She knew that Bill was not her daughter, but she believed that Bill's transition meant she would have a daughter again someday.

When Bill came out to his mother as polyamorous, she felt like she was losing the opportunity to have one emotionally bonded relationship with a daughter-in-law. She feared that she would be embarrassed in front of other family members if Bill brought multiple partners to visit for the holidays. Bill's mother worked hard to understand and accept Bill's relationships and she sought counseling to help her process what her future might look like. Eventually, she reached the conclusion that she could value the people Bill loved because her son loved and valued them. She reconciled her feelings of loss and found other ways to have girls' nights and connections with other women.

Molly

Molly's family (her ex-wife and daughter) continue to support Molly, but they experienced their own relational transition processes when Molly came out. Molly's daughter prided herself on being liberal and accepting. She found herself getting excited about the prospect of having two moms. Molly's wife worked a great deal and was away from home most of the time. Molly's daughter had always relied on Molly as a source of support, nurture, and stability. Molly's daughter told most people "it made sense" that Molly is and always had been her mother.

Molly's wife, Rebecca, was not delighted when Molly came out, but she supported Molly as well as she could. Personally, she loved Molly and she wanted nothing but the best for her. She knew she was not attracted to women and she identified pretty early that her relationship with Molly would have to end, but she had become so absorbed in her job that a split felt imminent anyway. Rebecca struggled most, not with her own reactions, but with the reactions of others (colleagues, people in her friend group). She lost most of her friends when she started standing up for Molly and trans issues by calling out microaggressions and by demanding insight and compassion from people in her life.

Rowan

Rowan has been in a romantic relationship for three years with Claudia, a 26-year-old lesbian cisgender woman. Claudia values her identity as a lesbian feminist, and she feels strongly about gender equality for people of all genders. When Rowan told Claudia that they identified as gender fluid, Claudia was kind and understanding. Claudia knew she would need to explore her lesbian identity as she continued to date Rowan, but she was glad that Rowan felt they could come out to her, and she found her love for Rowan deepening. As Rowan started taking masculinizing hormones to achieve a more androgynous look, Claudia was delighted to find that she was still very much attracted to Rowan's changing body.

Rowan also found that their love for Claudia deepened after they came out to her. Rowan felt closer to Claudia and they appreciated her support as they continued to explore their gender identity. They continued to be attracted to women (and to Claudia more specifically), but they began to realize that the term "lesbian" no longer fit for them. They began to identify as panromantic in order to capture their affection for people of a variety of genders.

Foundations and Key Concepts

Gender transition is a transition not only for your gender-expansive client; it is also a transition for everyone in their life. The people closest to a gender-expansive person may relate to them based on inaccurate assumptions for many years. In this chapter, we seek to provide tools that will help you support gender-expansive clients and their parents, children, siblings, partners, and other family members. We will revisit gender identity and how this may impact family and romantic relationship dynamics. Then we will discuss viewing gender transition as a process that impacts the family as whole, prompting the need to provide resources and support for those who are struggling to adjust to and support a family member or partner who comes out or is already out as gender expansive. We will also explore different types of romantic relationships, including monogamous and polyamorous relationships.

Throughout this chapter, we will primarily focus on biological family and romantic partners, but it is important to remember that gender-expansive people may also form families of choice or chosen family (see Milton & Knutson, 2021). Many gender-expansive and LGBQ people create family-like bonds with others to whom they are not biologically related. Because disconnection and estrangement from biological family is a common occurrence for many gender-expansive people, they create lasting connections with friends and community members to supplement or replace the support and love that would otherwise be received from biological family.

Deconstructing Negative Biases

Take a moment to reflect on what pops into your mind when you think about someone coming out as gender expansive to their family or to a romantic partner. You may automatically think the parents of a gender-expansive daughter will react negatively and force her to move out of the home. You may assume that the parents of a nonbinary teenager will start out meaning well, but will become distant because they don't understand their child's identity and don't take the time to learn on their own. You may figure that the children of a gender-expansive parent who comes out to them will break off communication with their parent. In general, you may find yourself expecting a negative outcome when a gender-expansive person discloses their identity to a loved one or friend.

If negative thoughts such as these pop into your mind (thoughts focusing on negative experiences and heartbreaking stories), you are not alone. Given the bleak ways that society and the media negatively characterize, depict, and treat gender-expansive people, it is no wonder that we expect something terrible or devastating to happen when a gender-expansive person comes out to the people in their life. One of the goals of this book is to help change the prevailing fatalistic narrative surrounding gender-expansive people. Yes, life can be incredibly hard for gender-expansive people, especially those early in their coming-out or transition process, but gender-expansive people also experience incredible acceptance, growth, connection, and resilience, as well as support from friends and loved ones.

The Power of Acceptance

We love hearing stories of gender-expansive teenagers crying tears of joy when their parents use the correct pronouns for the first time. Or when a brother or sister stands up for their gender-expansive sibling when someone says something inappropriate to them. Or when a gender-expansive woman is able to create an even more fulfilling relationship with her wife after coming out. Realistically, we know that some romantic relationships do end when a partner comes out, perhaps because their sexualities may prompt them to realize that they are no longer compatible when their relationship is redefined. It is important to provide resources and support to help partners amicably navigate the process when a partner comes out as gender expansive, regardless of whether the partners remain romantically involved.

Gender in Family Dynamics

You may be aware of the current "gender reveal" craze that has become popular when someone is expecting a baby. People bake cakes, shoot off fireworks, and light smoke bombs at gender reveal parties across the United States and in other countries as well. There are several assumptions in gender reveal parties that are worth noting, such as the genitals detected in an ultrasound determine gender, the colors blue and pink are synonymous with boy and girl, there are only two genders, and so on. We bring this up because it is a stark example of the incredible amount of focus and energy that people place on determining, establishing, and essentializing gender. The moment a child's supposed gender is revealed, people purchase gifts, make plans, and tailor their expressions consistent with their expectations. Babies are born under the proclamation, "It's a boy/girl!!"

Gender Fixation in Families

As family and friends, many of us become so invested in what we think a child's gender identity is that our worlds are shaken when they tell us that their gender is actually different from the gender they were assigned at birth. We may not even allow ourselves to consider that a child may come out as gender expansive at some point after they are born. In particular, parents' concepts of their child's gender identity may become so ingrained that they think they know their child's gender better than their child does.

When their child reveals to them that they are gender expansive, this may be the first time that the parent has been exposed to the idea of or entertained the possibility of having a gender-expansive child. The parent may then react negatively because they think their child is delusional or going through a phase or that gender transition violates their beliefs or values, among a variety of other potential reasons. Parents may go through a grieving process if they imagined their child's future and that future is dependent on their child being a certain gender. The parents may feel that the future they hoped for has died and/or is lost.

We focus a lot on parents in this chapter, because they play such an important role in a child's life, but other family members may be impacted by the coming out of a gender-expansive child. For example, cisgender siblings may go through a grief process if they were excited to have a brother/sister and then are informed that their sibling is a different gender. A cisgender sibling may express confusion about how to interact with their gender-expansive sibling and/or they may say that they feel they never really knew their gender-expansive sibling. Hearing such expressions of confusion and loss can be difficult for a gender-expansive person.

Components of the Family System

As we mentioned earlier, families are complex and working with them requires a great deal of empathy and awareness. Healing a family system after someone comes out can take time and perseverance, but families that reconfigure their expectations around gender are stronger for having done so. Families with transgender members can achieve incredible resilience, cohesion, and emotional health. The first step on the journey toward family wellness is to provide support for gender-expansive family members as they navigate their process of personal discovery and gender congruence.

Supporting Gender-Expansive Children

Many parents will likely not be experts regarding gender-expansive issues, and their reactions to having a gender-expansive child could range from very supportive to very hostile. We believe that most parents act with good intentions when it comes to their children, but good intentions can be harmful, especially in relation to gender transition. Because of this, a child may be taking a huge risk when they come out as gender expansive, whether they realize it or not. They may not know how their family will react, but, even more importantly, minors are also less likely to possess physical and emotion resources that may be needed to support themselves should their family reject them.

Even though gender-expansive people and issues are gradually becoming more commonly represented in the media, having a gender-expansive child will likely be the parents' first direct experience with a gender-expansive family member. The parents will likely be confused and will often consult medical and mental health professionals to determine how they can best support their child. If the child comes out as gender expansive in their teenage years (or later) and had not previously expressed any signs of gender variance from their gender assigned at birth, parents may question the validity of their child's trans identity. To such parents, it is important that you emphasize that while gender variance in childhood often does occur for people who later transition, this is not the case for all gender-expansive people. Another possibility is that a child may have hidden earlier signs of their gender-expansive identity from others for fear of negative reactions because coming out as gender expansive is often a stressful and scary process.

Parents who deny the validity of their child's trans identity can be challenging to address, especially if the child is younger than 18. Imagine being distanced from or being completely cut off from your parents, siblings, and other people who should be supportive but then reject you when you finally have the courage to reveal your complete self to them. Not only can this amplify the fear and dread of coming out to others because the experience was so negative, but this also often leads to having few resources and sources of support during gender transition, a process that is already incredibly emotionally and physically difficult in today's society. Working closely with the parents may be inevitable and the parents will most often have the final say in treatment decisions while their child is still under 18. Therefore, we recommend emphasizing to the parents the importance of supporting how their child self-identifies. This may be a good time to explore options, such as puberty blockers, that we discussed in Chapter 4.

Many gender-expansive children come out well after they reach adulthood. Research indicates that, regardless of age, children need the support of their parents (Milton & Knutson, 2021). Many of the recommendations above that are skewed toward younger children apply to adult children too. Although parents may exert less control over the decisions and access of adult children, their support, encouragement, and acceptance are invaluable. Learning to accept an adult gender-expansive child, learning new pronouns, and supporting their gender journey can be challenging, but it can also be rewarding. We often hear from parents that seeing their gender-expansive child happy and fulfilled (at any age) is incredibly fulfilling.

Supporting Gender-Expansive Parents

Just as a transitioning child affects the parents, a transitioning parent will have an impact on their children. Being a parent can be stressful enough without adding gender transition on top of that. Therefore, it will be important for you to address both stressors and concerns related to transitioning and to parenting. Gender-expansive-affirmative interventions, such as affirmation, validation, exploration of fears and concerns, and referrals for medical transition options will be just as important for a gender-expansive parent as for any other gender-expansive client.

Additionally, a parent may be concerned that their gender transition will negatively impact their children. Although research in this area is limited, children of all ages tend to eventually view the process of a parent transitioning, sometimes termed parental gender transition, in a neutral or positive light, but this may take time, supportive resources, and therapy (Veldorale-Griffin, 2014). Young children are generally viewed as being able to better handle and accept gender transition of their parents compared to adult children.

When the parent is married, gender transition can result in divorce, and it is typically the divorce, not the parent's gender transition, that puts the most stress on the children (Green, 1998; Hines, 2006). For parents who transition when their children are adults, parental gender transition can have positive or neutral effects on the closeness between parent and child (Veldorale-Griffin, 2014). There can even be a positive impact when a child has a gender-expansive parent, such as the opportunity to grow up in a household where parents are less likely to police gender or enforce gender roles (Bergstrom-Lynch, 2019). Overall, it may take time for children to accept their parent's gender-expansive identity; they may have confused or even hostile feelings toward a parent who comes out as gender expansive. Because this is also a transition period for the children, we recommend offering resources and providing a referral for therapy to the children, as appropriate.

Gender Transition and Romantic Relationships

When a partner comes out as gender expansive, their disclosure can impact all partners in the relationship. This may involve a renegotiation of gender roles and a reevaluation of sexual orientation labels—labels that may be very important or inconsequential depending on the individual. The partner who comes out will have the stress of navigating and trying to maintain a romantic relationship that may be in flux because the gender dynamics are now different from what they were at the outset of the relationship. They are also dealing with these relational stressors on top of all of the other stressors that come with transitioning genders.

Partners and Relationship Dynamics

Although gender identity and sexual orientation are not the same thing, gender can influence romantic and sexual attraction. Sexual orientation labels may dictate whether we are attracted to people of the same gender, a different gender, or multiple genders, and how we label our own sexual orientation is likely influenced by gender identity. For example, say that Emily identifies as a lesbian woman, meaning that she is a woman attracted to other women. Her identity as woman helps give meaning to her sexual orientation. Sexual orientation and gender identity are separate but often connected—a connection that can make for a complex process when someone in a romantic relationship comes out as gender expansive, and especially if they start transitioning.

As a gender-expansive person, embracing one's authentic self is an act of courage, self-love, and resistance in our cisnormative US society. Because simply existing as a gender-expansive person challenges gender norms and expectations, coming out to a romantic partner can be terrifying. This process can be complex, and even painful or invalidating, for both the individual who is transitioning and their partner or partners (Pulice-Farrow et al., 2017). For example, transitioning while in a relationship can significantly alter gender roles, intimacy, attraction, and labels placed upon the partners and the partnership as a whole (Platt & Bolland, 2018).

Transitioning in Close Relationships

In the case of Rowan, you can see that when one partner transitions, the entire relational system may change. In other words, the partner and even the relationship itself enters a phase of transition. The resulting dynamic can be difficult, filled with renegotiation of labels and roles. The process can involve many new, stressful experiences, some that are positive and some that are negative. Partners may stay together, they may end the relationship amicably, or the relationship may end with feelings of animosity.

The fact that relational transitions can be hard does not mean that they should be avoided. It is important to ensure that gender-expansive people have access to the gender-affirmative care that they need to meet their transition goals, and the needs of partners must be met too. For example, partners may need to see a therapist, and/or they may need validation for their powerful emotions, which may include anger, frustration, sadness, confusion, isolation. In the case of Molly, Rebecca did not anticipate Molly's transition and the dissolution of her romantic partnership with Molly. Both partners, then, must process their feelings of loss.

Molly's case does, however, illustrate the basic need for support and significant acts of affirmation for everyone impacted by the relational transition. An amicable separation can occur even if the relationship eventually dissolves, but this, unfortunately, is not always the case. A partner can feel betrayed, as if they have been lied to, when their partner comes out to them as gender expansive and begins gender transition. Clearly, the partner who is transitioning was not lying but may have been secretive about their identity because of the very real fear of stigma and rejection. As mentioned earlier, gender transition can be a brand-new, confusing, or even frightening process for the partner of a gender-expansive person. It is not uncommon for the partner to hurl insults or to behave in hurtful ways (Pulice-Farrow et al., 2017). Gender transition can be a difficult and stressful time for everyone, but it is very important to encourage mutual understanding and explore the sources of anger and pain.

Polyamorous Relationships

You may find yourself working with clients in relationships with more than one partner. In this book the term "polyamory," a form of consensual nonmonogamy, refers to a romantic, emotional, and/or sexual relationship involving more than two partners who have all consensually agreed to be in a nonmonogamous relationship (Rossman et al., 2019). We discuss polyamory more in Chapter 14, but it is also important to discuss briefly in this chapter on relationships.

The structures of polyamorous relationships can vary greatly, and different partners may seek different needs and experiences within the same relationship, but the important point is that all partners have consensually agreed to the dynamics of the relationship. You might be asking yourself, why is it important to know about polyamorous relationships? Research indicates that as much as 25% of the US population includes people who have been involved in a consensual nonmonogamous relationship at some point in their life (Haupert et al., 2017), and that the prevalence may be even higher in the gender-expansive community (Rossman et al., 2019).

Because gender-expansive people are already transcending gender norms, they may be more likely to also transcend other societal norms, including the concept of monogamous relationships. Unfortunately, just as is the case for gender-expansive people, people in consensual nonmonogamous relationships are often misunderstood and stigmatized, and receive inadequate affirmative health care (Vaughan et al., 2019). Therefore, we believe that it is important to explore current and possible future relationship dynamics when working with gender-expansive clients. Be sure to include the possibility for polyamorous relationships—and do so in a non-stigmatizing way. For those who are in or seek to be in a polyamorous relationship, there may be unique strengths to such relationships, such as having different needs met by different partners (Moors et al., 2017).

Summary and Recommendations

- Gender transition impacts the individual and everyone close to them.
- It is important to provide gender-affirmative care to your gender-expansive client, and to provide resources and support to family members, partners, and friends.
- It is important to identify and challenge cultural relationship and gender stereotypes.
- Fixation on gender assigned at birth by family members and partners is not only unhelpful but also often harmful to the gender-expansive client.
- Parents who have a gender-expansive child may feel lost, overwhelmed, and/or confused.
- It is important to both support and affirm a gender-expansive child while meeting the parents where they are.
- Gender-expansive parents may worry about how their coming out will impact their children.
- Generally, the parent-child relationship is eventually the same or even better following parental gender transition.
- Transition in a romantic partnership is a complex process. A renegotiation of labels and gender roles may be involved.
- The relationship may dissolve as a result of one of the partners transitioning, but it is still possible for the relationship to be a source of support and healing.
- Polyamorous relationships are subject to misunderstanding and stigmatization, and it is important to explore any biases you may hold toward nonmonogamous relationships.

Reflection Questions

1. What are ways you essentialize gender by making assumptions, based on the sex of a baby?
2. What are specific behaviors that you exhibit to reinforce the gender expectations placed on children (e.g., buying specific toys, disapproving of gender-expansive behaviors)?

3. Imagine your parent came out to you as gender expansive.

    - What feelings would you have?
    - What is at least one way you could support your parent?
    - What is at least one need you would have?

4. Imagine that a child or young adult in your life came out to you as gender expansive.

    - What feelings would you have?
    - What is at least one way you could support the child?
    - What is at least one need you would have?

5. Imagine that a current or potential future romantic partner in your life came out to you as gender expansive.

    - What feelings would you have?
    - What is at least one way you could support your partner?
    - What is at least one need you would have?

6. You may also want to imagine what it would be like if your best friend came out to you or if you came out to your family and friends. You can ask yourself about your feelings and reactions to a number of scenarios and experiences with friends, family, and partners.

References and Suggested Readings

Bergstrom-Lynch, C. (2019). Free to be you and me, maybe: Lesbian, gay, bisexual, and transgender parents doing gender with their children. *Journal of Gender Studies*, 1–13.

Green, R. (1998). Transsexuals' children. *International Journal of Transgenderism*, 2(4), 97–103.

Haupert, M. L., Gesselman, A. N., Moors, A. C., Fisher, H. E., & Garcia, J. R. (2017). Prevalence of experiences with consensual nonmonogamous relationships: Findings from two national samples of single Americans. *Journal of Sex & Marital Therapy*, 43(5), 424–440.

Hines, S. (2006). Intimate transitions: Transgender practices of partnering and parenting. *Sociology*, 40(2), 353–371.

Knutson, D., Kallo, E., & Hubbs-Tait, L. (2022). Parenting trans and nonbinary youth. *Oklahoma State University Extension*. https://extension.okstate.edu/fact-sheets/parenting-trans-and-nonbinary-youth.html

Milton, D. C., & Knutson, D. (2021). Family of origin, not chosen family, predicts psychological health in a LGBTQ+ sample. *Psychology of Sexual Orientation and Gender Diversity*. Advance Online Publication. https://doi.org/10.1037/sgd0000531

Moors, A. C., Matsick, J. L., & Schechinger, H. A. (2017). Unique and shared relationship benefits of consensually non-monogamous and monogamous relationships. *European Psychologist*, 22, 55–71. https://doi.org/10.1027/1016-9040/a000278

Parents, Families, and Friends of Lesbians and Gays (PFLAG). https://pflag.org/

Platt, L. F., & Bolland, K. S. (2018). Relationship partners of transgender individuals: A qualitative exploration. *Journal of Social and Personal Relationships, 35*(9), 1251–1272.

Pulice-Farrow, L., Brown, T. D., & Galupo, M. P. (2017). Transgender microaggressions in the context of romantic relationships. *Psychology of Sexual Orientation and Gender Diversity, 4*(3), 362–373. https://doi.org/10.1037/sgd0000238

Rossman, K., Sinnard, M., & Budge, S. (2019). A qualitative examination of consideration and practice of consensual nonmonogamy among sexual and gender minority couples. *Psychology of Sexual Orientation and Gender Diversity, 6*(1), 11–21. https://doi.org/10.1037/sgd0000300

Vaughan, M. D., Jones, P., Taylor, B. A., & Roush, J. (2019). Healthcare experiences and needs of consensually non-monogamous people: Results from a focus group study. *Journal of Sexual Medicine, 16*(1), 42–51. https://doi.org/10.1016/j.jsxm.2018.11.006

Veldorale-Griffin, A. (2014). Transgender parents and their adult children's experiences of disclosure and transition. *Journal of GLBT Family Studies, 10*(5), 475–501. https://doi.org/10.1080/1550428X.2013.866063

Groups

For gender-expansive people, group counseling may be one of the few places where they can share with others who truly understand what they are going through and benefit from feedback and support. For example, we are familiar with one LGBT center that is in an urban area, but people drive from all over the state to participate in gender support meetings weekly. From these meetings, people build friendships and community. We begin by discussing group dynamics in the experiences of Bill, Molly, and Rowan.

Bill

Bill has been leading gender-expansive groups for a couple of years now. His support group is an open/standing group, so people can join or leave the group as they wish, after they meet with Bill and agree to follow group guidelines. The time and location of the group is not publicly available because an anti-gender-expansive group in the area has a reputation for showing up at gender-expansive events when meeting details are posted online.

Bill works hard to make sure that the group remains welcoming and inclusive. In any long-term open group such as this one, cohesion may be hard to achieve because groups mimic the outside world where people feel rejected, cliques form, people come and go, and grudges are held. At the beginning of each group meeting, Bill reminds the group of the guidelines they agreed upon when they joined. The guidelines include statements about the power of inclusivity and the beauty of maintaining a healing, gender-affirming space. Keeping the focus on empowerment and empathy helps foster the supportive spirit that is the goal of any support group.

Molly

Molly does not have the time or resources to attend an in-person group in the city, but she does attend an online therapy group hosted by a local gender-affirming therapist. The therapist started the group for people in rural locations. Molly started attending the group because individual therapy was too expensive and she wanted more opportunities to connect with other trans women. She has grown a lot since she started attending, and she attributes that change to how thoughtful and active the therapist is in the group.

For example, Molly used to talk over other group members a lot. She was just so excited to participate, and she did not notice that she was upsetting other group members by cutting them off. During one session, the therapist stopped Molly after she had interrupted a different group member and the therapist asked the group member how she was feeling. The other member of the group shared that she felt silenced and hurt. Molly was shocked and embarrassed, and she started shutting down. The group members rallied around her and encouraged her to share her feelings. Molly finally opened up and, when she did, she realized it was the first time she felt safe to engage with other people without hiding aspects of herself. She felt as if she were connecting with others as a complete person, fully herself.

Rowan

Rowan loves Dungeons and Dragons. They would play D&D every day if they could. They were really excited when a local game shop owner started a gender-expansive D&D group. Rowan couldn't imagine anything better than a group for two things that were dear to them, their identity and their favorite game. Given that they were not out to extended family, friends, or their church community, the game shop quickly became their favorite place in the world. They looked forward to Wednesday night "game nights with the enby [nonbinary] crew."

Rowan particularly appreciated that the game shop owner was intentional about making the group a safe and affirming space. The owner started every game night with an affirming quote or by talking about an important gender-expansive figure who helped to shape history. He also invited attendees to take turns sharing "two wows and an ow." Rowan felt that hearing positive and negative things from their group members' weeks humanized them and made the group feel even more connected. Rowan honestly did not know what they would do without the group and was glad that the shop owner had found a way to make a small difference for gender-expansive people, making use of his space and his expertise.

Group Stages

In this chapter, we discuss ways that gender-affirmative work may extend to group settings in which human service professionals may be involved. Much of this book has focused on interaction patterns between professionals and individual clients and/or between professionals and client significant others (e.g., family, friends, partners); this chapter focuses on community building in settings that bring together groups of gender-expansive clients. It is important to note that, as with any marginalized group, individuals may be classified as existing within the same gender-expansive community while possessing very different characteristics, ideas, identities, and perspectives.

For example, an open, general gender-expansive group might include a 50-year-old nonbinary person who has been out for 20+ years, a person who is just "testing the waters" and is not out or comfortable disclosing any identities, and a 20-year-old trans man who has been on HRT for a year, as well as others. As we discussed in our chapter on intersectionality, the differences between individuals in the LGBTQ+ community are wide ranging. Likewise, group membership may include a wide range of ages, gender identities (if not specified by the group), religious identities, racial/ethnic backgrounds, socioeconomic statuses, and so on.

In this chapter, we draw on our experiences running groups and on current group therapy scholarship. Over the years, group theorists have named and defined the stages of group development differently (Alle-Corliss & Alle-Corliss, 2009, p. 64). The stages we outline borrow and/or modify labels from several frameworks but rely most heavily on Tuckman's (1965) approach: forming, storming, norming, and performing. We encourage readers to also check out Austin and Craig's research on benefits of cognitive-behavioral interventions with gender-expansive groups of youth (e.g., Austin & Craig, 2015).

Group Formation

Most gender-affirmative therapeutic approaches recommend connecting gender-expansive people with gender-expansive communities, either online or in person. The assumption is that gender-expansive people will receive support, encouragement, and vital information from fellow community members. This is a safe assumption on many levels, and in this kind of informal setting, individuals are given the opportunity to self-select into groups of similar or likeminded individuals with whom they feel safe. In formal group work, however, group members may have less involvement in the selection process because the human service professional is tasked with recruiting for and formulating the group.

Formal group work might include therapy groups, support groups, psychoeducational groups, and so on, specifically for gender-expansive people. Depending on the focus or intention of the group, a group may also focus on specific subgroups of gender-expansive people, such as gender-expansive people of color, transgender women, transgender men, or nonbinary people. Of course, in most cases, participation is voluntary and group members can leave at any time, but the groups are guided by theory, research, ethical guidelines, and best practices in group counseling.

Thus, gender-expansive-affirmative groups bring together individuals who possess a wide range of ideas and beliefs, and who may be in various stages of transition or identity integration. These differences may become heightened or more pronounced in the crucible of group work. It is important for gender-affirmative group practitioners to attend to all aspects of group process. Simply recruiting a group of gender-expansive people to populate a therapy group because they identify as gender expansive is not the best approach to creating an optimal, functional therapy group that adequately addresses the needs of all members. Attention should be given to how the group might function and/or dysfunction once it is formed. We want to note that this chapter should not substitute for formal training in group process and competence in leading therapy groups.

Group Member Selection

As with any group, it is important to select group members intentionally and with an eye to overall group function. We discussed in the assessment and diagnosis chapter that gender-expansive-identified individuals, like any other people, may come to therapy with a variety of disorders, life struggles, and presenting concerns. If the only criterion for group membership is one's gender identity, professionals may include individuals who are not ready for group, who have disorders that could damage group cohesion, and/or who may create an environment in which individuals feel excluded from a community they are "supposed" to feel aligned with.

For example, Heck and colleagues (2013) tried to argue that a wide range of individuals with various identities, including drag queens, drag kings, and cisgender men with feminine gender expressions are part of the gender-expansive community. Such broad-ranging definitions of gender-expansive identities are inaccurate; including cisgender drag queens in a gender-expansive therapy group could cause significant ruptures and problems. This is because drag performance is different from gender-expansive identity, and some gender-expansive people find drag performance to be upsetting or even disenfranchising. Of course, the conversations that arise from a mismatch between group members can be grist for the therapeutic process, but severe mismatches will not be therapeutically productive.

Forming

The term *forming* refers to the process of establishing group dynamics. As with any group, members will be most successful if they set appropriate goals when the group is formed that are measurable and achievable within the duration of the group. Given that gender-expansive people experience discrimination and possible social isolation, groups may provide a unique space for them to experience a variety of social tasks such as identifying interpersonal needs, sharing needs with others, navigating disagreement, or communicating in clear and direct ways. These are skills that anyone in society would benefit from learning, but they may carry unique utility or benefits for gender-expansive people, given the types of discrimination and interpersonal distress that gender-expansive people may face.

After group members have been screened and selected, group dynamics will require attention and monitoring in early stages of the therapy process. One early task is to establish trust, especially because gender-expansive people experience widespread discrimination and minority stress in their daily lives. They may have experienced rejection from families and loved ones. Gender-expansive and LGBTQ+ communities can be small, and information can travel fast. In gender-affirmative groups, clear guidelines for confidentiality, safety, and communication are important to establish. Of course, group members are not legally bound to confidentiality, but group leaders can establish clear guidelines and penalties for breaches of confidentiality between group members.

In this book, we have worked hard to establish that gender-expansive people should not be automatically lumped in with LGBQ+ people in many cases. However, gender-expansive people may also be a part of LGBQ+ communities. Given that LGBTQ+ communities tend to be small and close knit, group leaders should discuss the importance of keeping group work in the group, especially if subgroups of group members spend time together outside of group. For example, some group members may be involved in advocacy activities such as planning pride festivals, HIV awareness activities, or community events. Also, group leaders may themselves identify with the LGBTQ+ community and may encounter group members in social spaces. Given the complexity of these encounters and interactions, clear conversations about these possibilities need to take place early and often in group.

The need to establish clear boundaries and rules for confidentiality dovetails with another important early task: the need to build trust. Gender-expansive people may experience a wide range of breaches of trust that other individuals in society take for granted. For example, gender-expansive people may be kicked out of their homes, rejected by their families, fired from their jobs, or expelled from their friend groups after they come out. This means that gender-expansive people might not trust that typical rules or assumptions about family and interpersonal relationships apply to them. For this reason, it is important to establish constancy and trust at the early stages of the group. Creating an environment based on mutuality and trust allows for deeper work to occur.

One way to build trust and clear expectations for interpersonal interactions is to establish guidelines for addressing mistakes or ruptures. For example, some groups implement the "ouch" rule. When using the ouch rule, if an individual hurts or invalidates a fellow group member, the offended party is invited to say "ouch" as a signal that the slight has occurred. The offending party is then invited to say "I'm sorry" to the person who was hurt. After the offended party accepts the apology, they are invited to share why they were hurt. This turns the rupture into a reparative teaching moment. This entire exchange is, of course, built on trust and a desire for mutual understanding.

When a group is formed with a minority community that encompasses a broad range of identities (e.g., trans men, trans women, nonbinary individuals), group members may tend to "subgroup" or to align themselves with others who share their perspectives or similar identities (Heck et al., 2013). Groups may become microcosms of broader society. Gender-expansive individuals may already feel isolated in their daily lives. This possible group dynamic, as group members clump together and leave individuals with less represented identities isolated within the group, is something that needs to be addressed early on.

Storming

Storming refers to the renegotiation of group dynamics, interpersonal friction, or even ruptures between group members. Not all group differences can or should be accounted for in the early stages of group formation. In fact, within group differences may be fodder for rich conversations about identities, expectations, and limitations that are placed on gender-expansive people, even by other gender-expansive individuals. Group members will inevitably bring to group their assumptions, biases, and expectations about gender-expansive identities and about what it means to be gender expansive. These expectations may be explicitly stated by group members or may be acted out in group. One of the tasks of the storming stage is to unmask and push back against pressures to conform to idealized or community-endorsed norms around acceptable ways of being gender expansive (Heck et al., 2013).

For example, group members may possess different ideas of what it means to transition, acceptable approaches to transitioning, and about the coming-out process. Some group members may feel that coming out to everyone (e.g., work associates, friends, family, in online communities) is vitally important as a form of self and community advocacy. Group members who share this perspective may push others to come out, even if doing so would involve some level of risk or would generate distress. These expectations may be identified, explored, and therapeutically challenged as appropriate.

Furthermore, in gender-affirmative therapy, storming is not something that occurs only between group members. Group leaders may make assumptions, express biases, or foster dynamics that lead to ruptures. These ruptures may occur even when group leaders have the best of intentions. For example, a group leader who identifies as a cisgender man may say "we" to characterize the male-identified participants in the group in an effort to affirm the identities of masculine or male-identified group members. This act may actually marginalize some group members who identify as trans masculine and who feel as if their identities are erased by the group leader's attempt to over-identify with group members.

We suggest that these ruptures provide unique opportunities for healing and/or for corrective experiences. In daily life, individuals who use incorrect pronouns or who deadname gender-expansive people may become defensive or try to invalidate the other person when they are made aware of their incorrect behavior. In therapy, though, mistakes may become opportunities for learning new, different behaviors and experiences. Group leaders and group members may demonstrate appropriate remorse for their behaviors and may demonstrate that mistakes and ruptures do not have to result in distance or lasting disruptions in relationship. Rather, leaders and other members may demonstrate that relationships can thrive after ruptures occur. This can empower gender-expansive clients to correct others and to trust that affirming their own identity does not have to result in lasting disconnect.

Norming

Norming refers to the process by which the group works toward a state of stability and mutuality. As group members build trust, maintain cohesion despite conflict, and place trust in the group process, they may begin to reach their goals. However, group members may struggle with the generalizability of their skills to the world outside of the group. Whereas group members may be open to feedback, willing to navigate interpersonal friction, or willing to learn from fellow group members, individuals outside of the group may remain unyielding. For example, a group member may become very good at identifying and expressing their needs to fellow group members and they may experience receptivity in group when they express their needs. Yet, when that group member expresses their needs to family members or friends, they may experience rejection, frustration, or defensiveness.

During the norming stage, space can be made for group members to express their gratitude to fellow group members and their frustration that the rest of life cannot be reshaped to mimic the group. Although the group may feel compelled to be productive or to achieve individual and group goals, group leaders may remind group members that simply being together or providing support within the group is a productive act. In other words, the group may benefit from the awareness that being together may be just as powerful as doing together.

Another task of the norming stage is the affirmation of identities. Given that group members may feel marginalized or limited outside of the group, individuals may benefit from being reminded of how beautiful and valid their identities are. One of the most productive ways to combat invalidation is to validate another person's identity. Gender-expansive individuals are highly resilient and, when reminded of their beauty and strength, people can weather a variety of assaults and aggressions.

Performing

Performing refers to the process through which groups establish new interaction patterns and ways of being in relationship to others. As the group becomes more and more productive, a variety of tools may be used to help individuals reach their goals. Group members may benefit from engaging in role play, from writing down or scripting possible dialogues or exchanges with others, or from diagraming their transition or coming-out timelines. These are just a few of the many creative and/or structured tools that may be implemented in gender-affirmative groups. Some of the tools we provide for individuals may be completed in group settings as well.

At this stage of the group, a task orientation (or "fix it" approach) may take hold, and group leaders may need to remind group members to deepen and address emotional aspects of their experience. Given the many milestones, resource needs, and barriers that gender-expansive people may have, it is easy for groups to develop a problem-solving orientation. It will be important to remind group members that the emotions related to a given milestone are important to process as well.

As group members make progress within and outside of group as individuals, they may express a tendency or motivation to make collective progress as well. In other words, group members may feel compelled to come out or to transition according to a shared schedule. Group leaders may be faced with the task of helping group members to maintain appropriate autonomy so that individuals continue to meet their individual goals within their own contexts (Heck et al., 2013).

As participants explore and express their needs and as they make progress toward their goals, self-disclosure on the part of the group leaders may increase. As group leaders express care for the group and a desire for group members to live fulfilling and congruent lives, group members may take appropriate, therapeutically beneficial risks (such as coming out to a friend or scheduling a consultation with a medical professional). Heck and colleagues (2013) suggest that self-disclosure on the part of group leaders empowers group members to take action and to build greater confidence in their ability to navigate challenges and issues.

Termination

Termination refers to the process of ending the group's work in a way that supports continued progress for the group members beyond their involvement in the group. Heck and colleagues (2013) suggest that group members may fear or even avoid discussing termination of the group. Participation in group may provide a variety of valued benefits for gender-expansive individuals, and the thought of leaving or losing such a space may induce fear and resistance. Yet, given the number of painful ruptures, breaks, or abrupt ends to relationships that gender-expansive people may experience when they come out and/or transition, the opportunity to say "goodbye" in an intentional or therapeutic way may provide an opportunity for healing and a powerful corrective experience.

As extension of establishing trust that was important in the earlier stages of therapy, termination should be based on trust as well. Although group members may try to avoid discussions of termination, such discussions are an important part of establishing trust and they mark the therapeutic end of the therapeutic relationship. In many areas, there is a dearth of resources for gender-expansive people; and the end of group does not only mean the end of interpersonal connections, it also it marks the termination of a resource as well. Group members may benefit from planning what they will do after group, what sources of support they will access, and how they will replace or extend the emotional and interpersonal connections they established in group. Most of all, an abrupt end to group may damage the trust and confidence that group members began to place in the leaders and in each other.

Group leaders should be aware that gender-affirmative groups exist within a larger community as well. As with any group, gender-affirmative group members may wish to stay connected after the therapy group concludes. As we discussed earlier, group leaders may encounter group members in social spaces. Group members may wish to stay in contact with group leaders or may participate in future groups as appropriate. Group leaders should think through the possibility for dual relationships and should be prepared to set appropriate, therapeutically indicated boundaries.

General Suggestions

In this chapter, we discussed general group processes and dynamics specific to gender-affirmative group therapy. Given that this is a new and developing field, we encourage gender-affirmative group professionals to consult with colleagues engaged in similar work. Until more literature and guidance are produced to guide such work, shared knowledge and expertise will be important methods of quality control. This chapter provides some general guidance, but other gender-affirmative literature should be consulted, and professionals should not expect to become experts in gender-affirmative group therapy simply because they have read this book.

Because group therapy is comprehensive, relational, and interpersonally engaging, group professionals should possess awareness and a broad understanding of the issues facing gender-expansive people. Group members have their own expertise and insights, but group leaders in gender-affirmative group therapy may be called upon to push back when groups adopt unhelpful expectations for group members and/or for the group itself. For example, if the group begins to demand a specific transition timeline, group leaders should have the awareness necessary to provide psychoeducation about ways that transition timelines may differ and about the fact that some gender-expansive people may not transition at all.

Gender-affirmative therapy groups are not a replacement for individual therapy and should not be viewed as an easier version of individual gender-affirmative therapy. In other words, professionals who do not feel they have the training to provide effective individual gender-affirmative therapy should not provide group therapy with the assumption that the group will take care of itself. In fact, gender-affirmative group therapy may take more training and awareness than individual therapy in many cases.

These words of caution are not intended to dissuade practitioners from providing group therapy. On the contrary, given the benefits of group therapy for gender-expansive clients, we would encourage professionals to consider providing these services. We mentioned elsewhere that resources for gender-expansive clients are scarce, and providing group therapy may allow effective gender-affirmative professionals to provide support to more clients at a lower cost.

Group professionals are not likely to achieve a perfect level of preparedness; in gender-affirmative therapy, over-preparing can be problematic as well because gender-expansive identities are diverse and too much structure in group can be counterproductive. Group therapy provides a unique space in which gender-expansive clients can engage in relationships, experience acceptance from others, and experience value for and appreciation of their ideas and perspectives. Done well and with the right motives, gender-affirmative therapy can be transformative for clients and professionals alike.

Summary and Recommendations

* In general, best practices for providing group therapy apply to gender-affirmative groups.
* Leaders should give special consideration to screening and to membership in groups (e.g., trans men only? Anyone who is gender-expansive? Nonbinary over 50 group? etc.).
* Trust and clear guidelines for confidentiality, safety, and communication are important to establish as early as possible in the group process.
* Group members should discuss rules for the group, specifically addressing confidentiality and relationships outside of the group.
* Ruptures and conflicts may be seen as opportunities for learning and growth.
* Trust is an important component of any group, but is particularly crucial for therapy groups with gender-expansive people.
* Self-disclosure on the part of the group leader can empower group members to take action and to build greater confidence in their ability to navigate challenges and issues.
* Termination must be handled delicately and with skill.
* Group members may avoid discussions of termination, but given the number of painful ruptures, breaks, or abrupt ends to relationships that gender-expansive people may experience when they come out and/or transition, the opportunity to say "goobye" in an intentional or therapeutic way may provide an opportunity for healing and a powerful corrective experience.

Reflection Questions

1. What is one affirming group (e.g., employee support group, makeup tutorials, book club) that you could consider creating at your business and/or workplace?
2. What are your criteria for determining how well prospective members fit together?
3. What are skills or resources you will use if conflicts begin to arise within the group?
4. What referrals do you plan to use if someone needs more support than your group can provide?
5. How will you know when to end the group? How will you prepare group clients for the termination process?
6. What resources will you provide participants after the group ends?
7. How available will you be to past group participants?

References and Suggested Readings

Alle-Corliss, L., & Alle-Corliss, R. (2009). *Group work: A practical guide to developing groups in agency settings.* John Wiley & Sons.

American Group Psychotherapy Association: https://www.agpa.org/

Association for Specialists in Group Work: https://asgw.org/

Austin, A., & Craig, S. L. (2015). Transgender affirmative cognitive behavioral therapy: Clinical considerations and applications. *Professional Psychology: Research and Practice, 46*(1), 21. https://doi.org/10.1037/a0038642

dickey, l. m., & Loewy, M. I. (2010). Group work with transgender clients. *Journal for Specialists in Group Work, 35,* 236–245. https://doi.org/10.1080/01933922.2010.492904

Heck, N. C. (2017). Group psychotherapy with transgender and gender nonconforming adults: Evidence-based practice applications. *Psychiatric Clinics of North America, 40*(1), 157–175. https://doi.org/10.1016/j.psc.2016.10.010

Heck, N. C., Croot, L. C., & Robohm, J. S. (2013). Piloting a psychotherapy group for transgender clients: Description and clinical considerations for practitioners. *Professional Psychology: Research and Practice, 1,* 30–36. https://doi.org/10.1037/a0033134

Tuckman, B. W. (1965). Developmental sequence in small groups. *Psychological Bulletin, 63,* 384–399. https://doi.org/10.1037/h0022100

14

Sex, Sexuality, and Romantic Attraction
Dannie Klooster

Imagine you have a friend, Aron, whom you have known since high school. In high school, your friend went by "Erin" and she was an out lesbian woman. A few years after graduation, Aron shared with you that he identified as a man and was working on transitioning. He was still attracted to women, and so he identified as a straight man. Aron shared that this transition threw his family members for a loop.

Often, people get confused about the differences between gender and sexuality. This also contributes to barriers to adequate health access (Joyner & Bahng, 2019). Understanding the difference between these two concepts is vital when working with gender-expansive clients. Sexual orientation is more interpersonal in nature and involves the person or people the individual is physically, emotionally, or sexually attracted to. In contrast, a person's gender identity indicates their understanding of who they are internally, a man, woman, or other gender outside of the traditional gender binary. For a reminder of gender identity terminology, see Chapter 2. Before we discuss sex, sexuality, and romantic attraction further, we will discuss their role in the lives of Bill, Molly, and Rowan.

Bill

Like Aron, Bill's family was pushed to learn and grow each time he came out to them, first as lesbian at 15 and then as a heterosexual trans man at 20. Most recently, he came out to his mother as polyamorous, telling her about his romantic connections with multiple partners. While identifying as heterosexual, Bill engages in a range of sexual behaviors with his different partners. In his early twenties, Bill discovered that he was polyamorous when he noticed that he held romantic feelings for more than one person at a time.

Bill has had trouble explaining his sexual behaviors, polyamorous-style relationships, and gender identity to medical providers. When he first started gender-affirming hormone therapy, his doctor was hesitant to prescribe, telling Bill that starting testosterone would likely prevent him from having children in the future. Since then, Bill has had two pregnancy scares, despite not having menstrual cycles due to hormone therapy. He now relies on use of a copper IUD to prevent potential pregnancies. Bill gets anxious when interacting with professionals due to fears of being misunderstood.

Molly

Molly began exploring the kink community soon after she split up with her former wife, Rebecca. As a disabled trans woman, she enjoys the accepting and body-positive outlook of her friends in the kink community. As a dominatrix, she is able to re-create power dynamics with play partners, engaging in role plays and feeling comfortable with her sexuality. Because Molly lives in a rural area, most of her kink experiences of late have been through online community forums. Her feelings of isolation are countered by her participation in kink; however, her inability to attend in-person events has led her to further withdraw from this community. Molly feels a need to keep her kink membership a secret from most people. As a Latina woman, she fears that her kink membership might not be considered in line with some of her culture's more traditional values.

Rowan

Rowan formerly identified as lesbian, but now identifies as pansexual, a sexual orientation more aligned with their gender-fluid identity. Rowan identifies as both pansexual and panromantic. Rowan is generally more sexually attracted to people who present as feminine, or "femme." They identify as pansexual because who they are sexually attracted to is not dependent on a person's biological sex or gender identity. Their romantic affiliation, however, is panromantic: they may experience romantic attraction to individuals of any presentation or gender identity, although they may not feel sexually attracted to them.

For example, Rowan might be sexually and romantically attracted to a feminine-presenting trans woman, but only experience romantic attraction to a cisgender man. Additionally, these feelings are distinct from Rowan's gender identity of being gender fluid.

Historical Perspectives on Sexual Health

In the health-care system, transgender women have historically been treated as if they are heterosexual cisgender women. For trans women, sexual health efforts have been focused on a unidimensional conceptualization of trans women as having had a vaginoplasty (bottom surgery involving construction of a vagina) and as heterosexual (only having sex with cis male partners; Bauer & Hammond, 2015). In contrast, a recent study found that only 23% of trans women surveyed reported engaging in sexual activities with a cis male partner in the past year, and only 15% of the sample reported undergoing vaginoplasty (Bauer & Hammond, 2015).

Thus, sexual health efforts have largely overlooked the experiences of many trans women who do not fit into typically binary, heterosexual conceptualizations of women. Instead, sexual health care for trans women should be grounded in women's health care, but with a trans-affirmative outlook. For example, trans women should be granted equal access to fertility care, sexually transmitted infection (STI) screenings, bacterial vaginosis (BV) treatment, and birth control (Bauer & Hammond, 2015).

For transmasculine individuals assigned female at birth (AFAB) undergoing hormone therapy, sexual health likewise has become a unidimensional issue. When discussing hormone therapy, doctors may overemphasize their concerns about whether the individual will be able to conceive a baby in the future. Health-care providers should also consider other factors related to hormone use, such as positive outcomes of hormone therapy, sexual behavior, sexual orientation, human papillomavirus vaccination, and other relevant sexual health considerations (Grimstad & Garborcauskas, 2021).

Gender-Affirming Approaches

Thus, when approaching sexual health concerns with individuals of nontraditional sexual and affectional orientations and gender identities, professionals must extend beyond the historical approach rooted in the gender binary. Professionals should also keep in mind that clients' reported sexual behaviors may not align with their sexual orientation (Joyner & Bahng, 2019). Understanding terminology and avoiding assumptions are vital. Additionally, professionals are encouraged to ask clients how they refer to their own body parts and how they conceptualize sex when engaging in discussions around sexual health, in order to be as inclusive and understanding as possible (Joyner & Bahng, 2019).

Moreover, providers should restrict their questions to those that are only medically relevant in order to provide the best care possible. Avoiding questions that are inherently binary in nature, such as "do you have sex with men, women, or both?" can provide more insight into a client's sexual behaviors. For instance, a provider may ignore the possibility of anal sex if a client states he is only engaging in sex with women. As professionals, being sensitive to a client's understanding of how they define sex and sexual behavior is key to fostering a strong therapeutic relationship.

Similarly, professionals should avoid imposing their own assumptions on clients, especially when conducting intake sessions. Professionals can start with a thorough investigation of their own biases, expectations, and identities, and how they inform work with clients. Then they can reflect upon how to promote sex-positive, inclusive practices that celebrate gender diversity.

Gender-Expansive Clients and Sex Education Myths

A lack of adequate sexual health education in the United States has led to the perpetuation of harmful myths about what constitutes "safe sex." Furthermore, the phrase "safer sex" is considered to be more accurate than "safe sex" because no type of sexual activity can be guaranteed to be 100% safe. Given the lack of attention paid to sex in LGBTQ+ communities, myths surrounding the assumption of what constitutes safe/safer sex for gender-expansive individuals may be even more pervasive. For instance, testosterone for gender-affirming hormone therapy often causes changes in the menstrual cycle, resulting in no periods or menses. This can be misconstrued to mean that there is no possibility of pregnancy while on testosterone, when, in fact, this is not true.

Penetrative intercourse can result in pregnancy for individuals assigned female at birth, whether or not they are undergoing hormone therapy. Similarly, individuals assigned male at birth undergoing estrogen-based hormone therapy may experience sexual changes including increased difficulty getting or sustaining an erection. The possibility of impregnating a partner is still possible for some, but individuals assigned male at birth who are on estrogen-based hormone therapy may experience significant or complete suppression of sperm production (Jiang et al., 2019; Vereecke et al., 2021).

The overemphasis on possible loss of genetic fertility may originate from health-care providers' concerns about liability and being held responsible if someone later wants to conceive. As a result, gender-expansive folks considering hormone treatment are often alerted of potential fertility issues that may be encountered during hormone therapy, with less emphasis placed on the diverse sexual and romantic needs and desires that gender-expansive people can have. As professionals, understanding the various gatekeeping processes involved in attaining hormone therapy can help us to recognize the struggles that our gender-expansive clients endure, and how these can impact their health.

Toward a Sex-Positive Framework

In the face of the various hurdles to embracing sexuality, especially for gender-expansive people, embracing a sex-positive framework can help us to better empower and support our clients. The term *sex-positive* has evolved over time and encompasses various perspectives. As professionals, embracing a sex-positive framework when working with clients means emphasizing a body-positive, eroto-positive, kink-positive, and relationship-positive view of sexuality (Mosher, 2017). We expand on these terms and concepts below. Sex-positive professionals should also be intersectionality informed (see Chapter 3) when approaching client concerns by acknowledging the exclusion of people of color (POC) and people with disabilities from traditional conceptualizations of sexuality.

Body Positivity

Body positivity means emphasizing the beauty in all types of bodies and embracing or accepting bodies that are deemed unattractive or undesirable according to conventional beauty standards. Body positivity diverts from pervasive White hegemonic, patriarchal, fatphobic, ableist, and cissexist understandings of beauty. Proponents of body positivity often point to fatphobia as a major social hurdle, or the unidimensional view of thin, White, muscular bodies that is marketed as the universal standard of beauty. These Western standards of beauty exclude many communities, including gender-expansive people. Professionals cannot truly begin to embrace sex positivity in their work until they acknowledge their understanding of how beauty is constructed and begin to apply interventions to accept and empower individuals of all abilities, races, genders, and body types.

Eroto-Positivity

Eroto-positivity involves a mindset that embraces and accepts, rather than stigmatizes, the possibility of pleasure and joy in sexual interactions. A traditional view of sexuality includes erotophobia, which has historically ignored sexual pleasure beyond the orgasm of a straight cisgender man. In contrast, eroto-positivity flips the script by putting pleasure at the center of sexual interactions, placing an emphasis on a healthy sex life, masturbation, sexual exploration, and use of sex toys. For individuals who identify as asexual or on the asexual spectrum (e.g., demisexual, gray-asexual), a lack of engagement in sex should not be confused with erotophobia (Mosher, 2017). Asexuality can involve engagement in sexual acts for intimacy or partner pleasure, and individuals on the asexual spectrum can define pleasure in other ways. A sex-positive approach involves celebrating and normalizing a wide variety of sexual behaviors, desires, and exploration, while respecting a client's ability to make their own choices.

Kink Positivity

Along with focusing on body-positive and eroto-positive sexualities, engaging in sex-positive mental health work also calls for embracing a kink-positive mindset. Kink is an umbrella term often inclusive of bondage, dominance, submission, sadism, and masochism, also referred to as BDSM. However, kink is not limited to just these categories, and can extend to any type of fetishistic, voyeuristic, exhibitionist, role play, and/or other behavior that brings pleasure to an individual. While kink can be sexual in nature, it is important to acknowledge that kink behavior is not inherently sexual (Sprott et al.,

2020). For example, asexual people have reported that kink behavior can serve as a form of intimacy-building activity with partners (Winter-Gray & Hayfield, 2019), so it is important to not assume that asexual people do not engage or desire to engage in kink behavior. Kink can be identified as sensation-seeking, often involving intense scenes wherein a dominant partner(s) or "dom" interacts with a submissive partner(s) or "sub" in a previously negotiated, consensual manner. Various forms of kink can take place in private or community spaces, with groups of individuals, in dyads, or alone.

One psychological school of thought posits that membership in the kink community originates from a desire to work through childhood physical and/or sexual trauma. Recent studies suggest this assumption is incorrect (Brink et al., 2021; Pitagora, 2016) because this falsely pathologizes kink as originating from abuse and/or immoral desires. While some individuals in the kink community may have experienced trauma as children or adults, studies show that engagement in kink is associated with more secure attachment styles (Brink et al., 2021). In working with clients involved in kink circles, it is important to recognize that kink behavior fulfills an important role that is not inherently pathological, deviant, or even sexual.

Normalizing kink behaviors is especially important when working with gender-expansive clients; kink spaces can counter experiences of discrimination by providing affirmative and accepting community outlets. LGBTQ+ populations engage in kink more than cisgender heterosexual (cishet) populations (Speciale & Khambatta, 2020), likely due to a departure from heteronormative society fostered within kink spaces. There exists a large gap in accessible mental and physical health care for LGBTQ+ people involved in kink, because professionals are often uneducated about or unaware of kink behaviors altogether (Speciale & Khambatta, 2020). When working toward a kink-positive view of sexualities, especially for gender-expansive people, it is important to understand the positive impact kink membership can have on healing, community connection, self-actualization, resource acquisition, and belongingness.

Relationship Positivity

A relationship-positive view of sexuality is also essential when embracing clients of alternative sexual communities. Although heterosexual monogamy is often espoused as the ideal relationship form, many types of relationship constellations can occur outside of this archetype (see Chapter 12). The umbrella term consensual nonmonogamy encapsulates various relationship styles that do not adhere to traditional monogamy, such as seeking sexual and/or emotional connections outside of a dyadic relationship (Cohen & Wilson, 2017). The three main types of consensual nonmonogamy are swinging, open relationships, and polyamory. Swinging, also referred to as "the lifestyle," involves a couple (most often, a heterosexual couple) seeking sexual experiences outside of their relationship (Harviainen & Frank, 2018). Membership within swinging circles is often centered around trust, maintaining confidentiality, and connection to a primary romantic partner.

Open relationships involve a connection to a primary romantic partner, while seeking outside sexual relationships with others. In this case, a primary partner is the only source of emotional connection, while both partners permit outside sexual behaviors. In contrast to swinging, open relationships rarely involve membership to a specific group, and sometimes involve a "don't ask, don't tell" communication style allowing individuals to have outside sexual experiences without sharing the details of such ventures with their partner. Open relationships are more common with individuals in long-distance partnerships. Polyamory is centered on the belief that individuals are capable of loving and maintaining healthy relationships with multiple people simultaneously, with the consent of all partners involved (Klesse, 2018).

For professionals working with consensual nonmonogamous populations, understanding the differences between infidelity and consensual nonmonogamy is essential. Nonmonogamous relationships involve consent and communication between partners, whereas infidelity is defined by dishonesty. Nonmonogamous communities, in fact, often emphasize ethical considerations involved in emotional and sexual partnerships in order to maintain healthy relationships. Nevertheless, stigma against consensually nonmonogamous individuals can cause mental distress; studies indicate a strong social preference for monogamy, even among transitional-age youth (Thompson et al., 2020).

There exists considerable overlap between consensual nonmonogamy and kink community membership. Within kink circles, there are higher levels of acceptance of consensually nonmonogamous relationships, along with queer identities (Pitagora, 2016). Kink and polyamory in particular emphasize emotional and physical connectedness, consensual negotiation, and the establishment of healthy boundaries. Members of poly-kink (and other consensually nonmonogamous kink) communities may feel a need to keep these identities concealed due to social stigma and real-life implications of discrimination. As social stigma surrounding consensually nonmonogamous behaviors can result in depression, anxiety, and other mental health problems, it is vital that professionals provide a safe, affirming space for clients within such communities (Pitagora, 2016). Interventions connecting clients to their values can revitalize efforts for self-acceptance of behaviors often deemed negative by society. For instance, a values sorting activity, wherein clients rank which values are most important to them, can help clients recognize how their actions align with their sense of self.

A lack of information about engagement in kink and/or multiple relationships also results in the perpetuation of various myths. Some professionals may have a negative view of kink behavior and multiple relationships, conflating them with abuse and infidelity. In contrast, these behaviors include consent, communication, and honesty. Despite misinformation regarding what constitutes consensually nonmonogamous relationships and/or kink membership, involvement in one or both of these communities does not demonstrate pathology, moral deviance, or potential for negative outcomes. Common myths regarding consensually nonmonogamous and kink communitiesare below.

- **Myth:** Those with multiple romantic and sexual partners are more vulnerable to sexually transmitted infections (STIs).

  - **Counter:** Individuals in consensually nonmonogamous (specifically polyamorous) partnerships, as well as those who engage in sexual kink behaviors, get tested for STIs more often and do not have greater rates of STIs in comparison to monogamous partnerships (Pitagora, 2016). In fact, communication strategies utilized in alternative sexuality communities can lead to better sexual health outcomes for all partners involved, including higher levels of condom use and self-reported sexual fulfillment, and lower rates of sexual behavior under the influence of alcohol (Ka et al., 2020; Sizemore & Olmstead, 2018).

- **Myth:** Consensually nonmonogamous and/or kink relationships are maladaptive and unhealthy in comparison to "vanilla" monogamous relationships.

  - **Counter:** Individuals in polyamorous relationships exhibit higher levels of emotional and sexual satisfaction when compared to those in monogamous relationships (Ka et al., 2020). Research suggests that engagement in kink and consensual nonmonogamy is associated with more secure attachment styles (Brink et al., 2021; Ka et al., 2020), which are associated with more positive mental and physical health outcomes across the lifespan. Especially for gender-expansive populations, membership in a kink community can result in higher levels of acceptance, belongingness, and community engagement (Speciale & Khambatta, 2020).

- **Myth:** Engagement in kink behaviors and/or nonmonogamous relationships is unnatural for humans. These deviant behaviors should not be talked about.
  - ○ **Counter:** Contrary to popular belief, research demonstrates that humans are not evolutionarily wired to prefer monogamy (Brandon, 2011). Additionally, kink behaviors are a natural outgrowth of sexual exploration that are not associated with addiction, reenaction of abuse/trauma experiences, nor dangerous tendencies (Brink et al., 2021; Pitagora, 2016). Challenging traditional views on monogamy and sexual behavior in the treatment settings can lead to better mental and physical health outcomes for all individuals by destigmatizing nontraditional sexual and relationship patterns (Brandon, 2011; Pitagora, 2016).

Additional Considerations

Although a professional does not have to be queer, kinky, or consensually nonmonogamous to operate from a sex-positive framework, they should be able to embrace these identities in their clients. Even professionals who harbor more conservative personal values in their own life can be supportive of their clients by bracketing personal values and emphasizing a body-positive, eroto-positive, kink-positive, and relationship-positive view of sexualities in their clinical work.

Conclusion

Human service professionals should be as educated as possible without making assumptions about their clients' sexual health and sexualities. Professionals should have a good understanding of the historical oppression of sexually diverse people and the lack of sexual health education and information generally available. We encourage professionals to connect clients to resources when possible. As with other topics in this book, we also encourage professionals to examine their own biases and expectations with regard to working with clients of different sexual/affectional orientations, partnership styles, and gender identities.

Summary and Recommendations

- Gender-expansive populations have historically struggled to receive adequate sexual health resources.

- A lack of accurate sexual health education for gender-expansive clients can perpetuate harmful myths.
- It is important to be a sex-positive professional who is body positive, eroto-positive, kink positive, and relationship positive.
- It is important to recognize that Western beauty standards are based on White hegemonic, patriarchal, fatphobic, ableist, and cissexist understandings of beauty.
- Recognizing the negative impacts Western beauty standards have on us is vital to understanding gender-expansive clients.
- Professionals should question their assumptions regarding people of alternative sexualities and sexual communities.
- Providing a safe, open space for clients to discuss sexual concerns is vital to providing the best care possible.

Reflection Questions

1. How did you come to understand how you identify in terms of sexuality, partnership style, and romantic attraction?
2. Why might a gender-expansive client not want to discuss sexual health concerns?
3. What assumptions do you hold about individuals with more than one sexual partner? How might this impact your work with consensually nonmonogamous clients?
4. How can you empower clients to be more sex-positive in your work with them?
5. How have conventional Western standards of beauty impacted your own life?
6. How can you foster an accepting space that allows clients to be open and honest regarding their sexuality?

References and Suggested Readings

Bauer, G., & Hammond, R. (2015). Toward a broader conceptualization of trans women's sexual health. *Canadian Journal of Human Sexuality*, 24(1), 1–11. https://doi.org/10.3138/cjhs.24.1-CO1

Brandon, M. (2011). The challenge of monogamy: Bringing it out of the closet and into the treatment room. *Sexual and Relationship Therapy*, 26(3), 271–277. https://doi.org/10.1080/14681994.2011.574114

Brink, S. T., Coppens, V., Huys, W., & Morrens, M. (2021). The psychology of kink: A survey study into the relationships of trauma and attachment style with BDSM interests. *Sexuality Research & Social Policy*, 18(1), 1–12. https://doi.org/10.1007/s13178-020-00438-w

Cohen, M., & Wilson, K. (2017). Development of the Consensual Non-Monogamy Attitude Scale (CNAS). *Sexuality & Culture, 21*(1), 1–14. https://doi.org/10.1007/s12119-016-9395-5

Grimstad, F., & Garborcauskas, G. (2021). Clinicians perform incomplete sexual and reproductive health counseling in trans masculine adolescents. *Journal of Pediatric & Adolescent Gynecology, 34*(2), 247. https://doi.org/10.1111/j.1440-1584.2007.00859.x

Harviainen, J., & Frank, K. (2018). Group sex as play: Rules and transgression in shared non-monogamy. *Games and Culture, 13*(3), 220–239. https://doi.org/10.1177/1555412016659835

Jiang, D. D., Swenson, E., Mason, M., Turner, K. R., Dugi, D. D., Hedges, J. C., & Hecht, S. L. (2019). Effects of estrogen on spermatogenesis in transgender women. *Urology, 132*, 117–122. https://doi.org/10.1016/j.urology.2019.06.034

Joyner, A., & Bahng, J. (2019). Addressing the sexual and reproductive health needs of trans and gender nonconforming patients: Separate gender identity from sexual identity to allow for more comprehensive history-taking. *Ob. Gyn. News, 54*(5), 15.

Ka, W., Bottcher, S., & Walker, B. (2020). Attitudes toward consensual non-monogamy predicted by sociosexual behavior and avoidant attachment. *Current Psychology.* https://doi.org/10.1007/s12144-020-00941-8

Klesse, C. (2018). Theorizing multi-partner relationships and sexualities—Recent work on non-monogamy and polyamory. *Sexualities, 21*(7), 1109–1124. https://doi.org/10.1177/1363460717701691

Mosher, C. (2017). Historical perspectives of sex positivity: Contributing to a new paradigm within counseling psychology. *The Counseling Psychologist, 45*(4), 487–503. https://doi.org/10.1177/0011000017713755

Pitagora, D. (2016). The kink-poly confluence: Relationship intersectionality in marginalized communities. *Sexual and Relationship Therapy, 31*(3), 391–405. https://doi.org/10.1080/14681994.2016.1156081

Sizemore, K., & Olmstead, S. (2018). Willingness of emerging adults to engage in consensual non-monogamy: A mixed-methods analysis. *Archives of Sexual Behavior, 47*(5), 1423–1438. https://doi.org/10.1007/s10508-017-1075-5

Speciale, M., & Khambatta, D. (2020). Kinky & queer: Exploring the experiences of LGBTQ+ individuals who practice BDSM. *Journal of LGBT Issues in Counseling, 14*(4), 341–361. https://doi.org/10.1080/15538605.2020.1827476

Sprott, R., Vivid, J., Vilkin, E., Swallow, L., Lev, E., Orejudos, J., & Schnittman, D. (2020). A queer boundary: How sex and BDSM interact for people who identify as kinky. *Sexualities, 24*(5–6), 708–732. https://doi.org/10.1177/1363460720944594

Thompson, A., Moore, E., Haedtke, K., & Karst, A. (2020). Assessing implicit associations with consensual non-monogamy among U.S. early emerging adults: An application of the Single-Target Implicit Association Test. *Archives of Sexual Behavior, 49*(8), 2813–2828. https://doi.org/10.1007/s10508-020-01625-x

Vereecke, G., Defreyne, J., Van Saen, D., Collet, S., Van Dorpe, J., T'Sjoen, G., & Goossens, E. (2021). Characterisation of testicular function and spermatogenesis in transgender women. *Human Reproduction, 36*(1), 5–15. https://doi.org/10.1093/humrep/deaa254

Winter-Gray, T., & Hayfield, N. (2019). "Can I be a kinky ace?": How asexual people negotiate their experiences of kinks and fetishes. *Psychology & Sexuality,* 1–17. https://doi.org/10.1080/19419899.2019.1679866

15

Supervision

Some human service professionals pass on their skills and knowledge by providing supervision for professionals in training or for individuals who are in an applied academic program. Most of the literature or discussions about supervision are discipline specific (e.g., counseling, social work). Some research articles outline the benefits of specific supervision approaches (e.g., Knutson & Koch, 2021), but few focus specifically on the supervision process as it relates to providing services for gender-expansive clients. In keeping with the theme of this book, we take a broad approach to supervision in an effort to make this chapter useful for as many human service professionals as possible. We define supervision as oversight, one-on-one training, apprenticeship, and/or mentorship with the express purpose of increasing competence when working with gender-expansive communities. To simplify language in this chapter, we default to supervisor and supervisee terminology, but we encourage readers to apply this information to their own settings. The following are examples of the impact of supervision logistics on Bill, Molly, and Rowan, as well as a case example of a supervision dyad.

Bill

After running the gender-expansive support group at the LGBTQ+ center for two years, Bill is beginning to recognize his limitations. He hates having to cancel the group if he cannot attend and he realizes that he will not be able to run the group for the rest of his life. The group is growing, and it may someday split. Bill needs other group leaders who can stand in for Bill and who can eventually take over the group or spin-off groups. However, selecting someone to begin mentoring is easier said than done. As Bill begins thinking through the process, he notices that a lot rides on selecting the right supervisee.

For example, if Bill selects someone from the group itself, the group may view the new leader as an insider, but they will also have history with that leader and they may not take the supervisee seriously. If Bill selects someone from outside the group, the person may be easier for the group to look to for leadership, but there is no guarantee that the group will accept the new leader-in-training. Bill considered inviting a local mental health professional to colead the group, but most of the counselors he can think of identify as cisgender and he worries about the dynamic that would create with the group. Bill realized he needed advice, so he reached out to a friend who leads a support group in Dallas, Texas, to consult.

Molly

Molly has gotten a lot out of group therapy with her therapist in Fargo, North Dakota, but it is becoming increasingly apparent that Molly could benefit from individual therapy as well. Paying for group therapy and individual therapy is cost prohibitive for Molly, because of her limited, fixed income. As an advocate for Molly, her therapist started searching for individual therapists in the area who might be able to provide Molly with the care she needed, and the therapist found a professor at North Dakota State who maintained a private psychology practice. The professor agreed to provide co-therapy supervision for a student so that the student could gain experience and so that Molly could receive services free of charge.

At first, Molly was hesitant to meet with two therapists at the same time. She worried that she would be the odd person out or that the therapists would gang up on her. However, she found herself loving therapy. The counselors were open and caring, and they even joked about the uncommon supervision situation. Molly found it particularly helpful to get a couple of perspectives as she processed her emotions and reflected on relational dynamics. She also appreciated the fact that sessions did not have to be canceled if one of the therapists was unavailable. She felt safer knowing that two people were working to help her improve her life.

Rowan

As Rowan began preparing to graduate, they found themselves visiting their academic adviser more frequently. They worried about finding a job, about post-graduation plans, and that their parents were applying a lot of pressure for them to "finally move out [of the house]." They were particularly worried about being discriminated against by prospective employers, given that they had been on hormones for a few years. When they scheduled a meeting with their adviser two weeks ago, the adviser said, "I have a trainee shadowing me and I am wondering if it would be okay for them to be present when I meet with you?" Rowan agreed that the advisee could attend, and they were actually kind of excited that a future adviser would get to learn about working with a gender-fluid person who was about to enter the job market.

Rowan tried not to be aware that they were witnessing a supervision dynamic. They were meeting with their academic adviser for very important reasons, but they also could not help noticing how intentional their adviser was about involving their supervisee in the advising process. At their first meeting, the advisee just sat off to the side and listened, but in subsequent meetings, the supervisee started asking questions and offering possible solutions. Rowan took those opportunities to provide the supervisee with additional insights about their experience and their academic adviser made space for them to do so.

Lisa, LPC, and Austin, Master's Trainee

Austin is a second-year master's in counseling student at a university. He sees clients at the local domestic violence agency, which includes a shelter. He has a client, Susan, who is in her 40s and is beginning a social transition. Susan is worried about her partner's reactions when she comes out; her partner has been violent with her before. Susan also reports that her partner controls all of their finances, and she is unable to work currently because her partner likes her to stay home and says she shouldn't drive. She doesn't know where any of her important documents (social security card, birth certificate) are. She is only able to go to counseling because her partner thinks she is seeing someone about managing chronic pain. Austin would like the domestic violence agency to open space for Susan if she needs it at the shelter. Lisa tells him that isn't possible because the shelter is "only for women." Austin tries to explain that Susan identifies as a woman, but Lisa is adamant that the client cannot stay at the shelter. Austin comes to you for consultation and advice on how to approach this with his supervisor, Lisa, and whether to go to the director of the agency, because he feels this is discriminatory.

Supervision and Contextual Factors

In this chapter, we view supervision from several angles. On the surface, supervision may seem like a simple process of delivering information to a subordinate who is expected to learn that information and to behave accordingly, but we suggest that supervision with professionals who will work with gender-expansive clients is much deeper than that (see Hernández & McDowell, 2010). We begin by discussing contextual factors that surround supervision. Later, we will also talk about supervision as a relationship and as a profession.

Group Supervision

In this chapter, we assume that if you are someone who provides supervision, you will be working primarily with individual supervisees. Therefore, much of the content will assume a dyadic supervisory dynamic. However, many of the principles and ideas we discuss may be generalized to group settings. It is true that groups present supervisors with greater relational complexity and that groups take on their own characteristics and dynamics. However, the general principles discussed here should be sufficiently broad to inform general group work. For more about group dynamics, you may benefit from revisiting Chapter 13.

Supervisory groups have practical advantages such as saving time and resources, but they also enhance training by allowing supervisees to learn from each other and by exposing supervisees to a greater diversity of perspectives on gender-expansive care. Groups are also limited, though, because they may obscure deficiencies (e.g., biases, flawed assumptions) that would be exposed in deeper, one-on-one interactions. Individual supervision may not be as relationally rich, but it allows for more direct tracking of progress and targeted provision of feedback for supervisees. Where both are available, it is probably best for supervisees to receive a mix of both group and individual supervision as they prepare to care for gender-expansive clients.

Identity Differences

Most of this chapter, and even this book itself, assumes that readers identify as cisgender. However, supervisors and/or their supervisee(s) may identify as gender expansive. Unfortunately, very little has been written about the experiences of gender-expansive supervisees. Even if the supervisor and supervisee do not identify as gender expansive, supervisors may identify with a gender that is different from their supervisee and either individual may possess other marginalized identities (e.g., identifying as Black, bisexual, and so on) that are salient in the supervision space. It is important for the supervisor to be aware how identity similarities and differences may impact supervision (see Chapters 2 and 3).

We encourage supervisors to initiate a conversation about identities early in the supervisory relationship. Many identities are invisible, so supervisors should not assume that just because someone seems similar (such as skin tone), that they have a certain identity. A discussion of the many ways that intersectionality, power, and context impact the supervisory relationship is beyond the scope of this text, but readers are encouraged to consult additional scholarship as they explore complex relational dynamics in supervision (e.g., Hernández & McDowell, 2010).

We are not recommending that supervisors fixate on identity, but we do encourage supervisors to keep in mind that the diversity variables of the client(s) that the supervisee is working with are not the only salient ones. If a supervisee is struggling with a particular client, it may be because they under- or over-identify with the client. If a supervisor is struggling to provide feedback or is having a reaction to the work of a supervisee, it may be because of identity differences in the supervisee or even in the client with whom the supervisee is working.

Power Dynamics

Identities may play a role in power differentials. Some supervisors hold a lot of power over their supervisees. Some supervisors submit evaluations and grades, and/or determine when a supervisee is ready to work on their own. The gatekeeping function can put a lot of pressure on the supervisee to please their supervisor and to demonstrate competence. We bring attention to this dynamic because work with gender-expansive clients is not just about problem solving; it is also about building relationship and being present. If supervisees feel too motivated to fix, rescue, or do something with their clients, they may miss the important human element of gender-expansive work.

We talk about ways to counter power dynamics (e.g., self-disclosure, setting boundaries) in the next section. Supervisors may use a variety of tools to address the impact of power dynamics, such as demonstrating vulnerability and openness and sharing examples of their own developmental process. We do not recommend ignoring the power dynamics in supervision because doing so does not make power differentials disappear. In fact, acknowledging power dynamics is an important part of gender-expansive work because similar differentials exist between professionals and gender-expansive clients who may be in search of access to affirming care. For example, in the case of Austin and Lisa, above, the power differential is clearly creating difficulties in the supervision relationship and in Austin's ability to advocate for his client.

Constructive Feedback

If you struggle with giving constructive feedback as a supervisor, you are not alone. Some supervisors do not like conflict, and they experience the process of giving feedback as a conflictual process. If constructive feedback is viewed as painful or frightening, supervisors may avoid it and/or may pressure themselves into giving feedback in such a way that makes them come across as aggressive. In an effort to counter any fears about giving feedback, we encourage supervisors to view their feedback as a gift that they are giving to supervisees and, ultimately, to gender-expansive clients. Clients deserve excellence and you, as a supervisor, are uniquely situated to ensure that they receive the care they need.

The truth is that there are correct and incorrect ways of providing gender-expansive care. In our own practice, we have found that supervisees respect us more and value our expertise when we are able to provide them compassionately and directly with feedback about areas in which they can improve. If you are acting as a supervisor, you have skills that qualify you to hold that role. We encourage you to take pride in your ability to offer your knowledge to other future professionals in your field. As you prepare to give feedback to your supervisees about their work with gender-expansive clients, it may help to consult emerging texts about LGBTQ counseling standards and the evaluation of counselor readiness to work with LGBTQ clients (e.g., Dorn-Medeiros & Christensen, 2019).

Supportive Feedback

It is also very important to provide positive feedback to supervisees. You may find that supervisees are harder on themselves than you are when they, for example, misgender a client or when they make an inaccurate assumption about gender-affirmative work. As supervisors, we want our supervisees to be excellent gender-affirming professionals, but it is also important to take time to reinforce their passion for gender-expansive communities and to highlight their developmental progress. Given the power differential and the expertise possessed by supervisors, a kind word from a supervisor can make a huge positive impact on a supervisee. At the same time, as we have discussed throughout the book, it is crucial that supervisors are aware of their own biases, assumptions, and competence. We encourage supervisors to be open to learning from supervisees as well. As can be seen in the case of Lisa and Austin, above, Austin seems to have a more affirmative stance toward gender-expansive people than his supervisor, Lisa, does. In this case, Lisa might ask Austin to tell her more about why Austin thinks his client needs the shelter, or about how the shelter could be more inclusive of gender-expansive people.

The Supervisory Relationship

One theme you may have picked up on in this book is that gender-affirmative care is about building relationships. That dynamic extends to supervisory spaces, but there are some unique aspects of relationship building that show up in supervision (Bucky et al., 2010). We are unable to provide an exhaustive list in this chapter, but we highlight some of the more important dynamics that impact gender-affirming care. We also want to acknowledge that supervisors are human beings who possess important social skills that cannot be taught. We encourage supervisors to use their skills and to not lose their humanity when they enter supervision mode.

Self-Disclosure

Opinions about the appropriateness of self-disclosure with supervisees are mixed. Some practitioners believe that sharing their gender identity, sexual orientation, spiritual beliefs, and so on helps them to build a closer relationship with their supervisees. However, other supervisors suggest that sharing personal details may have negative implications for power differentials in supervision. For example, if a supervisee discovers that their supervisor is atheist, they may lose respect for or even develop concern for the supervisor. We suggest that each supervisee is different and that self-disclosure may impact various supervision relationships in various ways. We encourage you to use your best judgment and to share only what is comfortable for you.

As we suggested above, it may also be beneficial for supervisees to hear about their supervisor's developmental process. You may find that sharing about your mistakes helps supervisees to relax and to forgive themselves for their own errors. Again, however, we encourage you to be thoughtful about the information you disclose. It is not a good idea to model incorrect behaviors for supervisees and it is important to demonstrate competence as a supervisor. Too much self-deprecating humor or focus on supervisor mistakes can draw attention away from the performance of the supervisee.

Boundaries

As a supervisor, you likely already have experience with setting boundaries. However, there are some important boundaries to emphasize in the context of gender-expansive care. For example, some gender-expansive clients may present high risk (e.g., self-harm, suicidality). You will need to consider how available to be to your supervisee if they are seeing at-risk clients. You may want to provide supervisees with a backup supervisor, or you may need to set parameters around when you are available (e.g., regular business hours, until 7:00 in the evening).

As is the case with Molly, some clients may interact with you and/or your supervisee purely on electronic platforms. You may need to be clear with your supervisee and with their clients about which modes of electronic communication are appropriate to use. For example, it may be okay for your supervisee to text you, but they may also benefit from knowing that it is not okay to friend you or to contact you on social media.

Parallel Process

We encourage supervisors to keep an eye on parallel processes, or client dynamics that get replicated in the supervision space. For example, a supervisee may tell you that their client keeps avoiding talking about their gender identity. Every time the supervisee brings it up, the client redirects. You may notice that the same thing is happening in supervision sessions. Every time you bring up identity differences between you and your supervisee, the supervisee redirects the conversation. Bringing this up to the supervisee might produce important insight. The supervisee may realize that they feel afraid about how disclosure will impact their relationship with you. They may also realize that the client fears that they will not get the services they need if they disclose the details about their gender identity. Identifying parallel process can be a powerful tool in supervision.

Ruptures and Conflicts

It is important for supervisors to remain aware that conflicts may arise in the supervision relationship (Nelson & Friedlander, 2001). These may be used as a learning tool. For example, looking at the case of Lisa and Austin, it seems that Lisa was "adamant" and was not open to dialogue about their conflict. Another way she could have approached this is by saying, "Austin, it seems that you don't agree with the shelter policies. These policies have to be approved by our board, so they are difficult to change. But can you help me understand what you think should be changed?" Or "Austin, I know you are concerned about your client. Since this shelter is not an option right now, let's brainstorm what other local options we might have for her to keep your client safe." When disagreements about client treatment occur, supervisors may model conflict resolution and dialogue. If a rupture occurs, having dialogue about the conflict or misunderstanding can often make a supervisory relationship stronger. It is okay for a supervisor to be wrong, apologize, and figure out with the supervisee how to move forward.

Supervision as a Professional Role

Supervision is a space and a relationship, but it is also a professional role (Bernard & Goodyear, 2013). You likely became a supervisor because you demonstrated professional excellence and competence and are interested in mentoring others who are newer to the profession. Here, we hope to highlight some dimensions of professional supervision that are particularly salient in the context of gender-affirming care. Some of our recommendations overlap with the ethical and professional standards outlined in Chapter 8.

Qualification Compatibility

Consistent with ethical codes, you must limit your work to your areas of competence. That can be hard when it comes to gender-expansive care because there are few supervisors who are trained, experienced, and qualified in gender-affirming care. If you find that you are being asked to provide oversight for a supervisee who is working with a gender-expansive client and you fear that you lack some of the qualifications to do so, you may benefit from seeking your own supervision of supervision.

It is also important to consider the compatibility between your qualifications and those of your supervisee. Your supervisee may be very interested in learning how to provide excellent gender-affirming care, but they may lack important certifications or education to do so. Likewise, you may be qualified to supervise counseling students, but not other unlicensed professionals. Consider Bill's case and his search for a support group coleader. If Bill recruited a local counselor to colead the group, he would not be able to provide oversight of the counselor's clinical skills. Bill would only be able to focus on giving feedback about gender-affirming support group practice. The counselor would need to seek supervision if they wanted to improve their counseling practice with gender-expansive clients.

Consultation

When it comes to gender-affirming care, no single supervisor has all of the answers. The most effective gender-affirming supervision is collaborative. Excellent supervisors are aware of the limits of their knowledge, and they reach out to fellow professionals to consult as needed. We recommend maintaining a list of contacts you can reach out to when you are providing supervision of gender-affirming care.

Continuing Education

As we have noted in other chapters, the landscape of gender-affirming care is constantly changing. Identity terminology, definitions, and best practices are introduced, altered, and updated regularly. Supervisors are responsible for staying up to date with the most current gender-affirming practices and information. Of course, continuing education could include reading scholarly articles or attending seminars, but we also recommend following gender-expansive bloggers and YouTube influencers. Connecting with gender-expansive communities is a great way to keep learning and growing.

Future Developments

We noted earlier that this chapter is written primarily for cisgender supervisors and/or supervisees. At present, cisgender professionals and advocates make up the majority of supervisors, educators, and practitioners in the movement toward greater gender inclusion. Gender-expansive folks are conspicuously absent from many of the leadership positions in human service professional spaces. We hope, however, that those limited dynamics will change. We believe that it is the job of gender-affirming professionals to uplift and empower gender-expansive people to hold leadership positions that enable them to produce research, provide training, and offer supervision for gender-expansive people.

Cisgender allies are valuable and important, but they are also limited by the range of their experiences. Empowering gender-expansive people to hold leadership positions is a key part of successful supervision. Not only is it important to supervise cisgender students who are working with gender-expansive clients, it is also important to empower gender-expansive supervisees to obtain the certifications, endorsements, and experiences necessary to provide excellent care for the next generation.

Summary and Recommendations

- Many of the principles of individual supervision can be applied to group supervision.
- It is important to be aware of identity differences and similarities that exist between supervisors and supervisees.
- Initiating and expanding on discussions of identity, power, privilege, and oppression is critical to developing and maintaining a safe and effective supervisory relationship.
- It is very important to develop the ability to provide constructive feedback.
- Supportive feedback is an essential element of gender-affirmative supervision.
- Self-disclosure can be a powerful tool in supervision, but it should be used thoughtfully and sparingly.
- Relationship building is a part of both gender affirmative care and supervision.
- Conflict may occur in supervision. Conflict may be educational and may strengthen the supervision relationship if addressed appropriately.
- It is important to set thoughtful, clear boundaries with your supervisee, especially if they are working with at-risk clients.

Reflection Questions

1. What is something about yourself (e.g., an experience, identity) that it would be helpful to disclose to a supervisee?
2. What is something about yourself (e.g., an experience, identity) that would not be helpful to disclose to a supervisee?
3. What past experiences have you had with self-disclosure as a supervisee? How did these interactions go, and were there barriers to feeling comfortable or able to self-disclose?

4. How can you go about initiating discussions of identity, power, privilege, and oppression with a supervisee?
5. What can you do to minimize power differentials in the supervisory relationship?
6. How do you handle delivering constructive feedback and how could you handle it better?
7. If you have received supervision, what do you think makes a "good" supervisor?
8. How can you embody those qualities in work with gender-expansive supervisees or supervisees working with gender-expansive clients?
9. How much supportive feedback do you provide and how could you provide more/less?
10. What is one boundary that you think it is important to set with supervisees who are working with at-risk clients?
11. How have you handled conflict in supervision relationships?
12. What is one way you could work to uplift gender-expansive supervisees in an effort to encourage greater representation in leadership for gender-expansive supervisees?

References and Suggested Readings

Bernard, J. M., & Goodyear, R. K. (2013). *Fundamentals of clinical supervision* (5th ed.). Pearson.

Bucky, S. F., Marques, S., Daly, J., Alley, J., & Karp, A. (2010). Supervision characteristics related to the supervisory working alliance as rated by doctoral-level supervisees. *The Clinical Supervisor, 29*, 149–163. https://doi.org/10.1080/07325223.2010.519270

Dorn-Medeiros, C., & Christensen, J. K. (2019). Developing a rubric for supervision of students counseling LGBTQ clients. *Journal of LGBT Issues in Counseling, 13*(1), 28–44. https://doi.org/10.1080/15538605.2019.1565798

Hernández, P., & McDowell, T. (2010). Intersectionality, power, and relational safety in context: Key concepts in clinical supervision. *Training and Education in Professional Psychology, 4*(1), 29–35. https://doi.org/10.1037/a0017064

Knutson, D., & Koch, J. M. (2021). A cotherapy supervision approach using person-centered theory with a gender fluid client. *Clinical Case Studies, 20*(5), 368–384. https://doi.org/10.1177%2F15346501211003157

Nelson, M. L., & Friedlander, M. L. (2001). A close look at conflictual supervisory relationships: The trainee's perspective. *Journal of Counseling Psychology, 48*(4), 384–395. https://doi.org/10.1037//0022-0167.48.4.384

Nelson, M. L., Gizara, S., Hope, A. C., Phelps, R., Steward, R., & Weitzman, L. (2011). A feminist multicultural perspective on supervision. *Journal of Multicultural Counseling and Development, 34*(2), 105–115. https://doi.org/10.1002/j.2161-1912.2006.tb00031.x

Conclusion

If you read this book from cover to cover, thank you for embarking on this journey toward affirming care with us. If you read over a few chapters that were most pertinent to your work, we suggest that you keep this book and return to it as you continue to develop into an affirming professional. Either way, we encourage you to continue the work you started here. Becoming an affirming professional is not a journey with an end point. This text is intended to help you start the journey, but reaching the end does not mean that you can close the book on your gender exploration.

We hope you will continue to seek out opportunities to grow as an affirming professional. If your profession requires continuing education, we suggest that you look for gender-affirming training and education hours to meet your professional requirements. If your profession does not require formal continuing education hours, we urge you to set annual reminders on your calendar to participate in growth-fostering activities to improve your work. We also hope that you will incorporate gender-affirming practice into your daily life. We have found that the most effective gender-affirming professionals are lifelong learners who cultivate affirming spaces everywhere they go.

We also hope you will share your knowledge and experiences with others. As you learned while reading this book, gender-expansive people are negatively impacted by societies that do not embrace gender diversity. As a reader of this book, you have already joined us in our work to change professional spaces and to improve services for gender-expansive people. We invite you to join us in our mission to inspire greater gender affirmation in our communities, our countries, and, ultimately, in our world.

Resources Table

	Address	Phone	Website / Email	Website / Email
Counselors, couple therapists				
Endocrinologists or other physicians who will prescribe hormones (e.g., Planned Parenthood)				
Primary care providers / family providers				
Hospitals or medical centers that specialize in trans care				
Dentists				
Other mental health providers (e.g., psychiatrists, case managers)				
Voice coaches, communication specialists, speech therapists				
Gynecologists, urologists				
Electrologists, hair removal services				

	Address	Phone	Website / Email	Website / Email
Hairdressers, barbers, or salons				
Clothing stores				
Places to purchase wigs				
Places to purchase bras, lingerie, or breast forms				
Local PFLAG or other LGBT-friendly agencies or groups				
Gender support groups				
Support groups for partners, family members, children				
LGBT-friendly churches or religious groups				
Local public restrooms that are all-gender				
Friendly businesses (e.g., car repair shops, home repair services, etc.)				
Recreation spaces that are safe or friendly (e.g., public parks, gyms, nature reserves)				
Gender-affirming legal services (e.g., to help with legal name and gender marker changes)				
Other resources				

Letter of Recommendation for Hormone Replacement Therapy

DATE

DOCTOR
ADDRESS

Dear Dr. NAME,

I am writing this letter to recommend Hormone Replacement Therapy for my client, LEGAL NAME, aka CHOSEN NAME. I am a LICENSED PROVIDER in the State of FLORIDA and have worked with transgender clients for more than TEN years. I am familiar with the *WPATH Standards of Care*, participate in ongoing continuing education related to transgender issues, and am an active advocate for transgender clients, students, and personal friends.

NAME is a XX-year-old RACE client who was assigned GENDER at birth. XX HAS BEEN/NOT BEEN married for XX years and HAS/DOES NOT HAVE children. XX works and lives as a JOB in LOCATION. XX has had stable employment at the same employer for more than XX years.

XX and I have met weekly for hour-long individual therapy since DATE for a total of XX sessions. Informed consent was obtained at the beginning of therapy and has been re-established throughout our working relationship. Therapy has consisted largely of a humanistic, client-centered approach but has also included some cognitive behavioral techniques.

During this time, I have observed symptoms of XX [e.g., heightened anxiety and stress], but it is my professional opinion that these were due in whole to gender dysphoria. XX stated that XX has experienced gender dysphoria for as long as XX can remember, and the feelings of dysphoria have strongly heightened in the last XX years. Overall, I experience XX as QUALITIES HERE [e.g., highly intelligent, high functioning, and stable, with a positive attitude and motivation]—all of which will serve as strengths as XX transitions.

Diagnoses:
302.85 Gender dysphoria in adolescents and adults
OTHER DIAGNOSES

XX has followed the *WPATH Standards of Care* (7th Version) and has met the criteria for hormone therapy. In addition to meeting with me weekly or biweekly, XX has connected to a support network of other persons who identify as transgender in the XX area. XX has begun the process of coming out to family and friends and has received warm support from FAMILY MEMBERS. OTHER RELATIONSHIPS. XX has presented as a GENDER whenever possible in the last LENGTH OF TIME and anticipates presenting full-time as a GENDER in the next few months. XX and I will continue to meet as XX transitions. XX has engaged in considerable self-reflection and has given thorough consideration to XX transition plans and timeline. OTHER INFOR-MATION OR STATEMENTS TO MAKE STRONG CASE

It is my professional judgment that XX needs hormone therapy to assist with XX gender dysphoria, and I anticipate that XX will be compliant with treatment. I welcome a phone call to discuss XX case further if that would be helpful. My personal cell phone is PHONE.

Thank you,

Signature, credentials

CC: CLIENT

Note: Double exes (XX) and text in all caps indicate places that spe-cifics about the client should be entered. Other text may be changed as needed.

Letter of Recommendation for Surgery

DATE

DOCTOR
ADDRESS

Dear Dr. NAME,

I am writing this letter to recommend TYPE OF SURGERY for my client, LEGAL NAME, aka CHOSEN NAME. I am a LICENSED PROVIDER in the State of FLORIDA and have worked with transgender clients for more than TEN years. I am familiar with the *WPATH Standards of Care*, participate in ongoing continuing education related to transgender issues, and am an active advocate for transgender clients, students, and personal friends.

NAME is a XX-year-old RACE client who was assigned GENDER at birth. XX HAS BEEN/NOT BEEN married for XX years and HAS/DOES NOT HAVE children. XX works and lives as a JOB in LOCATION. XX has had stable employment at the same employer for more than XX years.

XX and I have met weekly for hour-long individual therapy since DATE for a total of XX sessions. Informed consent was obtained at the beginning of therapy and has been re-established throughout our working relationship. Therapy has consisted largely of a humanistic, client-centered approach but has also included some cognitive behavioral techniques. During this time I have observed symptoms of XX [e.g., heightened anxiety and stress] but it is my professional opinion that these were due in whole to the gender dysphoria. XX stated that XX has experienced gender dysphoria for as long as XX can remember, and the feelings of dysphoria have strongly heightened in the last XX years. Overall, I experience XX as QUALITIES HERE [e.g., highly intelligent, high functioning, and stable, with a positive attitude and motivation]—all of which will serve as strengths as XX transitions.

Diagnoses:
302.85 Gender dysphoria in adolescents and adults
OTHER DIAGNOSES

XX has followed the *WPATH Standards of Care* (7th Version) and has met the criteria for NAME OF SURGERY. In addition to meeting with me weekly or biweekly, XX has connected to a support network of other persons who identify as transgender in the XX area. XX has begun the process of coming out to family and friends and has received warm support from FAMILY MEMBERS. OTHER RELATION-SHIPS. XX has presented as a GENDER whenever possible in the last LENGTH OF TIME and anticipates presenting full-time as a GENDER in the next few months. XX and I will continue to meet as XX transitions. XX has engaged in considerable self-reflection and has given thorough consideration to XX transition plans and timeline. OTHER INFORMATION OR STATEMENTS TO MAKE STRONG CASE

It is my professional judgment that XX needs NAME OF SURGERY to assist with XX gender dysphoria, and I anticipate that XX will be compliant with treatment. I welcome a phone call to discuss XX case further if that would be helpful. My personal cell phone is PHONE.

Thank you,

Signature, credentials

CC: CLIENT

Note: Double exes (XX) and text in all caps indicate places that specifics about the client should be entered. Other text may be changed as needed.

"Carry Letter"

January 3, 2020

To Whom It May Concern:

I am a [license or qualifications] in the state of Iowa. [Client's full name], aka [Client's legal name], date of birth [date of birth], is under my care for gender dysphoria. [Client's full name] is currently transitioning to [her] true gender, which involves allowing [her] to live and present as a [woman] although [her] assigned/biological sex is [male] and [her] government-issued identification shows [her] to be [male].

It is imperative to the health and well-being of transgender persons that they be allowed to live life fully in the appropriate gender role. [Client's full name] should be allowed to use the [women]'s restroom and any other sex-segregated facility.

It also is imperative that [Client's full name]'s confidentiality and medical privacy be protected. Revealing [her] transgender status would compromise the confidentiality of [her] private medical history.

Thank you in advance for your assistance. If you have any questions or concerns, please do not hesitate to contact me at my cell phone number: [PHONE].

Sincerely,

Signature, credentials

Clinician Action Steps

See the table on the next page.

Action	What actions or changes will occur	Who will carry out these changes	By when they will take place, and for how long	What resources are needed to carry out these changes	Communication (Who should know?)
I will improve the intake paperwork at my agency to be inclusive of gender-expansive clients	Intake paperwork, informed consent, and initial interview will include trans-affirmative language	I will collaborate with the Director of Diversity and Outreach; will work with front office staff to make the changes	By June 1; will take place indefinitely	2–3 hours of my clinical time allocated to paperwork	All staff in the clinic; volunteers; other stakeholders
I will introduce myself using my pronouns	I will introduce myself with she/her/hers	Me	Today!	None!	Everyone!

Bibliography

Adelson, S. L. (2012). Practice parameter on gay, lesbian, or bisexual sexual orientation, gender nonconformity, and gender discordance in children and adolescents. *Journal of the American Academy of Child & Adolescent Psychiatry, 51*(9), 957–974.

Afrasiabi, H., & Junbakhsh, M. (2019). Meanings and experiences of being transgender: A qualitative study among transgender youth. *The Qualitative Report, 24*(8), 1866–1876.

Alle-Corliss, L., & Alle-Corliss, R. (2009). *Group work: A practical guide to developing groups in agency settings.* John Wiley & Sons.

American Academy of Child & Adolescent Psychiatry. (2018). *Conversion therapy.* https://www.aacap.org/AACAP/Policy_Statements/2018/Conversion_Therapy.aspx

American Association for Marriage and Family Therapy. (2015). *AAMFT code of ethics.* https://www.aamft.org/Legal_Ethics/Code_of_Ethics.aspx

American Counseling Association. (2014). *2014 ACA code of ethics.* https://www.counseling.org/resources/aca-code-of-ethics.pdf

American Group Psychotherapy Association: https://www.agpa.org/

American Psychiatric Association. (1952). *Diagnostic and statistical manual of mental disorders.* American Psychiatric Press.

American Psychiatric Association. (1968). *Diagnostic and statistical manual of mental disorders* (2nd ed.). American Psychiatric Press.

American Psychiatric Association. (1980). *Diagnostic and statistical manual of mental disorders* (3rd ed.). American Psychiatric Press.

American Psychiatric Association. (2013). *Diagnostic and statistical manual of mental disorders* (5th ed.). https://doi.org/10.1176/appi.books.9780890425596

American Psychological Association. (2009). *Resolution on appropriate affirmative responses to sexual orientation distress and change efforts.* https://www.apa.org/about/policy/sexual-orientation

American Psychological Association. (2015). Guidelines for psychological practice with transgender and gender nonconforming people. *American Psychologist, 70*(9), 832–864. https://doi.org/10.1037/a0039906

American Psychological Association. (2017). *Ethical principles of psychologists and code of conduct.* https://www.apa.org/ethics/code/

American Psychological Association. (2021). *APA resolution on sexual orientation change efforts.* https://www.apa.org/about/policy/resolution-sexual-orientation-change-efforts.pdf

American School Counselor Association. (2012). *ASCA National Model: A framework for school counseling programs* (3rd ed.). American School Counselor Association.

American School Counselor Association. (2016). *ASCA ethical standards for school counselors.* https://www.schoolcounselor.org/getmedia/f041cbd0-7004-47a5-ba01-3a5d657c6743/Ethical-Standards.pdf

Ansara, Y. G., & Hegarty, P. (2014). Methodologies of misgendering: Recommendations for reducing cisgenderism in psychological research. *Feminism & Psychology, 24*(2), 259–270. https://doi.org/10.1177/0959353514526217

Ashley, F. (2020). Homophobia, conversion therapy, and care models for trans youth: Defending the gender-affirmative approach. *Journal of LGBT Youth, 17*(4), 361–383. https://doi.org/10.1080/19361653.2019.1665610

Ashley, F., & Ells, C. (2018). In favor of covering ethically important cosmetic surgeries: Facial feminization surgery for transgender people. *American Journal of Bioethics, 18*(12), 23–25. https://doi.org/10.1080/15265161.2018.1531162

Association for Specialists in Group Work: https://asgw.org/

Austin, A., & Craig, S. L. (2015). Transgender affirmative cognitive behavioral therapy: Clinical considerations and applications. *Professional Psychology: Research and Practice, 46*(1), 21. https://doi.org/10.1037/a0038642

Bauer, G., & Hammond, R. (2015). Toward a broader conceptualization of trans women's sexual health. *Canadian Journal of Human Sexuality, 24*(1), 1–11. https://doi.org/10.3138/cjhs.24.1-CO1

Bem, S. L. (1974). The measurement of psychological androgyny. *Journal of Consulting and Clinical Psychology, 42*(2), 155–162.

Bergstrom-Lynch, C. (2019). Free to be you and me, maybe: Lesbian, gay, bisexual, and transgender parents doing gender with their children. *Journal of Gender Studies,* 1–13.

Bernard, J. M., & Goodyear, R. K. (2013). *Fundamentals of clinical supervision* (5th ed.). Pearson.

Bockting, W. O., Miner, M. H., Swinburne Romine, R. E., Hamilton, A., & Coleman, E. (2013). Stigma, mental health, and resilience in an online sample of the US transgender population. *American Journal of Public Health, 103*(5), 943–951.

Boskey, E. (2021a). Gender-affirming surgeries: Men, bottom. In A. Goldberg & G. Beemyn (Eds.), *The SAGE encyclopedia of trans studies* (Vol. 1, pp. 330–332). SAGE Publications, Inc. https://www.doi.org/10.4135/9781544393858.n116

Boskey, E. (2021b). Gender-affirming surgeries: Men, top. In A. Goldberg & G. Beemyn (Eds.), *The SAGE encyclopedia of trans studies* (Vol. 1, pp. 333–335). SAGE Publications, Inc. https://www.doi.org/10.4135/9781544393858.n117

Boskey, E., & Klein, P. (2021). Gender-affirming surgeries: Women. In A. Goldberg & G. Beemyn (Eds.), *The SAGE encyclopedia of trans studies* (Vol. 1, pp. 336–338). SAGE Publications, Inc. https://www.doi.org/10.4135/9781544393858.n118

Brammer, R., & Ginicola, M. M. (2017). Counseling transgender clients. In *Affirmative counseling with LGBTQI+ people* (pp. 183–212). American Counseling Association.

Brandon, M. (2011). The challenge of monogamy: Bringing it out of the closet and into the treatment room. *Sexual and Relationship Therapy, 26*(3), 271–277. https://doi.org/10.1080/14681994.2011.574114

Brink, S. T., Coppens, V., Huys, W., & Morrens, M. (2021). The psychology of kink: A survey study into the relationships of trauma and attachment style with BDSM interests. *Sexuality Research & Social Policy, 18*(1), 1–12. https://doi.org/10.1007/s13178-020-00438-w

Bucky, S. F., Marques, S., Daly, J., Alley, J., & Karp, A. (2010). Supervision characteristics related to the supervisory working alliance as rated by doctoral-level supervisees. *The Clinical Supervisor, 29,* 149–163. https://doi.org/10.1080/07325223.2010.519270

Budge, S. L., Thai, J. L., Tebbe, E. A., & Howard, K. A. (2016). The intersection of race, sexual orientation, socioeconomic status, trans identity, and mental health outcomes. *The Counseling Psychologist, 44*(7), 1025–1049.

Burnes, T. R., Singh, A. A., Harper, A. J., Harper, B., Maxon-Kann, W., Pickering, D. L., Moundas, S., Scofield, T. R., Roan, A., Hosea, J., & ALGBTIC Transgender Committee. (2010). American Counseling Association: Competencies for counseling with transgender clients. *Journal of LGBT Issues in Counseling, 4*(3–4), 135–159.

Canadian Counseling and Psychotherapy Association. (2015). *Standards of practice* (5th ed.). https://www.ccpa-accp.ca/wp-content/uploads/2015/07/StandardsOf Practice_en_June2015.pdf

Carpenter, C. S., Eppink, S. T., & Gonzales, G. (2020). Transgender status, gender identity, and socioeconomic outcomes in the United States. *ILR Review, 73*(3), 573–599.

Carpenter, M. (2016). The human rights of intersex people: Addressing harmful practices and rhetoric of change. *Reproductive Health Matters, 24*(47), 74–84.

Centers for Disease Control and Prevention. (2020, September 16). *Disability impacts all of us.* https://www.cdc.gov/ncbddd/disabilityandhealth/infographic-disability -impacts-all.html

Cohen, M., & Wilson, K. (2017). Development of the Consensual Non-Monogamy Attitude Scale (CNAS). *Sexuality & Culture, 21*(1), 1–14. https://doi.org/10.1007 /s12119-016-9395-5

Cohen-Kettenis, P. T., & Van Goozen, S. H. (1997). Sex reassignment of adolescent transsexuals: A follow-up study. *Journal of the American Academy of Child & Adolescent Psychiatry, 36*(2), 263–271.

Corey, G., Corey, M. S., & Corey, C. (2019). *Issues and ethics in the helping professions* (10th ed.). CENGAGE Learning Custom Publishing.

Crenshaw, K. W. (1989). Demarginalizing the intersection of race and sex: A Black feminist critique of antidiscrimination doctrine, feminist theory, and antiracist politics. *University of Chicago Legal Forum, 1989*(1), 139–167.

Davidson, S. (2016). Gender inequality: Nonbinary transgender people in the workplace. *Cogent Social Sciences, 2*(1), 1–12. https://doi.org/10.1080/23311886.2016 .1236511

Davis, G., & Evans, M. J. (2018). Surgically shaping sex: A gender structure analysis of the violation of intersex people's human rights. In B. Risman, C. Froyum, & W. J. Scarborough (Eds.), *Handbook of the sociology of gender* (pp. 273–284). Springer International Publishing.

Day, J. K., Perez-Brumer, A., & Russell, S. T. (2018). Safe schools? Transgender youth's school experiences and perceptions of school climate. *Journal of Youth and Adolescence,* 1–12.

Deogracias, J. J., Johnson, L. L., Meyer-Bahlburg, H. F., Kessler, S. J., Schober, J. M., & Zucker, K. J. (2007). The gender identity/gender dysphoria questionnaire for adolescents and adults. *Journal of Sex Research, 44*(4), 370–379.

de Vries, K. M. (2015). Transgender people of color at the center: Conceptualizing a new intersectional model. *Ethnicities, 15*(1), 3–27.

dickey, l. m., & Loewy, M. I. (2010). Group work with transgender clients. *Journal for Specialists in Group Work, 35,* 236–245. https://doi.org/10.1080/01933922 .2010.492904

Docter, R. F., & Fleming, J. S. (1993). Dimensions of transvestism and transsexualism: The validation and factorial structure of the Cross-Gender Questionnaire. *Journal of Psychology & Human Sexuality, 5*(4), 15–38.

Dorn-Medeiros, C., & Christensen, J. K. (2019). Developing a rubric for supervision of students counseling LGBTQ clients. *Journal of LGBT Issues in Counseling, 13*(1), 28–44. https://doi.org/10.1080/15538605.2019.1565798

Drescher, J. (2015). Queer diagnoses revisited: The past and future of homosexuality and gender diagnoses in *DSM* and *ICD*. *International Review of Psychiatry, 27*(5), 386–395. https://doi.org/10.3109/09540261.2015.1053847

Eliason, M. J., & Hughes, T. (2004). Treatment counselor's attitudes about lesbian, gay, bisexual, and transgendered clients: Urban vs. rural settings. *Substance Use and Misuse, 39*(4), 625–644. https://doi.org/10.1081/ja-120030063

Fausto-Sterling, A. (2000). *Sexing the body: Gender politics and the construction of sexuality*. Basic Books.

Fausto-Sterling, A. (2012). *Sex/gender: Biology in a social world*. Routledge.

Ferrara, M., & Casper, M. J. (2018). Genital alteration and intersex: A critical analysis. *Current Sexual Health Reports, 10*(1), 1–6.

Flores, A. R., Herman, J. L., Gates, G. J., & Brown, T. N. T. (2016). How many adults identify as transgender in the United States? http://williamsinstitute.law.ucla.edu/wp-content/uploads/How-Many-Adults-Identify-as-Transgender-in-the-United-States.pdf

Galupo, M. P., & Pulice-Farrow, L. (2020). Subjective ratings of gender dysphoria scales by transgender individuals. *Archives of Sexual Behavior, 49*(2), 479–488. https://doi.org/10.1007/s10508-019-01556-2

Galupo, M. P., Pulice-Farrow, L., & Lindley, L. (2020). "Every time I get gendered male, I feel a pain in my chest": Understanding the social context for gender dysphoria. *Stigma and Health, 5*(2), 199–208. https://doi.org/10.1037/sah0000189

Gay, Lesbian and Straight Education Network (GLSEN). https://www.glsen.org

Goldbach, C., & Knutson, D. (2021). Development and initial validation of the sociocultural gender dysphoria scale (SGDS). *Psychology of Sexual Orientation and Gender Diversity*. https://doi.org/10.1037/sgd0000548

Green, R. (1998). Transsexuals' children. *International Journal of Transgenderism, 2*(4), 97–103.

Griffiths, K. M., & Christensen, H. (2007). Internet-based mental health programs: A powerful tool in the rural medical kit. *Australian Journal of Rural Health, 15*(2), 81–87. https://doi.org/10.1111/j.1440-1584.2007.00859.x

Grimstad, F., & Garborcauskas, G. (2021). Clinicians perform incomplete sexual and reproductive health counseling in trans masculine adolescents. *Journal of Pediatric & Adolescent Gynecology, 34*(2), 247. https://doi.org/10.1016/j.jpag.2021.02.025

Grzanka, P. R., DeVore, E., Gonzalez, K. A., Pulice-Farrow, L., & Tierney, D. (2018). The biopolitics of passing and the possibility of radically inclusive transgender health care. *American Journal of Bioethics, 18*(12), 17–19.

Hakeem, A., Črnčec, R., Asghari-Fard, M., Harte, F., & Eapen, V. (2016). Development and validation of a measure for assessing gender dysphoria in adults: The Gender Preoccupation and Stability Questionnaire. *International Journal of Transgenderism, 17*(3–4), 131–140. https://doi.org/10.1080/15532739.2016.1217812

Harviainen, J., & Frank, K. (2018). Group sex as play: Rules and transgression in shared non-monogamy. *Games and Culture, 13*(3), 220–239. https://doi.org/10.1177/1555412016659835

Haupert, M. L., Gesselman, A. N., Moors, A. C., Fisher, H. E., & Garcia, J. R. (2017). Prevalence of experiences with consensual nonmonogamous relationships: Findings from two national samples of single Americans. *Journal of Sex & Marital Therapy, 43*(5), 424–440.

Heck, N. C. (2017). Group psychotherapy with transgender and gender nonconforming adults: Evidence-based practice applications. *Psychiatric Clinics of North America, 40*(1), 157–175. https://doi.org/10.1016/j.psc.2016.10.010

Heck, N. C., Croot, L. C., & Robohm, J. S. (2013). Piloting a psychotherapy group for transgender clients: Description and clinical considerations for practitioners. *Professional Psychology: Research and Practice, 1*, 30–36. https://doi.org/10.1037/a0033134

Hembree, W. C., Cohen-Kettenis, P. T., Gooren, L., Hannema, S. E., Meyer, W. J., Murad, M. H., Rosenthal, S. M., Safer, J. D., Tangpricha, V., & T'Sjoen, G. G. (2017). Endocrine treatment of gender-dysphoric/gender-incongruent persons: An endocrine society clinical practice guideline. *Journal of Clinical Endocrinology & Metabolism, 102*(11), 3869–3903. https://doi.org/10.1210/jc.2017-01658

Hendricks, M. L., & Testa, R. J. (2012). A conceptual framework for clinical work with transgender and gender nonconforming clients: An adaptation of the Minority Stress Model. *Professional Psychology: Research and Practice, 43*(5), 460–467. https://doi.org/10.1037/a0029597

Hernández, P., & McDowell, T. (2010). Intersectionality, power, and relational safety in context: Key concepts in clinical supervision. *Training and Education in Professional Psychology, 4*(1), 29–35. https://doi.org/10.1037/a0017064

Hines, S. (2006). Intimate transitions: Transgender practices of partnering and parenting. *Sociology, 40*(2), 353–371.

Hirschfeld, M. (1923). Die intersexuelle constitution. *Jarbuch Fur Sexuelle Zwischenstufen, 23*, 3–27.

Hoffman-Fox, D. (2017). *You and your gender identity: A guide to discovery*. Skyhorse Publishing.

Huang, H., & Davila, J. (2021). Social transition. In A. Goldberg & G. Beemyn (Eds.), *The SAGE encyclopedia of trans studies* (Vol. 2, pp. 791–795). SAGE Publications, Inc. https://www.doi.org/10.4135/9781544393858.n264

Hyde, J. S., Bigler, R. S., Joel, D., Tate, C. C., & van Anders, S. M. (2018). The future of sex and gender in psychology: Five challenges to the gender binary. *American Psychologist*. Advance online publication. https://doi.org/10.1037/amp0000307

InterACT & Human Rights Watch. (2017). *"I want to be like nature made me": Medically unnecessary surgeries on intersex children in the US*. Human Rights Watch.

Jackson, J. M. (2021). Black feminisms, queer feminisms, trans feminisms: Meditating on Pauli Murray, Shirley Chisholm, and Marsha P. Johnson against the erasure of history. In J. Hobson (Ed.), *The Routledge companion to black women's cultural histories* (pp. 284–294). Routledge.

James, S. E., Herman, J. L., Rankin, S., Keisling, M., Mottet, L., & Anafi, M. (2016). *The report of the 2015 U.S. Transgender Survey*. National Center for Transgender Equality.

Jiang, D. D., Swenson, E., Mason, M., Turner, K. R., Dugi, D. D., Hedges, J. C., & Hecht, S. L. (2019). Effects of estrogen on spermatogenesis in transgender women. *Urology, 132,* 117–122. https://doi.org/10.1016/j.urology.2019.06.034

Johnson, M. (2014). The It Gets Better Project: A study in (and of) Whiteness—In LGBT youth and media cultures. In C. Pullen (Ed.), *Queer youth and media cultures* (pp. 278–291). Palgrave Macmillan.

Jones, B. A., Bouman, W. P., Haycraft, E., & Arcelus, J. (2019). The Gender Congruence and Life Satisfaction Scale (GCLS): Development and validation of a scale to measure outcomes from transgender health services. *International Journal of Transgenderism, 20*(1), 63–80.

Joyner, A., & Bahng, J. (2019). Addressing the sexual and reproductive health needs of trans and gender nonconforming patients: Separate gender identity from sexual identity to allow for more comprehensive history-taking. *Ob. Gyn. News, 54*(5), 15.

Ka, W., Bottcher, S., & Walker, B. (2020). Attitudes toward consensual non-monogamy predicted by sociosexual behavior and avoidant attachment. *Current Psychology.* https://doi.org/10.1007/s12144-020-00941-8

Kessler, L. E., & Waehler, C. A. (2005). Addressing multiple relationships between clients and therapists in lesbian, gay, bisexual, and transgender communities. *Professional Psychology: Research and Practice, 36*(1), 66.

Klesse, C. (2018). Theorizing multi-partner relationships and sexualities—Recent work on non-monogamy and polyamory. *Sexualities, 21*(7), 1109–1124. https://doi.org/10.1177/1363460717701691

Knutson, D., & Goldbach, C. (2019). Transgender and non-binary affirmative approaches applied to psychological practice with boys and men. In K. Barber, T. Bridges, & J. D. Nelson (Eds.), Mitigating the harms of masculinity: A symposium on the APA Guidelines for Psychological Practice with Boys and Men. *Men and Masculinities, 22*(5), 921–925. https://doi.org/10.1177/1097184X19875174

Knutson, D., Kallo, E., & Hubbs-Tait, L. (2022). Parenting trans and nonbinary youth. *Oklahoma State University Extension.* https://extension.okstate.edu/fact-sheets/parenting-trans-and-nonbinary-youth.html

Knutson, D., Kertz, S., Chambers-Baltz, S., Christie, M., Harris, E., & Perinchery, R. (2020). A pilot test of a text message based transgender and non-binary affirmative cognitive behavioral intervention for anxiety and depression. Advance online publication. *Psychology of Sexual Orientation and Gender Diversity.* https://doi.org/10.1037/sgd0000438

Knutson, D., & Koch, J. M. (2018). Person-centered therapy as applied to work with transgender and gender diverse clients. *Journal of Humanistic Psychology, 62*(1), 1–19. https://doi.org/10.1177%2F0022167818791082

Knutson, D., & Koch, J. M. (2021). A cotherapy supervision approach using person-centered theory with a gender fluid client. *Clinical Case Studies, 20*(5), 368–384. https://doi.org/10.1177%2F15346501211003157

Knutson, D., Koch, J. M., Arthur, T., Mitchell, T. A., & Martyr, M. A. (2017). "Trans broken arm": Health care stories from transgender people in rural areas. *Journal of Research on Women and Gender, 7*(1), 30–46. https://digital.library.txstate.edu/handle/10877/12890

Knutson, D., Koch, J. M., & Goldbach, C. (2019). Recommended terminology, pronouns, and documentation for work with transgender and non-binary populations. *Practice Innovations, 4*(4), 214. https://doi.org/10.1037/pri0000098

Knutson, D., Matsuno, E., Goldbach, C., Hashtpari, H., & Smith, N. G. (2021). Advocating for transgender and nonbinary affirmative spaces in graduate education. *Higher Education, 83*, 461–479. https://doi.org/10.1007/s10734-020-00673-5

Koch, J. M., & Knutson, D. (2016). Transgender clients in rural areas and small towns. *Journal of Rural Mental Health, 40*(3–4), 154–163. https://doi.org/10.1037/rmh0000056

Kohlberg, L. A. (1966). A cognitive-developmental analysis of children's sex role concepts and attitudes. *The Development of Sex Differences*, 82–173.

Kosciw, J. G., Greytak, E. A., Zongrone, A. D., Clark, C. M., & Truong, N. L. (2018). *The 2017 national school climate survey: The experiences of lesbian, gay, bisexual, transgender, and queer youth in our nation's schools*. Gay, Lesbian and Straight Education Network (GLSEN).

Leikam, K. (2021). *Gender identity journal: Prompts and practices for exploration and self-discovery*. Rockridge Press.

McGuire, J. K., Anderson, C. R., Toomey, R. B., & Russell, S. T. (2010). School climate for transgender youth: A mixed method investigation of student experiences and school responses. *Journal of Youth and Adolescence, 39*(10), 1175–1188.

McLemore, K. A. (2015). Experiences with misgendering: Identity misclassification of transgender spectrum individuals. *Self and Identity, 14*, 51–74. https://doi.org/10.1080/15298868.2014.950691

Milton, D. C., & Knutson, D. (2021). Family of origin, not chosen family, predicts psychological health in a LGBTQ+ sample. *Psychology of Sexual Orientation and Gender Diversity*. Advance Online Publication. https://doi.org/10.1037/sgd0000531

Money, J., Hampson, J. G., & Hampson, J. L. (1957). Imprinting and the establishment of gender role. *AMA Archives of Neurology & Psychiatry, 77*(3), 333–336.

Moors, A. C., Matsick, J. L., & Schechinger, H. A. (2017). Unique and shared relationship benefits of consensually non-monogamous and monogamous relationships. *European Psychologist, 22*, 55–71. https://doi.org/10.1027/1016-9040/a000278

Mosher, C. (2017). Historical perspectives of sex positivity: Contributing to a new paradigm within counseling psychology. *The Counseling Psychologist, 45*(4), 487–503. https://doi.org/10.1177/0011000017713755

Movement Advancement Project. (2019). *Where we call home: Transgender people in rural America*. https://www.lgbtmap.org/file/Rural-Trans-Report-Nov2019.pdf

Movement Advancement Project. (2022). *Mapping transgender equality in the United States*. https://www.lgbtmap.org/mapping-trans-equality

Mulcahy, A., Streed, C. G., Jr., Wallisch, A. M., Batza, K., Kurth, N., Hall, J. P., & McMaughan, D. J. (2022). Gender identity, disability, and unmet healthcare needs among disabled people living in the community in the United States. *International Journal of Environmental Research and Public Health, 19*, 2588. https://doi.org/10.3390/ijerph19052588

Nahata, L., Chen, D., Moravek, M. B., Quinn, G. P., Sutter, M. E., Taylor, J., Tishelman, A. C., & Gomez-Lobo, V. (2019). Understudied and under-reported: Fertility issues in transgender youth—a narrative review. *Journal of Pediatrics, 205*, 265–271. https://doi.org/10.1016/j.jpeds.2018.09.009

Nahata, L., Tishelman, A. C., Caltabellotta, N. M., & Quinn, G. P. (2017). Low fertility preservation utilization among transgender youth. *Journal of Adolescent Health, 61*(1), 40–44. https://doi.org/10.1016/j.jadohealth.2016.12.012

National Association of Social Workers. (2021). *National Association of Social Workers code of ethics.* https://www.socialworkers.org/About/Ethics/Code-of-Ethics/Code -of-Ethics-English

Nelson, M. L., & Friedlander, M. L. (2001). A close look at conflictual supervisory relationships: The trainee's perspective. *Journal of Counseling Psychology, 48*(4), 384–395. https://doi.org/10.1037//0022-0167.48.4.384

Nelson, M. L., Gizara, S., Hope, A. C., Phelps, R., Steward, R., & Weitzman, L. (2011). A feminist multicultural perspective on supervision. *Journal of Multicultural Counseling and Development, 34*(2), 105–115. https://doi.org/10.1002/j.2161-1912.2006 .tb00031.x

Parents, Families, and Friends of Lesbians and Gays (PFLAG). https://pflag.org/

Perry, D. G., Pauletti, R. E., & Cooper, P. J. (2019). Gender identity in childhood: A review of the literature. *International Journal of Behavioral Development, 43*(4), 289–304. https://doi.org/10.1177/0165025418811129

Pitagora, D. (2016). The kink-poly confluence: Relationship intersectionality in marginalized communities. *Sexual and Relationship Therapy, 31*(3), 391–405. https:// doi.org/10.1080/14681994.2016.1156081

Platt, L. F., & Bolland, K. S. (2018). Relationship partners of transgender individuals: A qualitative exploration. *Journal of Social and Personal Relationships, 35*(9), 1251–1272.

Proulx, C. N., Coulter, R. W., Egan, J. E., Matthews, D. D., & Mair, C. (2019). Associations of lesbian, gay, bisexual, transgender, and questioning-inclusive sex education with mental health outcomes and school-based victimization in US high school students. *Journal of Adolescent Health, 64*(5), 608–614. https://doi.org/10.1016/j .jadohealth.2018.11.012

Puckett, J. A., Maroney, M. R., Wadsworth, L. P., Mustanski, B., & Newcomb, M. E. (2020). Coping with discrimination: The insidious effects of gender minority stigma on depression and anxiety in transgender individuals. *Journal of Clinical Psychology, 76*(1), 176–194. https://doi.org/10.1002/jclp.22865

Puckett, J. A., Matsuno, E., Dyar, C., Mustanski, B., & Newcomb, M. E. (2019). Mental health and resilience in transgender individuals: What type of support makes a difference? *Journal of Family Psychology, 33*(8), 954–964. https://doi.org/10.1037 /fam0000561

Pulice-Farrow, L., Brown, T. D., & Galupo, M. P. (2017). Transgender microaggressions in the context of romantic relationships. *Psychology of Sexual Orientation and Gender Diversity, 4*(3), 362–373. https://doi.org/10.1037/sgd0000238

Rachlin, K. (2018). Medical transition without social transition: Expanding options for privately gendered bodies. *Transgender Studies Quarterly, 5*(2), 228–244. https://doi.org/10.1215/23289252-4348660

Ratcliffe, M., Burd, C., Holder, C., Fields, A. (2016). *Defining rural at the U.S. Census Bureau* (US Census Bureau Report No. ACSGEO-1), US Census Bureau. https:// www.census.gov/content/dam/Census/library/publications/2016/acs/acsgeo-1.pdf

Rew, L., Young, C. C., Monge, M., & Bogucka, R. (2021). Puberty blockers for transgender and gender diverse youth—A critical review of the literature. *Child and Adolescent Mental Health, 26*(1), 3–14. https://doi.org/10.1111/camh.12437

Richards, C., Bouman, W. P., Seal, L., Barker, M. J., Nieder, T. O., & T'Sjoen, G. (2016). Non-binary or genderqueer genders. *International Review of Psychiatry, 28*(1), 95–102.

Ridgeway, C. L., & Kricheli-Katz, T. (2013). Intersecting cultural beliefs in social relations: Gender, race, and class binds and freedoms. *Gender & Society, 27*(3), 294–318.

Rossman, K., Sinnard, M., & Budge, S. (2019). A qualitative examination of consideration and practice of consensual nonmonogamy among sexual and gender minority couples. *Psychology of Sexual Orientation and Gender Diversity, 6*(1), 11–21. https://doi.org/10.1037/sgd0000300

Schank, J. A., Helbok, C. M., Haldeman, D. C., & Gallardo, M. E. (2010). Challenges and benefits of ethical small-community practice. *Professional Psychology: Research and Practice, 41*(6), 502. https://doi.org/10.1037/a0021689

Schulz, S. L. (2018). The informed consent model of transgender care: An alternative to the diagnosis of gender dysphoria. *Journal of Humanistic Psychology, 58*(1), 72–92. https://doi.org/10.1177/0022167817745217

Shepard, B. (2013). From community organization to direct services: The Street Trans Action Revolutionaries to Sylvia Rivera Law Project. *Journal of Social Service Research, 39*(1), 95–114. https://doi.org/10.1080/01488376.2012.727669

Sinclair-Palm, J. (2017). "It's Non-Existent": Haunting in trans youth narratives about naming. *Occasional Paper Series, 37,* 7.

Sizemore, K., & Olmstead, S. (2018). Willingness of emerging adults to engage in consensual non-monogamy: A mixed-methods analysis. *Archives of Sexual Behavior, 47*(5), 1423–1438. https://doi.org/10.1007/s10508-017-1075-5

Society for Human Resource Management. (2022). *Employing transgender workers.* https://www.shrm.org/resourcesandtools/tools-andsamples/toolkits/pages/employingtransgenderworkers.aspx

Speciale, M., & Khambatta, D. (2020). Kinky & queer: Exploring the experiences of LGBTQ+ individuals who practice BDSM. *Journal of LGBT Issues in Counseling, 14*(4), 341–361. https://doi.org/10.1080/15538605.2020.1827476

Sprott, R., Vivid, J., Vilkin, E., Swallow, L., Lev, E., Orejudos, J., & Schnittman, D. (2020). A queer boundary: How sex and BDSM interact for people who identify as kinky. *Sexualities, 24*(5–6), 708–732. https://doi.org/10.1177/1363460720944594

Stanley, J. L. (2017). Teaching ethics in relation to LGBTQ issues in psychology. In T. R. Burnes & J. L. Stanley (Eds.), *Teaching LGBTQ psychology: Queering innovative pedagogy and practice* (pp. 61–84). American Psychological Association. https://doi.org/10.1037/0000015-004

Stone, A. L., Nimmons, E. A., Salcido, R., Jr., & Schnarrs, P. W. (2020). Multiplicity, race, and resilience: Transgender and non-binary people building community. *Sociological Inquiry, 90*(2), 226–248. https://doi.org/10.1111/soin.12341

Stryker, S. (2017). *Transgender history: The roots of today's revolution.* Seal Press.

Testa, R. J., Coolhart, D., & Peta, J. (2015). *The gender quest workbook: A guide for teens and young adults exploring gender identity.* Instant Help.

Thompson, A., Moore, E., Haedtke, K., & Karst, A. (2020). Assessing implicit associations with consensual non-monogamy among U.S. early emerging adults: An application of the Single-Target Implicit Association Test. *Archives of Sexual Behavior, 49*(8), 2813–2828. https://doi.org/10.1007/s10508-020-01625-x

Tierney, W. G., & Ward, J. D. (2017). Coming out and leaving home: A policy and research agenda for LGBT homeless students. *Educational Researcher, 46*(9), 498–507.

Trans Employment Program. https://www.sfcenter.org/transgender-employment-program-tep/

Transgender Law Center. https://transgenderlawcenter.org/

Tuckman, B. W. (1965). Developmental sequence in small groups. *Psychological Bulletin, 63*, 384–399. https://doi.org/10.1037/h0022100

Turban, J. L., Loo, S. S., Almazan, A. N., & Keuroghlian, A. S. (2021). Factors leading to "detransition" among transgender and gender diverse people in the United States: A mixed-methods analysis. *LGBT Health, 8*(4), 273–280. https://www.apa.org/about/policy/sexual-orientation

Vance, S. R., Jr., Deutsch, M. B., Rosenthal, S. M., & Buckelew, S. M. (2017). Enhancing pediatric trainees' and students' knowledge in providing care to transgender youth. *Journal of Adolescent Health, 60*(4), 425–430. https://doi.org/10.1016/j.jadohealth.2016.11.020

Vaughan, M. D., Jones, P., Taylor, B. A., & Roush, J. (2019). Healthcare experiences and needs of consensually non-monogamous people: Results from a focus group study. *Journal of Sexual Medicine, 16*(1), 42–51. https://doi.org/10.1016/j.jsxm.2018.11.006

Veldorale-Griffin, A. (2014). Transgender parents and their adult children's experiences of disclosure and transition. *Journal of GLBT Family Studies, 10*(5), 475–501. https://doi.org/10.1080/1550428X.2013.866063

Vereecke, G., Defreyne, J., Van Saen, D., Collet, S., Van Dorpe, J., T'Sjoen, G., & Goossens, E. (2021). Characterisation of testicular function and spermatogenesis in transgender women. *Human Reproduction, 36*(1), 5–15. https://doi.org/10.1093/humrep/deaa254

Wesp, L. M., Malcoe, L. H., Elliott, A., & Poteat, T. (2019). Intersectionality research for transgender health justice: A theory-driven conceptual framework for structural analysis of transgender health inequities. *Transgender Health, 4*(1), 287–296. https://doi.org/10.1089/trgh.2019.0039

West, C., & Zimmerman, D. H. (1987). Doing gender. *Gender & Society, 1*(2), 125–151. https://doi.org/10.1177/0891243287001002002

Winter-Gray, T., & Hayfield, N. (2019). "Can I be a kinky ace?": How asexual people negotiate their experiences of kinks and fetishes. *Psychology & Sexuality*, 1–17. https://doi.org/10.1080/19419899.2019.1679866

Winters, K. (2006). Gender dissonance: Diagnostic reform of gender identity disorder for adults. *Journal of Psychology & Human Sexuality, 17*(3–4), 71–89. https://doi.org/10.1300/J056v17n03_04

World Health Organization. (2016). *International statistical classification of diseases and related health problems* (10th ed.). https://icd.who.int/browse10/2016/en

World Health Organization. (2018). *ICD-11: Classifying disease to map the way we live and die.* http://www.who.int/health-topics/international-classification-of-diseases

World Professional Association for Transgender Health. (2011). Standards of care for the health of transsexual, transgender, and gender-nonconforming people (7th ed.). *International Journal of Transgenderism, 13*(4), 165–232. https://doi.org/10.1080/15532739.2011.700873

abnormal, gender expansiveness as, 3–4
acceptance, power of, 150–51
access, 49, 65
  to care, 116, 155
  to competent providers, 66, 116
  to resources, 68, 69
action steps, clinician, 209–10
additional marginalized identities, of
    gender-expansive people, 4
adolescence, 49–50
adult children, gender-expansive parent
    and, 154
advertisement, of services, 75
advocacy, 102, 142, 143
affirmation, of identity, 169
affirmative care, 4, 7, 58, 66, 73
  gender dysphoria and, 116
  polyamorous relationships and, 157
  unpreparedness to provide, 96, 195
affirmative practice resources, 2, 7, 75,
    108, 124–25
affirmative providers, 5, 14, 15
affirmative work, 135–1356
affirming professionals, list of, 76
affirming surgeries, 126
  requirements for, 127
age, 42–43
all-gender bathrooms, 52
allies, cisgender, 197
alternative sexualities, assumptions
    about gender identity and, 185
ambiguous genitalia, 17
The American Counseling Association,
    107–8, 141
The American School Counselor
    Association (ASCA), 141
anti-gender-expansive laws, 59
anti-immigration rhetoric, 32
apprenticeships, 187
appropriate, labeling of behaviors as, 49
Aron (friend), 175
ASCA. *See The American School
    Counselor Association*

asexual people, 180, 181
assessment, 88–89
  diagnosis and, 85–86
assessment measures, formal, 89–90
assumptions, about gender identity, 15,
    19–24, 47–48, 79, 157
  alternative sexualities and, 185
  healthcare and, 178
Austin (Master's Trainee), 189, 193, 195
avoidance, of invasive questions, 78
awareness, of privilege, 27, 28, 191

ban
  on conversion therapy, 105
  on procedures on intersex babies in
    Europe, 17
bathrooms, all-gender, 52
BDSM. *See* bondage, dominance,
    submission, sadism, and
    masochism
Bem Sex Role Inventory, 90
best practices, 81
biases, 22–24, 28, 37, 81
  deconstruction of, 149–50
Bill (client), 6, 11–12, 16, 21, 23
  Boston and, 57
  experience as polyamorous, 147–48,
    175–76
  experience with VA of, 73, 86,
    99–100
  letter of support of, 123–24
  LGBTQ+ collaborative of, 111–12,
    119, 135
  military service of, 32, 86
  puberty and, 85–86, 93
  relationship with family of, 46,
    147–48
  romantic relationships of, 175–76
  support group of, 161, 187–88, 196
binary, gender, 12–14, 177–78
the binary and me exercise, 27–28
binary identities, focus of questionnaires
    on, 90

binary sections, gender-fluid people and, 138

biographical paragraph exercise, 38

biological families, reliance on, 50

Black Lives Matter, 33

Black women, 31

Blue Cross Blue Shield, 128

body
    dysphoria, 115
    positivity, 179–80, 185

bondage, dominance, submission, sadism, and masochism (BDSM), 180–81

Bostock v. Clayton County, Georgia, 52

Boston, Massachusetts, 6, 57

bottom surgery, 126

boundaries
    within group, 166, 172
    between supervisor and supervisee, 194, 197

breast augmentation, 127

breast removal, 127

broad-ranging definitions, of gender-expansive community, 165

California Lutheran University, 6–7

The Canadian Counseling and Psychotherapy Association (CCPA), 103

care. *See also* affirmative care
    access to, 116, 155
    gender-diverse, 2, 5–7
    teams of, 118, 120

carry letters, 128, 131, 207

case examples, 5–6

CCPA. *See Canadian Counseling and Psychotherapy Association*

challenges, to entrenched ideas, 53–54

change of mind, fear of, 93–94

chaplain experience, of author, 119

childhood, 48–49

children
    choosing own gender, 48
    gender-expansive people experience as, 47

chosen family, 149

cisgender, 13, 16
    allies, 197
    as considered normal by society, 23
    siblings of gender-expansive person, 151
    as umbrella term, 15
    use of by professionals when referring to self, 15, 19

cisgender heterosexual (cishet) population, 181

cisnormativity, 16–17, 23, 118, 155

Claudia (partner of Rowan), 148–49

client
    in the closet, 42
    confidentiality, 62
    as expert, 94
    high-risk, 194
    initial contact with, 73
    of Julie, 105
    legal name use of, 25, 100
    as out in certain situations, 114
    reluctance to let go of, 82
    steps before meeting, 75, 83
    story of, 79
    struggles unawareness of, 39

client-focused approach, 94

client-professional interactions, 39–40

clinical processes, 119–20

clinician action steps, 209–10

close relationships, 155

the closet, clients in, 42

Code of Ethics (American Counseling Association), 107–8

collaboration, with other professionals, 103, 104–5, 109, 119, 120
    group therapy and, 171

college or university counseling centers (UCCs), 142

colorblindness, gender, 95–96

coming-out process, 114, 153
    divorce after, 155–56, 157
    in rural areas, 65

common destructive beliefs, 22–23

communication, alternate forms of, 62

communication skills, 79

community, gender expectations and, 26

community building, 163
competence, 107, 131, 195
    domains of, 108–9
competence-building resources, 129
competent providers, access, to, 66
compliments to supervisees, importance
    of, 193
conception of babies, hormone therapy
    and, 177
concerns, discussion of, 92
confidentiality, in group, 166
conflict
    dialogue about, 195, 197
    fear of, 192
connection, with others, 38–39, 68
consensually non-monogamous
    relationships, as healthy, 183
consensual nonmonogamy, 156
    kink community and, 182–83
constructive feedback, 192
consultation, 196
contact, after end of therapy, 82–83
continuing education, 196, 199
continuum, gender as, 13–14
conversion therapy, 106
    ban on, 105
cost, of therapy, 61
COVID-19, 59
Cox, Laverne, 112
Crenshaw, Kimberle, 31
cross-discipline affirmative practice
    resources, 2
Cross-Gender Questionnaire, 90
cultural nuance, 58–59

daily life, gender-affirming practice and,
    199
deadnaming, 24, 168
decision-making, 103, 109
default diagnosis, 92
desire, to pass, 117–18
destructive beliefs, common, 22–23
detransition, 94
developmental disabilities, 35
developmental process, of supervisor,
    193–94

diagnosis, 92
    assessment and, 85–86
    as permission for treatment, 93–94
*Diagnostic and Statistical Manual for
    Mental Disorders, Fifth Edition
    (DSM-5)* (American Psychiatric
    Association), 87–88
dialogue, about conflict, 195, 197
differences, identity, 190–91, 197
different gender, space for, 77
disability status, 35–36
disabled people, inequities of, 35
disclosure, of identities, 39, 41
discomfort, with providing diagnosis,
    94–95
discretion, in urban areas, 62
discussion, of concerns, 92
discussion of termination, avoidance of,
    170, 172
distress, from treatment of gender-
    expansive people, 4
diversity, within LGBTQ+ community,
    163–64
divorce, after coming-out of one partner,
    155–56, 157
domains, of competence in counseling,
    108
drag performance, 165
*DSM-5. See Diagnostic and Statistical
    Manual for Mental Disorders,
    Fifth Edition*
dual relationships, of group therapy
    leaders, 170–71
dyadic supervisory dynamic, 190

early adulthood, 52–53
early awareness, of gender identity, 47, 54
early stages, of counseling, 73, 78–79
educational development, for gender-
    expansive people, 45
Emily (from relationships example),
    154–55
empathy, gender expectations and, 25,
    27, 43, 161
empowerment, of gender-expansive
    professionals, 196–97

Endocrine Society's Standards, 51
entrenched ideas, challenges to, 53–54
environment
    gender identity and, 24–25
    of therapy room waiting room and,
        77
erotophobia, 180
eroto-positivity, 180
ethical situations, 103, 109
Ethical Standards for School Counselors
    (ASCA), 141
ethics, 94–95, 99–100
ethics codes, 103–4
exclusion, of trans women by feminists,
    32
exercise
    the binary and me, 27–28
    biographical paragraph, 38
expectations, gender, 24–25, 48, 54,
    150–51
experience with gender-expansive people
    of parents, 151–52
    in rural areas, 66
expert, client as, 94
exploration
    of different sexual orientations, 41
    of gender identity, 21, 43, 78, 109
    of geographic culture of origin,
        67–68
    of identity, 21, 43, 78, 109

family
    gender expectations, 25, 68, 150–51
    members at appointments, 62
    of origin rejection from, 50
    proximity to, 63, 65
    system components of, 152–53
fatphobia, 180
fear
    of change of mind, 93–94
    of conflict, 192
    of unknown, 50
feedback
    as compassionate, 192
    constructive, 192
    viewed as gift, 192
female-to-male (FTM), 16

feminists, exclusion of trans women by,
    32
fight, for justice for gender-expansive
    people, 5
first appointment, 77–78
formal assessment measures, 89–90
formal group work, 164
forming, 165–66
forms, as inclusive, 77, 91–92, 140
front office staff, training of, 76, 83,
    120, 138–39, 143
frustration
    during group therapy, 168
    during transition process, 130
FTM. *See* female-to-male

gatekeepers, professionals as, 94, 125,
    179, 191
gender
    binary, 12–14, 177–78
    change of on government documents,
        105
    colorblindness, 95–96
    constellation, 14
    as continuum, 13, 14
    euphoria, 116–17
    expression, 11, 13–14, 114
    fixation, 151, 157
    journey, 22, 49, 54, 104, 199
    norms, 37
    as nuanced, 37
    overemphasis on during treatment,
        79
    pitch of voice and, 139
    reveals, 150–51
    sex and, 13, 48
    team of professionals, 104
    terminology, 12–13
    understanding of, 11, 27
    variance in childhood, 152
Gender 101, 11
gender-affirming
    action of other professions, 120,
        135–36
    approaches to healthcare, 177–78
    environments, 137–38, 139, 144
    hormones, 54

gender-affirming care, systemic approach
        to, 137
Gender Congruence and Life
        Satisfaction Scale, 90
"Gender Disorder," use of in *ICD 10*, 88
gender-diverse care, 2, 5–7
gender dysphoria, 87, 96, 97, 113, 115,
        120
    access to care and, 116
    assessments limitations of, 90
    inclusion of in medical manuals,
        88–89, 116
gender-expansive. *See specific topics*
gender-expansive entrepreneurs, support
        for, 143, 144
gender expectations, 24, 48, 54
    empathy, 25, 27, 43, 161
    family, 25, 68, 150–51
    violation of, 25
    workplace, 25–26
gender-fluid people, binary sections and,
        138
gender identity, 11–15, 19, 149
    across the lifespan, 45
    assumptions about, 15, 19–24,
        47–48, 79, 157
    early awareness of, 47–49
    exploration of, 21, 43, 78, 109
    of human service professionals, 37
    intersectionality and, 33
    problems with placing too much
        emphasis on, 79
Gender Identity/Gender Dysphoria
        Questionnaire for Adolescents and
        Adults, 89–90
gender inclusion, large companies and,
        143–44
gender-inclusive language, 75–76, 138
Gender Preoccupation and Stability
        Questionnaire, 90
generalist practice, 135
generalization, of skills, 168
genetic fertility, emphasis on, 179
geographic culture of origin, exploration
        of, 67–68
geographic location, 57
goodbyes, 82, 170

government agencies, LGBTQ+ people
        and, 73
grammatical correctness, of singular
        they, 18
gratitude, expression of, 168
grieving process, of parents, 151
groups, 161–62
group supervision, 190, 197
group therapy
    development stages of, 163–64
    dynamics of, 164
    formation of, 163–64
    frustration during, 168
    individual therapy and, 171
    member selection of, 164–65, 172
    plans for after, 170
    recruiting for, 164
group therapy leaders, dual relationships
        of, 170–71
group work, formal, 164
growth-fostering activities, 199

harm, avoidance of, 103–4, 109
healthcare
    assumptions about gender identity
        and, 178
    trans-affirmative, 177, 184
    trans women and, 177
Heck, N. C., 165
high-risk clients, 194
Hirschfeld, M., 85
homogenizing, of gender-expansive
        population, 96
honorifics, 139, 140
hormone replacement therapy, 203–4
hormone therapy, 51, 86–87, 115, 125
    conception of babies and, 177
    requirements for, 126
    sexual education and, 179
human service professionals, 1–2, 118–19
    intersectionality of, 36–37

*ICD. See International Classification of
        Diseases*
identity
    affirmation of, 169
    change therapy, 50

differences, 190–91, 197
disclosure of, 39
exploration of, 21, 43, 78, 109
gender, 15, 19–24, 33, 37, 45, 47–49, 79, 157
integration, 37, 43, 108, 164
interaction, 37–40, 191
intersectional, 37–38
ignorance about bonding with others, of professionals, 42
ignoring, of gender-expansive identities, 95–96
immigrants, 67–68
inclusivity, 2–3
individual journeys, of clients, 14, 17–18
individual supervision, 190
inequities, of disabled people, 35
infertility, hormone therapy and, 51
infidelity, consensual nonmonogamy contrasted with, 182
informal group work, 164
information-gathering, 77, 89, 97
informed consent, 107
initial contact, with client, 73
insurance companies, requirements of, 128
intake protocols, 91–92, 178
integration, of identity, 37, 43, 108, 164
interaction
    client-professional, 39–40
    of gender-expansive people with others, 118
    of identities, 37–40, 95–96, 97, 191
    in therapy group real world contrasted with, 168
intercourse, while on hormone therapy, 179
intermediate steps, in transition timeline, 130
International Classification of Diseases (ICD) 10, 88
international travel, for surgery, 128
internet access, in rural areas, 65
interpersonal growth, 62
interpersonal skills, development of, 165
intersectional gender identity, 37–38
intersectional identities, 37–38

intersectionality, 31, 191
intersex, 17–18
intersex babies, surgical procedures on, 17, 48
interview-based assessment, 91, 97
invasive questions, avoidance of, 78

Jennifer (client), 136–37, 141
job security, 40
Johnson, Marsha P., 5
Julie (colleague), 24–25, 64, 105–6
justice for gender-expansive people, fight for, 5

kink as trauma response theory, as incorrect, 181
kink behavior
    asexual people and, 181
    as natural, 184
    normalization of, 181
kink community, 180–85
kink positivity, 180–84, 185
kink relationships, as healthy, 183

language to describe self, access for child of, 49
large companies, 143–44
law officers, ID questions and, 128
laws
    anti-gender-expansive, 59
    about gender-expansive people, 27, 105, 141
leadership positions, gender inclusion and, 137–38
learning disability diagnoses, people of color and, 41–42
legal issues, of gender-expansive population, 102, 104–5
legal name of client, use of, 25, 100, 139
lesbian, gay, bisexual, transgender, and queer (LGBTQ+) rights movements, 5, 41
letters of support, 89, 94, 123–25, 127–31
    carry letter, 128, 131, 207
    college counselors and, 142–43

hormone replacement therapy, 203–4
refusal to write, 95
requirements for, 125–26
reticence to write, 93
surgery, 205–6
LGBTQ+. *See* lesbian, gay, bisexual,
transgender, and queer
LGBTQ+ resource centers, in urban
areas, 60–61
LGBTQ rights, 41
LGBTQ+ services, in Boston, 57
licenses, differences in, 1
limitations, of gender dysphoria
assessments, 90, 96
Lisa (LPC), 189, 193, 195
list, of affirming professionals, 76, 96,
119, 125, 131
local area, knowledge of, 59
local laws, impact of, 68–69
location specifics, 140–41

male-to-female (MTF), 16
marginalization, by LGB community,
35, 41
marginalizing questions, 40
medical interventions, 50–51
medical model, applied to gender-
expansive population, 102
medical transition, 113, 115
mental health, focus on, 3
mental health diagnosis, gender
expansiveness and, 4, 87–88
mental health providers, support for
surgery and, 127–28
microcosm of outside world, therapy as,
39–40
middle to late adulthood, 53–54
milestones, in therapy, 82, 169
Minnesota, 105
The Minnesota Multiphasic Personality
Inventory (MMPI), 41–42
minoritized racial status, 41–42
minority identities
of human service professionals,
36–37
in therapy, 31, 39–42
misgendering, 23–244

mispronouning, 23–24
mistakes, while working with gender-
expansive individuals, 22–24, 81
MMPI. *See* The Minnesota Multiphasic
Personality Inventory
Molly (client), 6, 12, 21–22, 24, 32
carry letter of, 124
hairstylist of, 126, 138
kink community and, 176
massage therapist of, 100
online therapy group of, 162, 188,
194
relationship with family of, 148,
155–56
search for therapist of, 74, 75, 100,
188
therapist in online group of, 162
transition experience of, 46, 86, 112
Money, John, 87
MTF. *See* male-to-female
multicultural practice, 108–9
multiple marginalized identities, 31–33,
108
multiple relationships, with client, 106
Mx. honorific, 18
myths
consensual nonmonogamy, 183–84
sex education, 178–79

National Model (ASCA), 141
nature, 64
negative outcome, expectation of, 150
neurodivergence, gender expansive
people and, 35–36
nonbinary, 16–17, 125
Nonmaleficence, 103–4
norming, 168–69
norms, conforming to, 167
North Dakota, 6, 58

older people, families and, 45
online store, pride flags on, 140
online support group, of Rowan, 112
open-ended questions, 91
open relationships, 182
operating systems, 140
oppression, gender expansiveness and, 4

othering, of gender-expansive
    individuals, 15–16
"other," problems with use of, 77
ouch rule, 166
overpreparation, 172

parallel process, 194
parents, reaction of, 151–52
partners, families and, 147–50
passing, 117, 120
    desire for, 118
performing, 169
pitch of voice, gender and, 139
pitfalls, 95–96
plan, for after therapy group, 170
polyamorous population, of US, 156
polyamorous relationships, 156–57, 182
population, of gender-expansive people, 2
positive aspects
    of kink community, 181
    of rural areas, 63–64
positive ethics, 101
poverty, of gender-expansive people, 36
power
    of acceptance, 150–51
    dynamics, 191–92
    privilege and, 34, 191–92, 197
practice concerns, 106
practices, before meeting client, 75, 83
prejudice, of mental health professionals,
    41–42
pressure, to "prove" gender, 50
prevention of problems, treating
    problems contrasted with, 101–2
preventive psychoeducation, 141
pride flags, on website of therapist,
    75–76
private practitioners, 143
privilege, 26–27, 39–40, 43, 191–92,
    197
    awareness, of, 27, 28, 191
professional organizations, 99
professional role, supervision as, 195–96
professionals
    collaboration, with, 103, 104–5, 109,
        119, 120
    as gatekeepers, 94, 125, 179, 191

human service, 1–2
    self-training of, 95
pronouns, 18
    change in, 114
    college professors and, 142
    gender identity contrasted with, 19
    mispronouning, 23–24
    sharing of when introducing self,
        79–80, 139
"pronouns," contrasted with term
    "preferred pronouns," 18
"prove" gender, pressure to, 50
psychoeducation, 142, 171
psychological benefits, of puberty
    blockers, 51
puberty, 50–51, 54
puberty blockers, 51, 153

qualification compatibility, 195–96
"queer," use of term, 43–44
questions. See also reflection questions
    as necessary, 178
    open-ended, 91

race, ethnicity and, 34–35
rapport, with client, 77
reaction
    of children, 153–54, 157
    of parents, 151–52, 157
Rebecca (ex-wife of Molly), 148
receptionist
    at salon, 136
    training of, 139
recovery, after misgendering, 23, 28
recruiting, for group, 164
reflection questions, 3
    assessment and diagnosis, 97
    ethics, 109
    exploring gender identity, 29
    family dynamics, 157
    geographic area, 69
    group therapy, 173
    intersectionality, 43–44
    letters of support, 131
    lifespan development, 54
    relationship building, 83
    sexuality, 185

supervision, 197–98
transitions, 120–21
understanding gender, 19–20
rejection, from family of origin, 50
relationship
    building, 73–74, 191, 197
    with family, of gender-expansive
        people, 47
    with family of client, 106–7
    with identity, change in, 37
    positivity, 181–82
    strengthening of, 79–80
religious symbols, 76
reluctance, to let client go, 82
renegotiation, of group dynamics, 167
renewed adolescence, 54
resentment, of older clients, 43
resilience
    focus on, 4–5
    of gender-expansive people, 82
resources, 68–69
    competence-building, 129
    transition care, 129–30
responsibility, levels of, 141, 144
retail settings, 138
rhetoric, anti-immigration, 32
Rivera, Sylvia, 5
role play, 169
romantic relationships, 149, 154–55, 157
Rowan (client), 6–7, 12, 22, 23, 32–33
    coming-out process of, 112–13, 118,
        136
    Dungeons and Dragons group of,
        162–63
    experience in Thousand Oaks of, 58
    experience with academic affairs
        coordinator of, 74–75, 101, 106,
        188–89
    game shop owner and, 162–63
    Planned Parenthood and, 87, 113
    pronoun change of, 49
    relationship with family of, 46–47
    romantic relationship of, 148–49,
        155
    school counselor and, 136
    sexual orientation of, 176–77
    transition timeline of, 124

ruptures, 81, 167–68, 195, 197
rural areas, 62
    coming-out process in, 65
    limiting aspects of, 64–65
    multiple relationships in, 107
    positive aspects of, 63–64

safer sex, 178
safe space, for sexual concern discussion,
    184, 185
Safe Zone trainings, 142
school, 51–52, 140–41, 144
school counselors, 141, 144
school environments, as toxic, 51–52
screening, of group members, 165
seclusion, 65
self-acceptance, 183
self-disclosure
    by group leader, 169–70, 172
    with supervisor, 193, 194, 197
self-exploration, 21, 27–28, 102, 104
self-training, of professionals, 94–95,
    108–9
semi-rural areas, 66–67
sensation-seeking, kink as, 181
services
    access to, 64
    advertisement of, 75
    expansion of, 59–60, 199
    for specific populations, 7
sex
    assigned at birth, 13–16, 19
    assignment decision of doctors as
        arbitrary, 17
    gender and, 13, 48
    sexuality and, 175–76
sex education myths, 178–79, 185
sex-positive framework, 179–80, 185
sex reassignment surgery (SRS), 18
sexual health, 177–83
sexuality, sex and, 14
sexually transmitted infections (STIs),
    consensual nonmonogamy and,
    183
sexual orientation, 35, 40–41
    exploration of, 41
    gender identity and, 155, 175–76

sexual pleasure, 180
shaping, of gender identity, 24–26, 28
shared language, for professionals, 119
Singh, Anneliese, 28
singular they, 18
skills
    communication, 79
    generalization of, 168
SOC. *See Standards of Care*
SOC 7. *See* Standards of Care, 7th
    edition
SOC 8. *See* Standards of Care, 8th
    edition
social dysphoria, 115
social justice practice, 108–9
social meetings, with client, 106, 166
social networks, 62
    in rural areas, 63, 65
social stigma, of polyamory, 182–83
social support of professionals, gender-
    expansive clients contrasted with,
    42
social transition, 50–51, 112, 113, 114
    diverse pathways of, 118
societal norms, 156
sociocultural context, 3–4
socioeconomic status, 36
    difference between client and
        professional, 40
space, for different gender, 77
special events, college counselors and,
    142
specialists, proximity to in urban areas,
    60
specific providers, information for, 92,
    97
sperm production, estrogen-based
    hormone therapy and, 179
SRS. *See* sex reassignment surgery
stabilization, 93
Standards of Care, 7th edition *(SOC 7)*
    (WPATH), 89. 93, 124–25
Standards of Care, 8th edition *(SOC 8)*
    (WPATH), 127
stealth, 117

STIs. *See* sexually transmitted infections
storming, 167–68
story, of client, 79
strengthening, of relationship, 79–80
student LGBTQ+ organizations, college
    counseling centers and, 142
subgroups, 166–67
supervisee
    as gender-expansive, 190–91
    required licenses of, 196
supervision, 187–88
    as professional role, 195–96
supervisor, developmental process of,
    193–94
supervisory dynamic, dyadic, 190
supervisory groups, 190
supervisory relationships, 193–94
support, for gender-expansive family
    member, 155–56
supportive feedback, 192–93
surgery
    bottom, 126
    international travel for, 128
    on intersex babies, 17, 48
    letters of support for, 205–6
    mental health providers and, 127–28
    top, 126, 127
Susan (client), 189
swinging, 182
systemic approach, to gender-affirming
    care, 137

task orientation, 169, 191
teletherapy, 59–60, 69
termination
    of group therapy, 170, 172
    of services, 81–82
terminology
    change in, 80
    gender, 12–13
TGNC. *See* TransGender and Gender
    Nonconforming
therapeutic alliance, 42
therapy
    access to, 68–69

contact after end of, 82–83
cost of, 61
minority identities in, 31, 39–42
as prestigious job, 42
struggles in, 164
therapy practice, change in, 129
Thousand Oaks, California, 6–7
Tim (colleague), 38
TNB. *See* transgender and nonbinary
top surgery, 126, 127
training, of front office staff, 76, 83, 120, 138–39, 143
trans-affirmative healthcare, 177, 184
trans broken arm, 79, 91, 116
transgender
    correct use of term, 16
    health concerns, 60
    nonbinary and, 16–17
    women, 31
    women of color, 41, 61
    youth, 45, 52
TransGender and Gender Nonconforming (TGNC), 11
transgender and nonbinary (TNB), 11
trans identity, denial of, 153
transition care resources, 129–30
transition process, 111–20, 157
    frustration during, 130
    at work, 53
transitions, 113
    according to schedule, 169, 171
    of parents, 152–53
transition timeline, 129–30
transmasculine individuals, 177
transportation, to therapy appointments, 61
transsexual, 18
"transvestitism," 87
trans women, healthcare and, 177
travel
    to Fargo, 58
    to resources from rural areas, 65–66
treatment decisions, of parents, 153

trust
    breaches of in lives of gender-expansive people, 166
    establishment of, 165, 166, 170, 172

UCCs. *See* university counseling centers
umbrella term
    cisgender as, 15
    gender-expansive as, 19
unique stressors, of transitioning, 54
university counseling centers (UCCs), 142
unknown, fear of, 50
urban areas, 59–60
urbanized areas, 60
Utrecht Gender Dysphoria Scale, 89

VA. *See* Veterans Affairs
vaginoplasty, 177
values sorting activity, 183
variance, across geographic locations, 59
veracity, 102
Veterans Affairs (VA), 73
violation, of gender expectations, 25
violence, against trans people, 41, 61, 94
vocational issues, 40
voice pitch, gender and, 139

wall example, 27–28
ways to transition, variety of, 118–19
web-based resources, 130–31
website of therapist, pride flags on, 75–76, 140
Western beauty standards, 180, 185
workplace
    coming out in, 52–53
    gender expectations and, 25–26
    protections lack of, 52–53
The World Professional Association for Transgender Health (WPATH), 89, 108, 126

younger professionals, acceptable terms and, 43

About the Authors

Douglas Knutson (he, him), PhD, LHSP, is assistant professor in the School of Community Health Sciences, Counseling and Counseling Psychology at Oklahoma State University. He serves as director of the Diversity and Rural Advocacy Group (DRAG), a consortium of international researchers and advocates who focus on health and resilience in LGBTQ+ populations. Dr. Knutson has published 38 peer-reviewed articles, book chapters, professional papers, and encyclopedia entries. He has coauthored 74 presentations delivered at international, national, and local conferences and professional meetings. His work has been referenced in *USA Today*, *Stateline*, and *NPR News*. He currently serves on the editorial boards of *The Counseling Psychologist* and *Psychology of Sexual Orientation and Gender Diversity*. Dr. Knutson's work is focused on the development and implementation of transgender- and nonbinary-affirming interventions with an emphasis on rural populations.

Chloë Goldbach (she/her/hers), MS, MA, is a White, lesbian, transgender woman and PhD candidate in counseling psychology at Southern Illinois University Carbondale (SIUC). She organizes community-wide events on transgender and nonbinary issues as an officer of the SIUC Women, Gender, and Sexuality Studies organization, serves as an associate researcher of the Diversity and Rural Advocacy Group (DRAG) at Oklahoma State University, teaches courses on LGBTQ+ and workplace diversity issues, leads a YouTube channel on transgender and nonbinary topics, and is a therapist-in-training with a focus on serving LGBTQ+ clients and clients with eating and body image concerns. Chloë has published 10 peer-reviewed articles, encyclopedia entries, and professional papers, all related to issues impacting LGBTQ+ individuals. She has delivered more than 40 presentations at international, national, and local conferences, training workshops, and professional meetings. She is currently conducting research on barriers to health-care access for transgender and nonbinary people, experiences of LGBTQ+ people during the COVID-19 pandemic, and centering the voices and experiences of transgender and nonbinary people in the treatment and conceptualization of gender dysphoria.

Julie M. Koch (she/they), PhD, is professor of counseling psychology in the College of Education at the University of Iowa. She/they has extensive experience with clinical practice with LGBTQ+ rural populations. Dr. Koch is a former high school teacher and school counselor. Dr. Koch enjoys working with schools and international collaborations. She/they was a Monbusho Scholar at University of Hokkaido and received a Fulbright Specialist Grant to work with the LGBT Centre in Mongolia.